Freestaters
The Republic of Ireland Soccer Team
1921-1939

DESERT ISLAND FOOTBALL HISTORIES

Club Histories

	ISBN
Aberdeen: A Centenary History 1903-2003	978-1-874287-57-5
Aberdeen: Champions of Scotland 1954-55	978-1-874287-65-0
Aberdeen: The European Era	978-1-905328-32-1
Bristol City: The Modern Era – A Complete Record	978-1-905328-27-7
Bristol City: The Early Years 1894-1915	978-1-874287-74-2
Bristol Rovers: The Bert Tann Era	978-1-905328-37-6
Cambridge United: The League Era – A Complete Record	978-1-905328-06-2
Cambridge United: 101 Golden Greats	978-1-874287-58-2
Carlisle United: A Season in the Sun 1974-75	978-1-905328-21-5
The Story of the Celtic 1888-1938	978-1-874287-15-5
Chelsea: Champions of England 1954-55	978-1-874287-94-0
Colchester United: Graham to Whitton – A Complete Record	978-1-905328-35-2
Colchester United: From Conference to Championship	978-1-905328-28-4
Coventry City at Highfield Road 1899-2005	978-1-905328-11-6
Coventry City: The Elite Era – A Complete Record	978-1-874287-83-4
Coventry City: An Illustrated History	978-1-874287-59-9
Derby County: Champions of England 1971-72, 1974-75	978-1-874287-98-8
Dundee: Champions of Scotland 1961-62	978-1-874287-86-5
Dundee United: Champions of Scotland 1982-83	978-1-874287-99-5
History of the Everton Football Club 1878-1928	978-1-874287-14-8
Halifax Town: From Ball to Lillis – A Complete Record	978-1-874287-26-1
Hereford United: The League Era – A Complete Record	978-1-874287-91-9
Hereford United: The Wilderness Years 1997-2006	978-1-905328-22-2
Huddersfield Town: Champions of England 1923-1926	978-1-874287-88-9
Ipswich Town: The Modern Era – A Complete Record	978-1-905328-24-6
Ipswich Town: Champions of England 1961-62	978-1-874287-63-6
The Old Farm: Ipswich Town v Norwich City	978-1-905328-12-3
Kilmarnock: Champions of Scotland 1964-65	978-1-874287-87-2
Leyton Orient: A Season in the Sun 1962-63	978-1-905328-05-5
Luton Town at Kenilworth Road: A Century of Memories	978-1-905328-10-9
Luton Town: The Modern Era – A Complete Record	978-1-874287-90-2
Luton Town: An Illustrated History	978-1-874287-79-7
Manchester United's Golden Age 1903-1914: Dick Duckworth	978-1-874287-92-6
The Matt Busby Chronicles: Manchester United 1946-69	978-1-874287-96-4
Motherwell: Champions of Scotland 1931-32	978-1-874287-73-5
Northampton Town: A Season in the Sun 1965-66	978-1-905328-01-7
Norwich City: The Modern Era – A Complete Record	978-1-874287-67-4
Peterborough United: The Modern Era – A Complete Record	978-1-874287-33-9
Peterborough United: Who's Who?	978-1-874287-48-3
Plymouth Argyle: The Modern Era – A Complete Record	978-1-874287-54-4
Plymouth Argyle: 101 Golden Greats	978-1-874287-64-3
Plymouth Argyle: Snakes & Ladders – Promotions and Relegations	978-1-905328-34-5
Portsmouth: The Modern Era	978-1-905328-08-7
Portsmouth: From Tindall to Ball – A Complete Record	978-1-874287-25-4
Portsmouth: Champions of England – 1948-49 & 1949-50	978-1-874287-50-6
The Story of the Rangers 1873-1923	978-1-874287-95-7
The Romance of the Wednesday 1867-1926	978-1-874287-17-9
Seventeen Miles from Paradise: Saints v Pompey	978-1-874287-89-6
The Southend United Chronicles 1906-2006	978-1-905328-18-5
Stoke City: The Modern Era – A Complete Record	978-1-874287-76-6
Stoke City: 101 Golden Greats	978-1-874287-55-1
Potters at War: Stoke City 1939-47	978-1-874287-78-0
Swansea City: Seasons in the Sun	978-1-905328-02-4
Third Lanark: Champions of Scotland 1903-04	978-1-905328-03-1
Tottenham Hotspur: Champions of England 1950-51, 1960-61	978-1-874287-93-3
West Bromwich Albion: Champions of England 1919-1920	978-1-905328-04-8
West Ham: From Greenwood to Redknapp	978-1-874287-19-3
West Ham: The Elite Era – A Complete Record	978-1-905328-33-8
Hammers Through the Looking Glass	978-1-905328-23-9
Wimbledon: From Southern League to Premiership	978-1-874287-09-4
Wimbledon: From Wembley to Selhurst	978-1-874287-20-9
Wimbledon: The Premiership Years	978-1-874287-40-7
Wrexham: The European Era – A Complete Record	978-1-874287-52-0

World Cup Histories

England's Quest for the World Cup – A Complete Record	978-1-905328-16-1
Scotland: The Quest for the World Cup – A Complete Record	978-1-897850-50-3
Ireland: The Quest for the World Cup – A Complete Record	978-1-897850-80-0

Miscellaneous

Blinded by the Lights: A History of Night Football in England	978-1-905328-13-0
Red Dragons in Europe – A Complete Record	978-1-874287-01-8
The Book of Football: A History to 1905-06	978-1-905328-00-4
Football's Twelve Apostles: The Making of the League 1886-1889	978-1-905328-09-3
Football's War & Peace: The Tumultuous Season of 1946-47	978-1-874287-70-4
Freestaters: Republic of Ireland 1921-39	978-1-905328-36-9

Freestaters

The Republic of Ireland Soccer Team 1921-1939

Series Editor: Clive Leatherdale

Donal Cullen

DESERT ISLAND BOOKS

First published in 2007
by
DESERT ISLAND BOOKS LIMITED
7 Clarence Road, Southend-on-Sea, Essex SS1 1AN
United Kingdom
www.desertislandbooks.com

© 2007 Donal Cullen

British Library Cataloguing-in-Publication Data
A catalogue record for this book is available from the British Library

ISBN 978-1-905328-36-9

All rights reserved. No part of this book may be reproduced or utilised in any form or by any means, electronic or mechanical, including photocopying, recording or by any information storage and retrieval system, without prior permission in writing from the Publisher

Printed in Great Britain
by
Biddles Ltd, King's Lynn

Contents

	Page
ACKNOWLEDGMENTS AND DEDICATION	6
INTRODUCTION	7
1 THE SPLIT	11
2 A RECORD OF THE FULL INTERNATIONAL SOCCER MATCHES PLAYED BY THE IRISH FREE STATE 1926 TO 1939	67
3 STATISTICS	153

Acknowledgments

My first thanks have to go to my wife and daughter, to whom this book is dedicated. My wife, Denise, is Canadian and as such understands little about the greatest game in the world but she has never let me live it down that she picked Brazil to win the 2002 World Cup while I picked Argentina or Portugal.

In order to produce a book without (too many) errors you have to rely on a good proofreader and preferably someone with some knowledge of the game. I found both in my brothers Raymond and Aiden, who could be honest and blunt if need be. I would also like to thank my publisher and friend Clive Leatherdale.

To the following, who have helped me directly, I send my thanks: Mark Baber, Stephen Bridge, Daniel Burtinshaw, Denis Byrne, Mary Cullen, Robert Cullen, Paul Days, Sean DeLoughry, Steve Flanagan, Roy France, John Galvin, Tom Greig, Mark Griffin, Paul Haynes, David Hillam, Frank Holt, Neil Jacques, Amy Kinsella, Bronagh Kinsella, Bryan Kinsella, Louise Kinsella, Antonia Lacey, Mark Lamb, John Litster, Paul McKew, Bob McPherson, Ru O'Reilly, Kevan Platt, David Reid, Gavin Reardon, Keith Roe, Jake Rookes, Davide Rota, Armanda Santos, Tony Scholes, Phil Sherwin, Greg Stock, Remco van Dam, Ian Watts, Gary Wolstenholme, David Wood.

Dedication

This book is dedicated with love to the two females in my life:
Denise Cullen, my wife and best friend 'I love you more'
and Grace Clare Yvon Cullen, my daughter and my life 'Dawgin'

and also to the memory of Katie Byrne who, like her distant relation Roger Byrne of Manchester United, was taken from us at an early age.

Introduction

At the time of writing, the Split in Irish soccer is long-established and relations between the governing body in the South (the Football Association of Ireland, FAI) and that in the North (the Irish Football Association, IFA) were never more cordial. The differences of the past are long forgotten. It was not always so. The 20th century had arrived with a united Irish Football Association, which controlled the game within the whole country, as befitted a united Ireland under British rule. Few could have anticipated the problems that would split the organisation in two, with even fewer foreseeing the impact both sides of the Split would have on the world game. With the passage of time both Irelands would reach the quarter-finals of a World Cup that in 1900 had not yet been conceived. Both Irelands would also some day host the best nations in the footballing world and sometimes beat them. That, too, back in 1900, was unimaginable.

The Irish Football Association was formed in Belfast in 1880, at a time when Association Rules Football was just one of many sports played in Ireland. But as happened almost across the globe, soccer caught the public imagination like no other. There is an old saying that 'Football is a gentleman's game played by ruffians while Rugby is a ruffian's game played by gentlemen'. For the working classes the simplicity of the gentleman's game was perhaps the main reason it became the people's game.

The first competition introduced by the IFA was the Irish Cup, which began in 1880-81 and was won 1-0 by Moyola Park against Cliftonville, which in its early years was a top club in Belfast. Ireland's second city became the home of Irish soccer. That in itself was unusual, because almost every other sport in Ireland was based in the capital, Dublin. It would be another ten years before an Irish league was set up, by which time Distillery had become top dogs in Irish soccer with four wins from five IFA Cup final appearances.

On February 18th, 1882 Ireland played its first international and suffered what is still its heaviest defeat. The match was played at Bloomfield Park in front of 2,500, and England, the opposition, scored thirteen goals without reply. The team representing Ireland that day was: James Hamilton (Knock), John McAlery (Cliftonville), Don Rattray (Avoneil), David Martin (Cliftonville), John Hastings (Knock), James Buckle (Cliftonville), Billy McWha (Knock), John Davison (Cliftonville), John Sinclair (Knock), Andy Dill (Knock), Davy McCaw (Malone).

Eight of that side was retained against Wales in Wrexham a week later. Another heavy defeat ensued, but at least Sammy Johnston from Distillery had the honour of scoring Ireland's first goal on his debut. Wales, however, scored seven. Ireland's third international was against England in Liverpool and the English again trounced the Irish. On St Patrick's Day, 1883, the Irish gained their first draw when William Morrow, who had scored in the first Irish Cup final, scored Ireland's first goal at home in a 1-1 draw with Wales.

The Irish League, which got underway in 1890-91, was won by the team that was to dominate Irish football from the late 19th century – Linfield. The Belfast club, formed just four year previously, did the double and did so again for the next two seasons. Of the 27 League titles up for grabs before the Split, Linfield won twelve as well as thirteen Irish Cups.

On the international front, Ireland's elusive first victory came in Belfast at the sixteenth attempt, 4-1, and was at the expense of Wales. Up until now, the Irish team was largely staffed with home-based players. That was to change, but results did not improve. Ireland would play nine more games before their next win, and ship 60 goals. On February 7th, 1891 Ireland achieved its biggest win before the Split and it was again the Welsh who suffered. A team of entirely home-based players, six of them from Linfield, ran out 7-2 winners.

Two years later saw the birth of the Irish League representative team. A side containing seven Linfielders beat the Scottish League 3-0 at Ulsterville. They would not win again for another six years, when the Scottish League were again their victims. In all, before the Split, the Irish League played 48 times, losing all but eight.

In 1899, for the match against Wales in Belfast and for the first time, the IFA picked four men playing their club football in England. Ireland triumphed 1-0 but, predictably, lost their next match, 1-9 in Glasgow against a rampant Scottish side. Archie Goodall netted Ireland's goal and became the first English League player to score for Ireland.

Despite the influx of professional Irish players from the 'mainland', Ireland would not score for another six games and then Preston's Andrew Gara notched a hat-trick in a 3-0 win over the Welsh, again, in Cardiff. Ireland and Wales were the cannon fodder for the big guns of England and Scotland, who regularly fought it out for the Home Championship. Wales had the odd success against the top two, but Ireland had not beaten England or Scotland until 1903, when goals by Maurice Connor (Brentford) and John Kirwan (Tottenham) gave Ireland a shock win in Glasgow.

The amateur internationals started for Ireland in 1906. These offered the chance for southern-based players to gain international recognition. Ireland played England at Dalymount Park on December 15th with a team entirely composed of players from the two leading amateur clubs in Ireland at the time – Bohemians and Cliftonville. Ireland lost 1-2 in front of a small crowd. Ireland played eleven amateur internationals before the Split, all bar one against England, and recorded three wins, one draw and seven defeats.

England were at last beaten in a full international after 32 attempts, when Ireland's greatest player of the 1920s, Billy Gillespie (Sheffield United) scored twice on his debut in a 2-1 win in Belfast on February 15th, 1913. It was the start of a golden period in Irish soccer, which culminated with the winning of the Home International championship for the first time. Wins over Wales and that first over England, as well as a draw with the Scots, brought the biggest international prize then existing home to Ireland. And there it stayed for six years as football was suspended following the outbreak of the First World War in August 1914. Seventy years later the Home International championship trophy returned to Belfast for the last time and as far as anybody knows it is still there!

The First World War ended in November 1918 and international football in Britain resumed the following year but the Irish team was to play only six more games before the Split. Ireland's last international was on April 9th, 1921 when the following team lost 1-2 to Wales in Swansea: Elisha Scott (Liverpool), Davy Rollo (Blackburn Rovers), William McCandless (Glasgow Rangers), Billy Lacey (Liverpool), Michael Scraggs (Glentoran), John Harris (Cliftonville), Pat Robinson (Blackburn Rovers), John Brown (Glenavon), Robert Chambers (Distillery), Allan Mathieson (Luton Town), Louis Bookman (Luton Town). Perhaps fittingly, a Distillery man, Robert Chambers scored Ireland's goal, as Ireland's first ever goal had also been scored by a man from the Grosvenor Park club. It was Ireland's 103rd international since 1882.

Soccer in Ireland had taken root in Belfast and its main power base was there. However, it was a growing sport and it was not long before the capital, Dublin, got in on the act. Most sports at the time, bar Gaelic games, were played and administered by the upper and middle classes. Soccer, or Association Football as it was known, was different. It was truly the 'People's Game' and remained so for its first 100 years or so until, in the 1990s, it suddenly became fashionable among higher social circles. Despite its grass-root support in the working and lower class, it was in the universities that the game first blossomed in Dublin.

A group of Dublin Students at Trinity College formed a team called the Dublin Association. The Dublin University side was formed some time later and both teams regularly contested the Irish Cup. In fact, both managed to get to the semi-finals in their time but no further. The game became so popular in Dublin and its surrounds that the IFA decided that it needed a body to control the game in Leinster. On October 27th, 1892, with a £50 donation from the IFA, the Leinster Football Association was formed and the game in that Province began to expand. In time its membership would be the biggest in Ireland and the LFA began to flex its muscles by requesting international football for Dublin.

At that time it was accepted that Windsor Park in Belfast was the best venue in Ireland for representative fixtures. All Dublin had to offer before the 20th century was Lansdowne Road as an alternative. The headquarters of Irish rugby (which, like most sports in Ireland, did not split in 1921) was used once, but Lansdowne Road was generally unsuitable for soccer, as various rugby matches were scheduled more or less to coincide with the Home Championship games. Dublin's Dalymount Park opened in 1901 and hosted its first full soccer international when Scotland won 1-0 on St Patrick's Day in 1906. Since that time it hosted three of the fifteen home games for Ireland, as well as six IFA Cup finals, two amateur internationals, and one Inter-league game.

The Leinster Football Association were not satisfied, however, and felt that they remained the poor relations within the IFA. Looked at from Dublin's perspective, it seemed the Irish team was more representative of Ulster than Ireland, and that the Leinster FA were only fed crumbs to placate its growing demands for more big games and a more powerful identity within the IFA.

The 1916 rising and the subsequent War of Independence curtailed the use of Dublin as a venue for major soccer fixtures. Yet accusations of Belfast-bias from those in the South persisted. The issue came to a head in the 1921 IFA Cup. Shelbourne from Dublin had reached their tenth Cup semi-final and were drawn to meet Belfast's Glenavon in Belfast. It was now that events outside football in Ireland began to impact upon the Irish game.

The Split

With Irish nationalism eating into every aspect of life on the island of Ireland, football – the game of the people – was exploited for political ends by all warring parties. This hastened the geographical split in the administration of the game, largely through brutal scenes at certain football grounds. Surprisingly, it was not the clubs from the South that witnessed turbulence, rather it was a Belfast club that was to mirror the events unfolding across Ireland.

Belfast Celtic, which had been a member of the Irish League since 1896-97, became an obvious outlet for Irish nationalism in that city and as such attracted its fair share of violence. Having won the League twice and the Cup once, the club was thrown out of the League following trouble at the 1920 IFA Cup semi-final with Glentoran. A player from Belfast Celtic was sent off, sparking mayhem on the terraces. A pitch invasion ensued, to the accompaniment of Irish nationalist flags and rousing songs. There was even a report of shots fired into the terraces where the Glens fans were housed. The tie was suspended, with Glentoran awarded a place in the final. Yet discrepancies in their paperwork meant Glens too were expelled from the competition. The 1920 IFA Cup was therefore awarded by default to Shelbourne, who had beaten Glenavon in the other, quieter, semi-final. So it was that the Reds brought the IFA Cup back to Dublin for the fourth and last time.

Dublin clubs had been competing in the Irish League since 1902-03 and in the Irish Cup since its inception. Even so, Ulster dominated the League and the Cup to the extent that one or other Belfast club had contested every Cup final until 1908. Success for clubs from other provinces were few. The first occasion any non-Ulster team touched the heights had been when Limerick reached the final of the 1892 IFA Cup. Their team, however, was in fact a British Army Regiment, the Black Watch, which lost the final to Linfield. Three years later there was excitement in Dublin when Bohemians, only four years in existence, marched to the final to meet the powerhouse of Linfield, who had contested the previous five Cup finals. Linfield won by a record score of 10-1.

Another British Army side from the South – the Sherwood Foresters from the Curragh in Dublin – reached the 1897 Cup final, only to be beaten by another Belfast club, Cliftonville. The 1900 final was again won by Cliftonville, overcoming Bohemians who had reached the semis of the last three IFA cups. Freebooters, another Dublin amateur side, were in the following year's Cup final but they too lost to Cliftonville.

Bohemians' reward for reaching the semi-final of the 1902 Cup was election to the Irish League for the following season. The 1902-03 campaign was special for the Dalymount Park club, for it would host the IFA Cup final for the first time. Bohs finished next to bottom in their debut League season but reached the Dalymount final where they lost 1-3 to Distillery.

In 1904-05 Bohs were joined in the Irish League by another side from Dublin – Shelbourne, who likewise reached the IFA Cup final and likewise lost to Distillery. 1905-06 saw both Dublin clubs reach the semi-finals, in which Shels – who had turned professional – beat Derry Celtic to contest the final with Belfast Celtic, the 2-0 victors over Bohs. Two goals from James Owens, who had top-scored for Shels in the League, brought the Cup to Dublin for the first time. A year later Shels were runners-up to Linfield in the League and to Cliftonville in the Cup.

A year later the same two Dublin clubs overcame Belfast opposition in the semis to stage the first all-Dublin final. Shels were favourites, but the amateurs of Bohs prevailed after a replay. James Owens again scored for Shels, but two goals from Dick Hooper and another from Willie Hopper gave Bohs the Cup. Bohs would get to the final in 1909 and the semi-final in 1910 before the next all-Dublin clash in the 1911 final. This time Shels came out on top, again after a replay.

Neither Bohs not Shels seriously threatened in the Irish League prior to the Great War and, immediately after it, in 1919-20, Shelbourne finished fourth and Bohemians last. Shels won the Cup by default but this would be the last occasion that both Dublin clubs competed as an Irish League club.

Down South, the Leinster Senior League flourished. The Leinster Senior Cup was as important for Dublin as the IFA Cup was for Ireland. Bohemians had won the LSC on fifteen occasions and Shelbourne ten. The League was predominately Dublin-based, but teams from Athlone and Dundalk also competed. It was the Leinster Senior League that provided the teams when the Free State League was formed in 1921. Elsewhere, football was predominately a 'garrison' game, played by the various regiments of the British Army dotted around Ireland. Limerick, Athlone and, especially, Cork housed British Army units and it was there that a further soccer powerbase was established.

Soccer had its roots in England and Scotland and the game's global expansion followed in the wake of soldiers, sailors and settlers. This was also the case in Ireland. By 1900 the British Army had a number of Irish units within its ranks, and soccer inevitably spread.

Soccer ran counter to the ethos of the Gaelic Athletic Association (GAA) – set up four years after the establishment of the Irish Football Association to 'prevent the decline of native pastimes'. The GAA imposed restrictions on soccer, rugby, hockey and cricket, lumping them under the derogatory title of 'foreign games'. The fact that GAA sports (principally hurling and Gaelic football) would remain largely confined to Ireland, whereas the 'foreign' games, especially soccer and rugby, would be at the forefront of promoting Ireland on a world stage, was of little account. Indeed, the GAA would portray itself as the flag-bearer of Irish identity and culture, condemning the 'foreign sports' as being imposed on Ireland by outsiders.

This was far from the case. Ireland's first Olympians were soccer players, most of whom had played Gaelic games in school, but that did not deter the GAA from imposing bans on members playing, or even attending 'foreign games'. This attitude would sour Irish sport for over a century. Not until 2007 was international soccer and rugby permitted to be staged at the cradle of the GAA, Croke Park.

The GAA had been greatly strengthened by the events of 1916. The Easter Rising had not been widely popular within Ireland but the subsequent execution of its leaders by the British reignited the Irish Independence movement. This resistance permeated all fields of Irish society and found an outlet in soccer. Clubs like Bohs and Shels were lumped together with Belfast Celtic and Cliftonville as promoting of the ideal of Irish independence and, by association, the IRA.

The GAA became the sports organisation most supportive of Irish nationalism, even though the independence movement also found voice in soccer. Despite quitting the Irish League in 1920, Bohs and Shels still entered the 1921 Irish Cup. Shelbourne, the holders, drew 0-0 in the semis with Lurgan side Glenavon. The replay was scheduled for St Patrick's Day but Glenavon refused to travel because of disturbances in and around Dublin. And who could blame them? The War of Independence had by March 1921 claimed almost 1,000 lives and tension was high following the hanging of six IRA men in Mountjoy Prison three days before the scheduled replay.

Viewed from Belfast, Dublin was 'too hot' to stage an important soccer match and so the Irish Football Association ordered the replay to be switched to Belfast. Shelbourne protested that Belfast was equally dangerous and was, in fact, under military curfew. They would also be financially out of pocket, not to mention being denied home advantage. When the IFA refused to reconsider, Shels withdrew, which incurred expulsion from all further competitions. Shelbourne, the only professional club in Dublin, were out in the cold.

A month earlier the Irish amateur team had travelled to Paris to take on France for the first time. The selection of the XI raised hackles down South. This was Ireland's thirteenth amateur international. Most of the previous twelve had been represented by just two clubs, Bohemians and Cliftonville. So when the team announced contained just a single Bohs (Jack McCarthy, who would later play for the Free State in Italy in 1926), allegations flew of 'Northern bias'. Although two other Dublin clubs, St James's Gate and UCD, had players included, Northern players formed a huge majority. Tension carried over onto the field. As the teams emerged, Sinn Fein banners and Irish tricolours were spotted in the crowd and the Irish team was ordered back inside until the offending flags were removed. As reported by Peter Byrne in *The Football Association of Ireland: 75 Years*, it was only years later that 'a letter to the

Irish Times revealed that the offending flags had been carried by African students of the Royal College of Surgeons in Dublin'.

All this called to mind an incident years later. The Republic of Ireland were due to play a World Cup qualifier at Windsor Park when a Unionist politician protested at the flying of the Irish tricolour inside the ground. It was politely pointed out that the flag was indeed a tricolour, but was blue, white and red, acknowledging the French referee!

The Intermediate Cup was also hit by controversy. The Cup, one of the top prizes in amateur football, was held by Dublin side St James's Gate and its final was scheduled for Dublin in 1921. When the IFA demanded moving the game to Belfast the Brewery club promptly withdrew.

In fact, only one sporting event in Ireland had been directly affected by the Troubles. That was the GAA match between Dublin and Tipperary at Croke Park when the Black and Tans, in retaliation for the shooting dead of fourteen British agents in Dublin, had locked up the ground and shot at the patrons inside, killing at least twelve. But then the IRA opened fire at a cricket match in Dublin and injured a girl. Viewed with hindsight, the possibility of an attack on a high-profile soccer match was not inconceivable, especially if it involved a team from the North.

The Leinster Football Association upped the ante by proposing to form its own association and play within its own competitions, perhaps even forming an international side. However, political events overtook this proposal and, following a truce in the War of Independence in June 1921, the Irish Free State, minus six counties in Ulster, was born. Ireland was split in two and most sporting organisations now had to decide whether to follow suit.

THE FORMATION OF THE IRISH FREE STATE FOOTBALL ASSOCIATION

There were various sporting organisations in Ireland in 1921. The biggest, by far, was the Gaelic Athletic Association which, as a sporting (and sometime political organisation), had allied itself to the nationalist cause. The Irish Rugby Football Union (IRFU) had been founded ten years earlier than the GAA and was generally regarded as elitist. Hockey might also fall into this category, but not the third 'foreign' sport, soccer, which was viewed as the working man's game. The other notable sporting bodies represented boxing, swimming, golf, bowling, rowing, tennis, and badminton, but it was only in soccer that the split between North and South occurred. Why?

The chief reason was that it was the only major sport in Ireland – governed by the Irish Football Association (IFA) – that had its headquarters in Belfast. When the island was split in 1921, the IRFU and the IFA faced the same dilemma and both hoped to remain united. The IRFU's largely upper-crust membership also harboured conflicting views on the future of rugby in Ireland, but with its headquarters in Dublin it did not face the same pressures as the IFA and quickly decided to keep its organisation intact.

The IFA did not have that luxury. Even prior to the split it was in trouble internally, feuding with the Leinster branch, and the simple fact of being based in Belfast was bound to present upheavals when the Free State was granted independence.

(For non-Irish readers it should be explained that historically Ireland was divided into 32 counties and four provinces – Leinster to the east, radiating out from Dublin; Munster to the south, with Cork its largest city; Connaught to the west, furthest from Britain and where the Gaelic language is most often heard; and Ulster to the North. Most, but not all, of historic Ulster became Northern Ireland.)

Ironically, despite being branded by some a foreign sport, soccer had been at the forefront of Irish independence. The Dublin clubs in the Irish League had attracted nationalist backing, as had Belfast Celtic. This was countered by Northern clubs like Linfield, Glentoran and Glenavon becoming havens for unionist support, so sectarianism was already embedded. The IFA had always been viewed from the South as biased towards Belfast players and clubs, and the events of the past two years had only hardened attitudes. The Leinster Association of the IFA, with support from Munster – another hot-bed of Irish soccer – started by seeking concessions but ended with dreams of forming their own association.

At the Irish Football Association's AGM in Derry on Saturday, May 14th, 1921 it was proposed that should any Dublin club reach the semi-final and final of the IFA Cup, Dublin would host those games. Thereafter they would alternate between Belfast and Dublin every year a Dublin club was involved. Shelbourne, still smarting at the handling of their semi-final the previous season, argued that the Cup be removed from IFA control and passed to a committee of senior clubs. Needless to say, interpreting this as a motion of censure, the IFA refused.

That same day, in Dublin, the Leinster and Munster Football Associations met to consider the future of Irish football. The timing was curious, because the chairman of the Leinster FA, Mr R E Richey, was in Derry. This left it to a previous chairman, Mr J A Ryder, now secretary of the LFA, to set out what was at stake:

'It is in the best interests of football that the association should continue its connection with the IFA Ltd [but] during the present season, the principal rounds of the Irish Cup and the Intermediate Cup were forbidden to be played in Dublin and the Irish Junior Cup was not played. In fact no matches with Northern clubs took place, thus the IFA Ltd cut themselves adrift from our association. It is considered that if the association had a free hand, a lot could be done to develop and popularise the game, rules being drawn up on the lines suitable to clubs without any restrictions.'

Perhaps blinded by patriotic zeal, most clubs backed the formation of a new association. This was before, it must be remembered, the country was split. The risks were huge. The parent body, the IFA, might cut them adrift, and while the prospect of a competition within Dublin was welcome, the appeal might soon wane. Then there was the problem of having no international football of any type. The cessation of senior internationals for Dublin would be financially disastrous.

On the other hand, the troubles had already seen a curtailment of Dublin games and the paltry sums coming from the IFA had not really compensated. It was the Juniors who had most to lose. Southern players had been well represented in the annual Junior international joust with the Scots, but the split would deny them the chance of further international honours. A photograph purporting to show the first ever international Free State team was in fact the last Junior international team fielded by the whole of Ireland, which won 1-0 at Celtic Park in 1921. The Free State's first Junior international would have to wait another eight years.

Potentially the most damaging aspect of a split was that the IFA would refuse to recognise any Free State FA and, by extension, so would the English, Scottish and Welsh governing bodies. This would not only rule out international fixtures against the four British nations but would also ban the transfer of players from a Free State club to one under British control.

The long-term effects could not be foreseen, but any all-LOI team for internationals would be weak for the simple reason that if full-time professional clubs could not sustain themselves, then the entire League of Ireland would revert to an amateur structure. Against this, a Free State XI regularly being trounced at international level might be preferable to an Ulster XI representing the whole of Ireland. Mind you, these considerations were some way down the road when the principals met in the Molesworth Hall on Wednesday, June 1st, 1921.

The proposal was simple – the establishment of a new organisation to take control of the game in the South. This, of course, was well before the Treaty, which separated the island into North and Southern Ireland, and the War of Independence still had another bloody month to run before the truce. So the proposed organisation was in reality a breakaway body from the association that governed the game in the whole of Ireland. Had the whole island gained independence, then the IFA would still have controlled soccer in the country and the breakaway organisation would have jurisdiction only over a part of it. So, when the proposed body was duly set up it was political developments in the country that shaped its future.

The IFA was furious, turning its back on the breakaway body and any clubs that saw fit to join it. The threat of secession had been simmering for two seasons, yet the concessions granted by the IFA had not been enough to satisfy the men from the South.

On the political stage, on July 11th, 1921, a truce was declared in the War of Independence to determine the future of the island of Ireland. This truce led to a treaty which unleashed civil war and brought eventual partition. Partition, which saw the Free State control 26 counties and Britain the other six, was the defining act that determined the future of soccer in Ireland. It is doubtful whether the breakaway Southern Association would have survived within a united Ireland (under British or Irish rule).

Go it Alone: Season 1921-22

Soccer in Ireland was carved into two and the lines of demarcation seemed straightforward. The IFA would govern the sport in the Six Counties, or the Province, Ulster, or Northern Ireland (whichever name suited at the time), while the Football Association of the Irish Free State would take control in the newly formed Free State. Simple, right? Wrong! This is Ireland and things are never as easy as they seem. For instance, the IFA still controlled soccer in the whole of Ireland, while the Free State FA had within its jurisdiction clubs in Belfast who had signed up with the Southern body. Then there was the squabbling over who actually presided over soccer as a whole. The IFA had the mandate but the Free State FA was in some places described as the 'All-Ireland FA'. A week before the new League of Ireland kicked off, a friendly match in Dublin warranted this report in the *Irish Times*:

'Association football in Dublin entered on a new phase on Saturday [September 10th] when a League team from Falls and District [Belfast], who have thrown in their lot with the recently formed All-Ireland Football Association, played … Bohemians at Dalymount Park. The institution of the All-Ireland Association marks a clean break with the governing body, the Irish Football Association, whose headquarters have always been in Belfast. The intention of the new association is to take control of "soccer" in Leinster, Munster, and Connaught, and to welcome to the fold any Northern clubs that may decide on "joining up". Among those who have done so are a number from the Falls road and district.'

By going ahead with the match, the Falls and District League was outlawed by the IFA, along with every other club which had joined the new body, including those in the South. Bohemians, 2-1 victors, played a return match in Belfast in October and also won 2-1.

On Saturday, September 17th, 1921 the League of Ireland (as distinct from the Irish League) kicked off with three fixtures. Bohemians defeated the YMCA 5-0 at Dalymount Park, Shels beat Frankfort 4-0 at Richmond Park, and there was a 5-1 home win for St James's Gate over Dublin United. It is not recorded who scored the first ever goal in the League of Ireland, it being either Frank Haine of Bohs or a player called Cannon (sometimes spelt Canning) from Shels.

The 'go it alone' policy gained momentum, with the bans imposed by the IFA dismissed as petty and vindictive. The League of Ireland was up and running, albeit with just eight Dublin clubs. Shelbourne and Bohemians became the linchpins around which the League would function. The past two winners of the Leinster Senior Cup – Dublin United and St James's Gate – as well as Frankfort, Jacobs, Olympia and the YMCA, all took part in the new league. Week One had begun with heavy defeats for all the away sides and by week two there was another type of split, when it was clear that Bohs, Shels and the Gate were far superior to the rest. By week three, Bohs topped the league after beating Shels 2-0 at Dalymount Park, which to all intents was now the 'home' of Irish soccer.

Up North, the rump of the Irish League was left with just six clubs, all but one from Belfast. The season's first representative fixture coincided with the Bohs v Shels match. The Irish League was expected to struggle for players to take on the English League at the Oval in south London. Naturally, League of Ireland players were off-limits, yet the Irish League only went down 0-1. The small nation now controlled by the IFA would continue to post extraordinary results in the years to come.

The first hurdle for both Irish associations was not long in coming. The opening Home International was scheduled for Belfast. Ireland (the name would be disputed for years) would host England. The IFA considered all Irish players (even those in the banned South) to be eligible, which meant it could call upon a bigger pool of players than could the Free State. In fact the IFA could also select Irish players on the 'mainland', whereas the Free State was restricted to those who operated in the League of Ireland and other local leagues, and who were born in the 26 counties comprising the Free State.

More than 60 Irish players played in Britain. Hypothetically, some twenty of those might have been eligible for the Free State FA, had it been in a position to play anyone, but even this was not clear-cut. The Free State's head of Foreign Affairs, Arthur Griffith, was in London. Amongst the issues under discussion was the composition of Ulster. Historically, Ulster comprised nine counties, of which three wished to be part of the Free State, three to remain loyal to Britain, and three others – Tyrone, Fermanagh and Armagh – were disputed. This left some Ulster-born players with a dilemma which, happily, was solved before the Free State played its first full international.

The players chosen for what is described as Northern Ireland's first international match were Belfast-born, with three exceptions: Louis Bookman, formerly of Belfast Celtic, was winning his fourth cap, despite being born in Lithuania; Billy Lacey, ex-Shelbourne, hailed from Wexford and was winning his 21st cap. The star of the team was a Donegal man, Billy Gillespie, who had scored four goals in his previous seven games for Ireland. Gillespie, like Lacey, was eligible to play for the Free State but never did, despite being one of the hottest forwards in England in the 1920s. In fact, the IFA would continue to cap men from the South until the 1950s. The Free State would also loosen its attitude and, in time, would call upon the services of men from Ulster. This meant players could, and did, win international caps for both Irelands.

However, on Saturday, October 22nd, 1921 at Windsor Park, the team representing Ireland was Northern Irish. They scored after 25 minutes through Billy Gillespie, only for Billy Kirton to equalise five minutes later. The press noted: 'The Irish forwards failed badly and only the Irish defence allowed the home side to escape with a draw.' England had not won in Ireland since 1912 and would not do so until 1929. These were good days for Irish international football, despite the split.

Next up was the first of the season's amateur internationals, against England, set for November 12th at Leicester. The most recent of these, in February 1921 in Paris, had been spoiled by the tricolour incident, as noted earlier. The team now announced by the IFA comprised ten players from the Irish League and one from England. Bohemians, and every other club in the 'breakaway association', were out in the cold. The match was played a day late in Leicester due to fog and the English won 4-1.

There was recognition of sorts for one Southern-born player when Kilcock's Mick O'Brien was selected to play for the English Football League against the Army. O'Brien scored twice in a 4-1 win and would, in time, become one of the first players to be capped by both the IFA and the Free State FA.

Free State League of Ireland final table 1921-22:

	P	W	D	L	F	A	Pts
St James's Gate	14	11	1	2	31	8	23
Bohemians	14	10	1	3	35	13	21
Shelbourne	14	8	2	4	31	21	18
Olympia	14	5	4	5	20	21	14
Jacobs	14	4	4	6	23	27	12
Frankfort	14	3	5	6	22	32	11
Dublin United	14	5	0	9	25	39	10
YMCA	14	0	3	11	17	43	3

By Christmas 1921 the League was done and dusted, with St James's Gate the first champions of the League of Ireland. Shelbourne won the Shield title, which commenced as soon as the League campaign was over. Gate won a second trophy when they defeated Jacobs in the Leinster Senior Cup, which left only the 'big one' to be decided.

The FAI Cup would in time become the glamour event in Irish soccer. At first the Leinster Senior Cup was the 'blue riband' Cup, but that would soon change. The FAI Cup had commenced in November with the Leinster League sides battling it out in the preliminary rounds. Among them was a team from Ringsend called Shamrock Rovers. They played and beat UCD in front of a small crowd at Windy Arbour. From these humble beginnings, Rovers would emerge to become one of the finest clubs in Irish soccer. They reached the first round proper, and victories over Olympia, Dublin United and Bohemians pitched them into the final against League Champions St James's Gate on St Patrick's Day, March 17th 1922. The final ended 1-1, with Gate winning the replay 1-0 to complete a double.

That FAI Cup final was not without incident. Charlie Dowdall and Bob Fullam, opposing inside-lefts, conducted an ongoing feud, and at the final whistle Rovers' Fullam – a tough Dublin docker – led a mob into the dressing room to confront Dowdall, a fitter at the Guinness brewery and just as tough. One ugly incident was averted by another, which was in keeping with the times. Dowdall's brother, Jack, on active service with the IRA while the Treaty was being thrashed out, aired a revolver but did not fire.

At season's end a team representing the League of Ireland met one representing the Leinster Senior League in two games. The League of Ireland won both with a side which the papers said was 'thoroughly representative of the [League]'.

For the purposes of this book, the Six Counties which remained part of the United Kingdom will now be called Northern Ireland. Its governing body, the Irish Football Association, will sometimes be shortened to the IFA. The Football Association of the Irish Free State would later become the Football Association of Ireland. Its controlling body is the FAI or, on occasions, the Free State FA. As the controlling bodies are now firmly established under the names Northern Ireland (IFA) and the Republic of Ireland (FAI), these names are used when appropriate.

GALLIA ARE HERE: SEASON 1922-23

As the League of Ireland's second season commenced, the fledgling Free State was in trouble. The Treaty, signed in December 1921, had divided political opinion into the pros and antis. Five days after St James's Gate won the first FAI Cup, Anti-Treaty forces occupied the Four Courts, Ireland's legislative home, which was just across the Liffey from the Brewery where most of the Gate players worked. Fears of civil war prompted a general strike, and sectarian killings once again flared up in Belfast and Cork. The British demanded an end to the occupation of the Four Courts or suffer the consequences – the dissolution of the Free State. On June 28th, 1922 the Irish Army fired on the Four Courts with British artillery, thereby sparking the civil war that was to shape Ireland's politics for the rest of the century.

By the time the League of Ireland resumed, on Saturday, September 16th, the fighting in Dublin was over, although parts of the city, notably O'Connell Street and the Four Courts, were in ruins. Elsewhere the Anti-Treaty forces appeared to have been routed and were in retreat. The country returned to a fragile normality.

The League of Ireland had lost two clubs (Frankfort and the YMCA) but was up to twelve with the introduction of six more, including the first from outside the Pale, Athlone Town. The big game that first Saturday was Shels v Bohs in Ringsend, which ended 1-1. Champions St James's Gate won 3-1 in Athlone, while Shamrock Rovers lost at home to fellow new boys Shelbourne United. Bohemians were the early pace-setters, clear of the pack by the time they met Shamrock Rovers in October. In a foretaste of one of the League's fiercest rivalries, Rovers won 2-0 and never looked back, recording an unbeaten run of 21 games that brought the first of many titles to the Milltown club.

Free State League of Ireland final table 1922-23:

	P	W	D	L	F	A	Pts
Shamrock Rovers	22	18	3	1	77	19	39
Shelbourne	22	15	4	3	72	14	34
Bohemians	22	14	4	4	72	23	32
Shelbourne United	22	12	3	7	43	37	27
St James's Gate	22	11	3	8	49	35	25
Athlone Town	22	11	3	8	46	33	25
Jacobs	22	6	8	8	38	34	20
Pioneers	22	8	3	11	38	65	19
Midland Athletic	22	7	2	13	30	68	16
Dublin United	22	4	3	15	30	70	11
Olympia	22	2	7	13	13	57	11
Rathmines Athletic	22	2	1	19	21	74	5

Northern Ireland called up Tom Farquharson, Cardiff City's Dublin-born goalkeeper, for the international against Scotland in March. The IFA had previously used five players born in the Republic and Farquharson, the sixth, would become only the second to make his debut since the split – the first being another goalkeeper, Frank Collins. Farquharson only got the call because Alfie Harland, the ex-Linfield keeper at Everton, lay concussed in a London hospital. Although Harland recovered, he would only earn one more cap, while Farquharson would establish himself as Ireland's No 1 and perhaps the finest custodian for either Ireland in the 1920s. Farquharson's chief rival was Elisha Scott, now in his tenth year as a professional. Scott would guard Northern Ireland's posts for a further six years, which would curtail Farquharson's international career. Otherwise the Dubliner might well have won more then the seven caps awarded by the IFA.

The big news down South was the visit of French side Gallia to Dublin. The French FA had made overtures to the Free State FA regarding a first international game but nothing had yet materialised. However, the French were actively supporting the Free State's bid for admission to FIFA, a French-inspired organisation established in 1904. The British Associations had joined in 1905 only to withdraw in 1920, rather than accept the membership of former belligerents from the Great War. FIFA was trying to entice the British to return, which placed the French FA in a quandary. The President of FIFA, the Frenchman Jules Rimet, while sympathetic to the Free State, knew that the admission of an association banned by the British Associations would hamper the bigger objective of getting them back on board.

Jules Rimet gave his name to the first World Cup, in honour of FIFA's attempts to organise a worldwide international football competition. By 1923 this dream was uppermost in his mind. If the British Associations adamantly stayed out, FIFA had nothing to lose in supporting the Free State, or indeed any other worthy applicant to boost membership. When the British nations pulled out in 1920, FIFA was left with 21 members. The aim was to increase that number leading up to the 1924 Olympic Games, after which the British Associations might be tempted to rejoin.

French lobbying on Ireland's behalf continued but, in the meantime, the French FA sanctioned a visit by one of their club sides, despite the ongoing civil war. Like the Troubles of the 1970s and 80s in Northern Ireland, the violence was sporadic and the Free State FA, like the IFA in that later period, used their persuasive powers to encourage sporting visits. And so the Athletic Club Gallia of Paris arrived to take their place in Irish history.

Gallia was not one of the leading clubs in France, though they had won the French Championship (or what passed for a championship) in 1905. They had not done much since, and were for that reason possibly ideal low-key visitors to a state that craved recognition. The reception accorded to the French side was akin to a visit by Brazil today. Gallia were scheduled to play two games, one against Bohemians and the other against a League of Ireland selection. The Free State FA initially intended to pick a team representing all of Ireland, but restricting it to a League of Ireland selection allowed the selectors to showcase the best of Free State soccer. The French FA demurred, given the delicate political nature of Irish soccer, so the Free State League team was renamed Pioneer FC Selected XI. In reality, it was the same eleven.

On Saturday, March 31st, Gallia played a 1-1 draw with Bohs at Dalymount Park. The following day, at the same venue, they drew 0-0 with the Pioneer XI. Sunday was in those times an unusual day for football – although it would become familiar – and it was interpreted as a slap in the face to the IFA, which insisted on playing weekend games on Saturdays. It would be eight more years before an Irish representative team would play at home on a Sunday. For the record, the side chosen by the Free State was: Frank Collins (Jacobs); Paddy Murphy (St James's Gate), Stephen Boyne (Jacobs); Ernie McKay (St James's Gate), Johnny McIlroy (Bohemians), Frank Connell (Shelbourne); John Sweeney (Athlone Town), Charlie Dowdall (St James's Gate), Ned Brooks (Bohemians), Bob Fullam (Shamrock Rovers), Christy Robinson (Bohemians). Gallia's visit set Ireland off on the road to international football.

There now arose a further complication in the already tangled mess of Irish soccer. Some Northern clubs had entered the FAI Cup, and one of these,

Alton United from Belfast, had advanced to the final by beating non-Leaguers Fordsons. Alton United were a Junior club from the Falls and District League, and from such humble roots they left their mark on Irish football history. Against the odds they beat favourites Shelbourne in the St Patrick's Day final. The Dublin press noted the private joy felt by the IFA in Belfast, that a local club had walked off with the biggest Cup prize within the Free State. Alton United's impact on Free State soccer was short lived and they would never defend the trophy. It would take another 66 years before the FAI Cup would cross the border again.

Meanwhile, the standoff between the Irish Football Association and the Free State FA remained unresolved. The IFA sought, and got, a ban on transfers and games between the 'breakaway' Association and the rest of the British Associations. However, cracks were appearing. The Welsh FA wrote to the Irish Football Association requesting permission for one of their clubs to play friendlies against Bohemians and Shelbourne. The IFA refused the request until 'those clubs were affiliated with the Irish Football Association'.

THE CONFERENCE

The first attempt to break the ice came from the IFA, whose council met on a cold Tuesday, eleven days before Christmas 1922 to request a meeting with their Free State counterparts. As a sweetener, Linfield FC offered to play a friendly in Dublin 'with a view to bringing about a return of the relations that once existed between Northern and Southern clubs'. Although these initiatives were welcomed in Dublin, the planned conference was doomed to failure before it even began.

By the end of 1922 the Football Association of the Irish Free State had been in existence for just over a year. In that time it had gained control of soccer in the 26 counties of the Free State as well as parts of Northern Ireland. The first season of the League of Ireland had been so successful that membership had increased. For all the troubles that had accompanied the partition of Ireland, it could be said that soccer had flourished both North and South. However, there was still the question of who actually controlled the game in the country. The Free State FA governed soccer in the South, which produced the unusual situation of the IFA not recognising the border while the Free State FA did.

So, when the IFA offered to negotiate, each side misread the other's intentions. The IFA sought reunification under Belfast authority, albeit with (minor) concessions to the South. The Free State FA had a different agenda and looked upon the meeting as confirming recognition of their separate Association.

For some reason, the Free State FA sat on the invitation over Christmas, which gave rise to much speculation. For example, the New Year's edition of the *Irish Independent* expressed the hope that 'all will be working under the one banner' adding, 'The new Football Association of Ireland ... had in its first year of existence shown wonderful results. It has, nevertheless, graciously lent its ear to the overtures from the North. With characteristic candour, the Northern critics aver that the game in Belfast and Ulster is in a parlous state, and that Dublin's help is needed, as well as the help of other provincial organisations affiliated to the new Football Association, if the North is to carry on.'

The idea that Northern Irish football was on its last legs was untrue, but it encouraged the sense that the IFA was coming cap in hand to plead for salvation. In fact, soccer in Northern Ireland was flourishing. The Irish League might only have had six clubs for seasons 1921-22 and 1922-23, but all six were, in most departments, stronger then the eight that formed the League of Ireland in its first season. Although crowd figures do not exist for either League, it can be assumed that attendances in the Irish League remained constant, while in the South they would be lower, given the poor state of most grounds in and around Dublin. The League of Ireland's initial eight clubs could boast an average attendance of possibly 8-10,000, while the Irish League could almost double that. In the absence of reliable attendances, these estimates will have to suffice.

There was also another consideration – international football. This was barred to the Free State FA, but a total of 50,000 spectators had attended the two games Northern Ireland had staged at Windsor Park since the split. The Free State would not better the 30,000 who packed Windsor Park in October 1921 for the visit of England until 35,000 saw the Free State take on Spain in December 1931. Northern Ireland's biggest pre-1939 home attendance would be 45,000 for the visit of Scotland in 1936. In short, Northern Ireland did not need the Free State clubs to survive, and its conciliatory overtures were misinterpreted in the South as weakness.

A possible reason for the delayed reply from the South was internal division on what course of action to take. They had two choices — stay out or rejoin. The latter option was surely the better for the Irish game as a whole, and should that be their direction then some concessions could be wrung from Belfast. Staying separate carried risks, though these were reduced by the first successful season of the League of Ireland. Eventually a conciliatory reply was sent, and the IFA duly despatched a delegation to Dublin for talks on Saturday, February 3rd, 1923 which would decide the future of the game in Ireland.

The Irish League table since the split:

1921-22	P	W	D	L	F	A	Pts
Linfield	10	7	3	0	18	6	17
Glentoran	10	5	3	2	14	7	13
Distillery	10	5	1	4	18	17	11
Glenavon	10	3	2	5	11	14	8
Queen's Island	10	3	2	5	9	16	8
Cliftonville	10	1	1	8	3	13	3

1922-23	P	W	D	L	F	A	Pts
Linfield	10	7	2	1	20	5	16
Queen's Island	10	5	2	3	17	21	12
Glentoran	10	4	3	3	14	9	11
Distillery	10	4	2	4	12	13	10
Cliftonville	10	2	2	6	11	19	6
Glenavon	10	2	1	7	12	19	5

STUPENDOUSLY IMPERTINENT

The train bearing the delegates from the North arrived in Amiens Street station to be greeted by an enthusiastic crowd, in addition to members of the Free State FA. Most of the Northern party were old friends and there was much laughter and backslapping as the parties headed for the Shelbourne Hotel, where a year earlier the constitution for the new Irish Free State had been drafted under the chairmanship of Michael Collins. It was a historical venue to try and heal the rift in Irish soccer. As always, at the request of the Northern delegates, the press were excluded.

The meeting, euphemistically described as 'of a harmonious nature', broke up in failure after three hours: 'The Conference between the representatives of the IFA Ltd, and the FAI failed to come to an agreement.' The Northern delegates had proposed: (1) The Southern portion of Ireland to be given more representation on the Council; (2) Dublin should have a fair share of international matches; (3) Council meetings should be held alternately in Belfast and Dublin.

The Free State's demands had hardened, however, and went way beyond those previously expressed. They had ten proposals of their own, which they kept up their sleeve, to be unleashed on the unsuspecting Northern delegates: (1) All clubs and other organisations having their headquarters within the Free State to be under the control of the Football Association of Ireland; (2) Any club or organisation with its headquarters outside the Irish Free State to be eligible for membership of the FAI on the usual conditions; (3) The Present IFA to become the North of Ireland Football Association or similarly named body; (4) The relations between the FAI and the North of Ireland FA to be, except as hereinafter provided, similar to the relations existing between the Football Association of England and the Army Association; (5) Except in competitions in which clubs from both Associations participate, the North of Ireland FA to have full control over all clubs and other organisations directly affiliated to it; (6) In competitions open to and participated in by clubs from the two Associations, and in all international matters, the controlling bodies to consist of representatives of the two Associations on a scale to be arranged; (7) Suspensions of clubs, organisations, players, officials, etc by the Assoc-iation to which they are affiliated to be recognised and maintained by the other Association within its jurisdiction; (8) All funds securing to other Associations, by reason of membership or competitors entirely within its own control to be the property of that Association; (9) All funds securing from competitions, etc dually controlled to be shared by the two Associations on a scale to be arranged; (10) The North of Ireland FA to have the right to nominate members on all international selection committees on a scale to be arranged.

Old friends or not, the IFA's proposals saw some lively exchanges:

Murphy (South): 'I, for one, would never agree to the entire control of football being run from Belfast as we might as well give up altogether.'

Wilton (North): 'Then what would be your suggestion?'

Murphy: 'Dual control!'

Wilton: 'The International Board has laid it down. There would be only one body recognised in Ireland.'

Murphy: 'We might as well be plain and straight in this business, and I wish to state that unless the headquarters be in Dublin, if there is one controlling body, we could not hold the clubs in the South we have got since leaving the IFA. They would go over at once to another game.'

When the Northern party were handed the South's counter-proposals the mood turned sour. Wilton glanced through them but hadn't got far before throwing them on the table.

'Impossible!' he said. 'There is not even a basis of discussion in them.'

And that was that. Wilton thanked his colleagues for keeping their tempers in check, dismissed the South's demands as 'stupendously impertinent', and insisted any future overtures must come from Dublin. Paragraphs (3) and (10) had particularly riled him: 'The IFA,' he said, 'with its forty years history, was to efface itself and its name in favour of a body two seasons old.'

RECRIMINATIONS

The *Belfast Telegraph* pointed the finger: 'Although it was only hoping against hope that the conference would produce harmony and agreement, the result at the same time comes more or less as a disappointment. There is no good blinking the fact that the political aspect dominates the position so much in Dublin that even had the Leinster delegates as individuals been willing to come to an understanding, the fear is entertained that they would have been obliged to sink their personal views. The IFA and the North are not responsible for the present partition in Association football, and those who are always crying about the evils of partition in other respects have deliberately brought about the partition in this important branch of sport, and Saturday's conference shows that they are deliberately perpetuating it.'

This was true. In political terms the Free State hoped to ignore the border while the opposite was true for the North. However, accusations of political interference did not go down well in the South. Chairman Harrison replied:

'There was no ground for that statement [of political interference], but, on the contrary, I consider that the IFA officials had come down in the interests of Belfast alone. We had acted in the interests of all Ireland, and went as far as we could go. The wish of the IFA to delegate their powers to local associations was a confession of their inability to govern and foster the game. The FAI purposely refrained from going into the grievances of the past. We came to the conference with practical proposals. With regard to the claim that the IFA's 40 years control of the game entitled them to anything, the FAI in its two years existence had spread the game farther than it ever before extended.'

Hopes of soccer union in Ireland were dashed and, in fact, the gap had widened. Paradoxically, the impasse would benefit the game both in the South and the North. The Irish League asked the bad boys to return to the fold, as they now needed a bigger, more competitive, league. Belfast Celtic, who had been expelled, were invited back on board. The club hesitated, but when it did return, in 1924-25, it dominated football north of the border until further crowd trouble forced them out for good.

Robert Murphy had represented the South's case with such force that the Free State FA recruited him as its chief negotiator. It was his efforts that led to the visit of Gallia, the supportive lobbying by the French FA within the corridors of FIFA, and eventually a first international match, against Italy in 1926. Before that, however, Irish soccer was given an unexpected opportunity on the world stage.

Lugh of the Long Arm: Season 1923-24

By the start of the League of Ireland's third season, the troubles in Ireland were practically over. The civil war terminated on May 24th and the infant nation began the process of establishing itself internationally. In these turbulent early 1920s, soccer broadly reflected the changes reshaping Ireland. From the patriotic zeal that had provoked the split, to the ending of hopes of a united Ireland, the people's game mirrored the events unfolding within the Free State. In September 1923 the Irish Free State was admitted to the League of Nations: a month earlier its Football Association had been admitted to FIFA.

FIFA's annual meeting convened in Geneva on Monday, May 21st, 1923. Delegates from 57 members would determine the admission of the Free State and Turkey, both of whom presented related problems (Turkish football was also divided between two associations, in Ankara and Constantinople).

The Free State's application presented particular difficulties. For one thing, England, Scotland, Wales and Ireland (IFA) were outside FIFA. Inside or out, however, the British — especially the Football Association — carried huge weight within FIFA. They could also influence the votes of Commonwealth Associations. Added to which, FIFA knew that an organisation shorn of its strongest members (England were perhaps the best side in the world, with Scotland not far behind) lacked credibility. Therefore, FIFA was bending over backwards to lure them back in. If the British said 'no', that would not be good for the Freestaters. And the British did say 'no'.

The following day the Irish press reported that the Freestaters' application had been rejected by 'a large majority'. In those days, newspapers relied on cablegrams and someone had goofed. It was left to the *Freeman's Journal* to clarify a cablegram from the Irish delegates: 'The Emergency Committee of the International Federation was ordered by the Congress to grant recognition before 1st Sept, on confirmation of the Free State status by the British Foreign Office.'

The confusion was understandable, as the Freestaters' application hung by a thread. The original message was suspected of stemming from a mischievous IFA source: 'No person intimately connected with the affairs of the FAI found any difficulty in solving the problem of the origin of the Geneva telegram. The two words "Dublin body" contained in its last paragraph gave the whole show away.'

The source of the first telegram was never unearthed, but if it had emanated from the IFA then it hinted at sour grapes. The British Associations had gone to the conference bent on discrediting the Freestaters. The English FA appeared tetchy. There was no hiding the fact that they regarded FIFA as an upstart body, in the same way that the IFA regarded the Free State FA. The Secretary of the (English) FA, Mr F J Wall, gave every impression of wanting to be anywhere else.

The Irish question, however, needed to be nipped in the bud. Wall presented FIFA with three grounds for rejection: The FA would not intervene in the Irish dispute; English clubs would not play those of the FAI; and admission of the Football Association of Ireland would be detrimental to the FA's own readmission.

These were high stakes. FIFA was faced with losing, perhaps permanently, the oldest associations and strongest teams. The Freestaters stressed their country's independence and that the FAI controlled the game within the 26 counties and parts of Northern Ireland. They cited the example of Canada, likewise a Dominion within the British Commonwealth, but also a member of FIFA since 1912. There followed a question and answer session, at the end of which FIFA recommended: (1) If the Irish Free State possessed the political status claimed by the delegates, the Federation would grant membership to its national Association; (2) The Federation would not allow the FAI to claim any membership within the Six County area, nor would it permit the Irish Football Association, Ltd to encroach on the Irish Free State territory; (3) Subject to satisfactory assurances on the first two parts, the Federation would continue its relationship with the Irish Football Association, Ltd and would admit the Football Association of Ireland to membership as the national Association of the Irish Free State. In the meantime, the Free State would be granted provisional membership, with full membership awarded before September 1st.

This was a victory against the odds. FIFA had backed the Free State, which could now anticipate international football. Almost immediately, offers of matches came from sympathetic nations – Italy, Switzerland, Norway, Finland and Sweden – but for the moment minds concentrated on the 1924 Olympic Games, which is where the Free State planned its international debut.

In August 1923 the Irish Free State became one of eleven newcomers joining FIFA. From Europe they were accompanied by Estonia, Latvia, Lithuania, Poland, Portugal, Romania and Turkey. Egypt became the first African member, and two powerhouses from South America also joined – Brazil and Uruguay. These eleven would soon be joined by Bulgaria, raising FIFA's membership to 68 by the time of the Olympic soccer tournament in Paris at the season's end.

Back home, the League of Ireland kicked off on the second Saturday in September with just ten teams. Dublin United and Olympia had failed to be re-elected, while Rathmines Athletic had folded. Dublin club Brooklyn were the only newcomers, and they quickly lost 1-5 to Shelbourne.

Shels and Bohs were the early pacesetters and when they met at Dalymount Park in October it was the Gypsies who topped the table, thanks to English centre-forward Dave Roberts. Thereafter Bohs were uncatchable, winning fifteen out of fifteen on their way to their first League of Ireland title.

Free State League of Ireland final table 1923-24:

	P	W	D	L	F	A	Pts
Bohemians	18	16	0	2	56	20	32
Shelbourne	18	13	2	3	55	21	28
Jacobs	18	11	2	5	36	21	24
Athlone Town	18	8	5	5	34	24	21
St James's Gate	18	9	2	7	38	27	20
Shelbourne United	18	8	3	7	30	31	19
Shamrock Rovers	18	7	3	8	35	32	17
Brooklyn	18	4	2	12	23	37	10
Pioneers	18	2	1	15	15	60	5
Midland Athletic	18	2	0	16	13	62	4

To ease tensions between North and South, two 'Olive Branch' games were played. Bohemians travelled to Belfast to play Linfield in December, while Glentoran came to Dublin to face Shelbourne. The Bohs agreed with their hosts to play annually for the Condor Cup, which remained on the soccer calendar until 1932, when the FAI stepped in to call a temporary halt.

On the international front, despite its new status the Free State struggled to find opponents whereas Northern Ireland still had the Home Internationals and the Irish League still had the Inter-League series. Regarding the coming Northern Ireland v England international in October, the *Irish Independent* on September 15th, 1923 noted that 'there are, roughly, 60 Irishmen registered in the four big English Leagues and the Scottish League Division 1. Of these, 31 assisted in their clubs' opening engagements.' Come the day, Northern Ireland enjoyed another famous win. Dubliner goalkeeper Tom Farquharson fumbled a corner for England's opener, but Billy Gillespie headed level and set up the winner for Queen's Island's Tom Croft.

In December the Welsh League accepted an invitation to play in Dublin. For the Welsh, this offered a welcome addition to their fixture list as they had only recently started competing in Inter-League games. The Welsh League, of course, was amateur, so it did not technically breach the suspension imposed by the British Associations. However, the side picked was far from amateur, with most of the players from the three Welsh clubs in the Football League. The Irish eleven comprised the best within the League of Ireland. It was the first chance for the South to pit themselves against quality opposition.

The selectors chose their team from a hastily arranged trial. Come Saturday, February 9th all other fixtures were cancelled and several Government officials were present. Val Harris, Shels' centre-half, would have captained the side but he could not play, so his place was taken by Bohs' young Johnny McIlroy. All the players, bar two, were from the Free State. Of the others, McIlroy was an Ulsterman and Dave Roberts was English. The team that lined up in front of a good crowd at Dalymount Park was: Frank Collins (Jacobs), Bertie Kerr (Bohemians), Stephen Boyne (Jacobs), Ernie McKay (St James's Gate), Johnny McIlroy (Bohemians), Mick Foley (Shelbourne, captain), Jimmy Harvey (Jacobs), Christy Robinson (Bohemians), Dave Roberts (Bohemians), Harry Willits (Bohemians), Jack Fagan (Shamrock Rovers).

The weather was miserable. The Irish tricolour and the Welsh flag were hoisted and the St James Brass and Reed Band played *Men of Harlech* and the *Soldier's Song*. The LOI wore green shirts with shamrocks, white shorts and orange stockings (in those days the Irish team up North wore St Patrick's blue, and would so until the 1930s).

Star of the match was 'Kruger' Fagan. Fagan had not had the best of seasons with Shamrock Rovers, who never really recovered from the sale of Bob Fullam and John Joe Flood to Leeds. From a Fagan cross, Ernie McKay shot the Irish into the lead after only two minutes, but moments later a mistake by Bertie Kerr allowed Jack Nock to equalise. Nock was one of four Cardiff City reserves in the Welsh side. Another, Jimmy Jones, put the visitors ahead before half-time. The home side levelled late in the second half when another cross by Fagan was headed home by Dave Roberts. With five minutes to go, Jack Kneeshaw fumbled a Fagan centre and Roberts bundled the ball into the net. A minute later Collins saved from Billy Taylor but could not hold the ball and Jimmy Jones tapped it in to make it 3-3, which was how it finished. The crowd ran on and shouldered off all the players they could find.

Hard on the heels of the Welsh League came Glasgow Celtic, the Scottish Cup holders. Another sell-out was expected. The match was conceived by the Olympic Organising Committee of the FAI to raise funds to compete in Paris in May. The Celtic game was used to try as many players as possible, leaving only three from the earlier match. The team was: Bill O'Hagan (Fordsons), Paddy Kavanagh (Shelbourne), Jack McCarthy (Bohemians), Ernie McKay (St James's Gate), Val Harris (Shelbourne, captain), Mick Foley (Shelbourne), Jack Simpson (Shelbourne), Alec Kirkland (Shamrock Rovers), Jim O'Flaherty (University College Dublin), Charlie Dowdall (St James's Gate), Jack Fagan (Shamrock Rovers).

A crowd of 22,000 crammed into Dalymount, enjoying brighter weather than that for the Inter-League game a fortnight earlier. Most of the 22 players on show were well known to the crowd but there was one on whom most attention was focused – Celtic's inside-forward Patsy Gallagher. Gallagher was then 30 and already a legend. Born in Donegal, he had been playing for Ireland since the end of the First World War and had won practically everything that could be won with Celtic. He alone could put an extra couple of thousand on the attendance.

Celtic, clad in their famous green hoops, lined up against the Irish in royal blue or, as it was diplomatically referred to, St Patrick's blue. After nine minutes Alec Thomson shot against a post and Joe Cassidy seized on the rebound to put Celtic ahead. The lead was doubled with a rocket from Andy McAtee. Celtic's 3-0 win was completed near the end when Cassidy added a second. The receipts from the game exceeded £1,000.

The season would be crowned by participating in the Olympic Games for the first time, with the Irish soccer team becoming the first independent Irish Olympians. Three months after returning home it briefly looked like they might play a full international too. The GAA had revived the Tailteann Games to coincide with the Olympics and invited athletes with a Celtic connection from around the world to participate. The Tailteann Games dated back to 632 BC and were organised by the High King of Ireland, Lugh of the Long arm, in honour of his mother Queen Tailte. France hoped to send a soccer side to Croke Park, but were rebuffed. The games took place in August 1924 with all sorts of sports bar two, soccer and rugby. So the opportunity to play its first full international was lost by the Free State FA through no fault of its own. It also set them on a collision course with the GAA which would endure well into the next century. It would take the old High King's games to bring the matter to the fore, once again, but Lugh of the Long arm would have been proud when eleven men walked out on a foreign field in May to launch Ireland on a world sporting stage, to continue the tradition he started all those years ago.

The 1924 Olympic Games

It was the newly formed Irish Olympic Council which extended an invitation to the Football Association of the Irish Free State to send a team to Paris. Soccer would be the opening event of the Games. Ideally, the team should have been all-Ireland, but this was impractical. The Northern body turned its back, and the South seized the chance to gain more international recognition. The team would be Irish, but from the Free State only, and all the players had to be amateur.

The selection process commenced in April with a series of trials. In total, 33 players were tried, from whom a squad of sixteen was chosen for the tournament: Paddy O'Reilly (Athlone Town), Jack McCarthy (Bohemians), Bertie Kerr (Bohemians), John Thomas (Bohemians), Tom Murphy (St James's Gate), Ernie McKay (St James's Gate), John Joe Dykes (Athlone Town), Tommy Muldoon (Athlone Town), Paddy Duncan (St James's Gate), Mickey Farrell (St James's Gate), Frank Ghent (Athlone Town), Johnny Murray (Bohemians), Dinny Hannon (Athlone Town), Charlie Dowdall (St James's Gate), Christy Robinson (Bohemians), Joe Kendrick (Brooklyn).

The players were waved off on Saturday, May 24th to embark on the first great adventure in Free State sport. They would be gone for two weeks and when they returned it would be to more cheering crowds. Their trainer, Charlie Harris, who would be associated with the Irish team for many years, said afterwards that the players did their best and Ireland should be proud of their conduct. It was a fitting tribute to a bunch of Irishmen who made friends wherever they went and set the standard for the Irish athletes to follow after they returned.

The 1924 Olympics were the biggest so far. There were 44 nations present, with 3,000 athletes and 124 events. The games would be famous for launching the acting career of American swimmer Johnny Weissmuller (who would find fame as *Tarzan*), Harold Abrahams' 100 metres win for Britain, later immortalised in the film *Chariots of Fire*, and for the unveiling of the official Olympic moto 'Citius, Altius, Fortius' (Faster, Higher, Stronger). The Games began on Sunday, May 25th with the soccer tournament.

Soccer at the Olympic 'summer' Games had always been the poor relation. There had been an unofficial soccer tournament at the first modern Games of 1896 in Athens but little is known about it. The 1900 tournament was merely a demonstration event outside the Games itself. Upton Park from Great Britain won first prize, but no medals were awarded as it was not an Olympic event.

The third modern Olympics were held in the United States in 1904. Again the soccer tournament was a demonstration event, but every Canadian of a certain age will tell you they won the gold medal for soccer thanks to Galt FC. Yet again there were no medals. There was an unofficial football tournament at the fourth modern Games in Athens in 1906 but this time medals were awarded. The gold medal went to Denmark, the silver to Turkey and the bronze to Greece.

The first real Olympic soccer tournament took place at the 1908 Olympics in London and involved eight teams. Great Britain won the gold, Denmark the silver and the Netherlands the bronze. Four years later, eleven teams took part and again Great Britain claimed gold, Denmark the silver and the Netherlands bronze. The next Olympics were held in 1920, fourteen teams participated, and the hosts, Belgium, won gold, albeit by default when the Czechs stormed off in protest at the referee. Spain took silver and the Dutch yet again the bronze.

The soccer tournament in these, the Eighth Olympic Games, would be the biggest yet, and was seen by FIFA as a dress rehearsal for a proposed 'Worlds Cup'. The Olympic soccer tournaments since the First World War had been dogged by controversy over what was condemned as 'shamateurism'. The Olympics had long held up the ideals of amateurism, but domestic soccer was relentlessly switching to professionalism, whose ethos was slowly creeping into the Olympic movement. Great Britain refused to send an amateur soccer team to the 1924 Games in protest at the shamateurism practised by others. Indeed, of the 22 teams taking part, at least half had a minimum of one professional player within their ranks. The Irish team was completely amateur.

The tournament would be staged on straight knock-out lines, which meant a preliminary round was needed to eliminate six teams. This would reduce the field to sixteen for the first round. All the teams were put in a 'hat' and Ireland were one of ten lucky sides to receive a bye into the first round. Their opponents would be Bulgaria, who had also enjoyed a bye. For both countries it would mark their debuts on the World stage.

Olympic Games   *Wednesday, May 28th, 1924*   *Paris*
BULGARIA (0) 0   IRELAND (0) 1
    Duncan 70

Ref: H Henriot (France)   *Colombes Stadium*   *1,659*

IRELAND (2-3-5)   BULGARIA (2-3-5)
Paddy O'Reilly (Athlone Town)   Petar Ivanov (Levski Sofia)
Bertie Kerr (Bohemians)   Aleksandr Hristov (Levski Sofia)
Jack McCarthy (Bohemians)   Simeon Yankov (Levski Sofia)
Ernie McKay (St James's Gate)   Ivan Radoev (Levski Sofia)
John Joe Dykes (Athlone Town)   Boian Bianov (Ticha Varna)
Tommy Muldoon (Athlone Town)   Geno Mateev (Levski Sofia)
Mickey Farrell (St James's Gate)   Dimitar Mutafchiev (Levski Sofia)
Dinny Hannon (Athlone Town)   Nikola Mutafchiev (Levski Sofia)
Paddy Duncan (St James's Gate)   Todor Vladimirov (Slavia Sofia)
Joe Kendrick (Brooklyn)   Konstantin Maznikov (Levski Sofia)
Johnny Murray (Bohemians)   Kiril Iovovich (Levski Sofia)

MANAGERS: Committee   Leopold Nitsch
CAPTAINS: John Joe Dykes   Todor Vladimirov

The early history of Bulgarian football was in many ways similar to that of the Freestaters who lined up against them in an eerily empty Colombes Stadium. Having gained their independence from the Ottoman Empire in 1908, Bulgaria endured years of turmoil in which soccer was given a low priority. Bulgaria were one of the last nations to be admitted to FIFA, joining just in time for the 1924 Games and, like the Irishmen they faced, their squad was entirely amateur.

Their coach was an Austrian, Leopold Nitsch. While journeying to Paris the team stopped off in Vienna to play Austria, in what would be Bulgaria's first ever international. Austria, one of the top teams in Europe at the time, would not send a team to the Olympics and extended little pity on their visitors. A full-strength Austrian side thrashed them 6-0. Nine of the beaten Bulgarians would face the Irish, with Vladimirov, like Athlone's Dykes, captaining his side on his debut. Bulgaria's top club at that time was Levski, who provided most of the players.

The Irish selectors faced the problem of where to play Paddy Duncan. Popularly known as 'Dirty', Duncan was one of the most versatile players in the League at a time when positions were more or less rigid. The Irish side basically picked itself but Duncan's abilities in any position could not be ignored. He had played in attack and defence in the trial games preceding the Games and was used anywhere and everywhere for his club, St James's Gate. This season he had mainly occupied the left-half position for the Brewery team but he was also an effective forward. The selectors decided to let him lead the attack, with Dinny Hannon dropping back to inside-left, allowing Tommy Muldoon to come in at left-half.

As for the game itself it was, frankly, poor. Bulgaria started the better and caused O'Reilly problems in the Irish goal. However they lacked a finisher and by half-time the Irish defence had their opponents' measure. Ireland's attacks were sporadic in that opening period and Ivanov didn't have any serious shot to save.

The second half saw Ireland began on the offensive and bombard Ivanov's goal. The Bulgarian goalkeeper never buckled and single-handedly saved his side from a heavier defeat.

The only goal, when it came, was fortuitous. When Murray's cross found Duncan, the centre-forward appeared to be well offside as he banged the ball into the net. The aggrieved Bulgarians lost their discipline after that and it wasn't long before the referee gave a penalty-kick to Ireland. Dinny Hannon, who had been capped at both amateur and senior level by Ireland, took the spot-kick but failed to beat Ivanov, despite being initially reprieved and having a retake.

The *Irish Times* noted pessimistically: 'On this afternoon's display the opinion was expressed that the Irishmen would stand little chance against the crack teams in the competition.'

Olympic Games   *Monday, June 2nd, 1924*   *Paris*
NETHERLANDS (1) 2   IRELAND (1) 1 (aet)
Formenoy 6, 104   Ghent 32
Ref: H Retschury (Austria)   *Pershing Stadium*   500

IRELAND (2-3-5)	NETHERLANDS (2-3-5)
Paddy O'Reilly (Athlone Town)	Gejus van der Meulen (HFC)
Bertie Kerr (Bohemians)	Harry Denis (HBS)
Jack McCarthy (Bohemians)	Hans Tetzner (Be Quick Gr.)
Ernie McKay (St James's Gate)	Andre Le Fevre (Kampong)
John Joe Dykes (Athlone Town)	Evert van Linge (Be Quick Gr.)
Tommy Muldoon (Athlone Town	Peer Krom (RCH)
Mickey Farrell (St James's Gate)	Ber Groosjohan (VOC)
Dinny Hannon (Athlone Town)	Ok Formenoy (Sparta)
Paddy Duncan (St James's Gate)	Joop ter Beek (NAC)
Frank Ghent (Athlone Town)	Gerrit Visser (Stormvogels)
Johnny Murray (Bohemians)	Jan de Natris (Ajax)

MANAGERS: Committee   Bill Townley
CAPTAINS: John Joe Dykes   Harry Denis

Of the 22 starters, the soccer tournament was now down to eight survivors. There was some confusion as to the identity of Ireland's opponents in the quarter-finals. Believing that they would face the winner of the Sweden v Belgium tie, the Irish squad watched in horror as the Swedes tore the Belgians apart. However, that was not how it worked. Instead, all eight teams were put in a 'hat' again and paired off again. Ireland came out with the Netherlands, who had won the bronze medal at each of the previous three Olympic Games.

This was an experienced Dutch side. Three of the team that faced Ireland had been part of the Dutch squad at the previous Olympics and only two of their players were now making their debuts – Ocker 'Ok' Formenoy and Joop ter Beek. The Dutch, like the Irish, had received a bye into the first round where they slaughtered Romania 6-0. Surprisingly, Cor Pijl, who scored four goals, and Albert Snock-Hurgronje, who got another, were dropped in favour of the two debutants. Again, the team that faced Ireland was composed entirely of amateurs.

In the closing stages of the ill-tempered Bulgaria match, Joe Kendrick had received a knock which, although not serious enough to warrant him leaving the field at the time, was serious enough for the selectors to rest him now. His natural replacement was Charlie Dowdall but for some reason the selectors opted for winger Frank Ghent at inside-left. This meant that there were now five Athlone Town players in the eleven, which was the most one club would ever provide for Ireland.

In time, the Dutch would become known for their passing game, which had people in the 1970s raving about 'total football'. However, the passing game was nothing new to the Dutch. They had been playing that way since their international debut in 1905. To the untrained eye, their game lacked a clinical finish. To the Irish players, used to a different philosophy, their opponents' keep-ball tactics were frustrating and misunderstood. It only took the Dutch six minutes to drag the Irish defenders out of position and allow Ok Formenoy to beat O'Reilly. The Irish responded with an equaliser when a corner from Farrell was put away at the far post by Ghent.

The Dutch dominated the second half but never really got behind the Irish defence as they had done for the opening goal. In fact there were few chances, and when the referee blew at the end of 90 minutes it meant extra time for only the fourth time in Olympic history. It was a first for Ireland. With both sets of players being amateur, the prospects for a thrilling half-hour were slim. The Dutch secured the decisive goal just before the turnaround from what was described as a soft free-kick. The rest of the game petered out and the Dutch progressed to their fourth semi-finals in a row.

Ireland were out of the competition but far from disgraced. With most teams invited to stay on until the final, Free State officials were busy networking. With Estonia also idle, a friendly was hastily arranged for the following day. The Colombes Stadium was free and permission given to play there. A bigger then expected crowd turned up.

Friendly	*Tuesday, June 4th, 1924*	*Paris*
ESTONIA (1) 1	IRISH FREE STATE (1) 3	
Upraus 37	Duncan 15, Robinson 48, Ghent 69	
Ref: Y Mohamed (Egypt)	*Colombes Stadium*	*3,000*

IRISH FREE STATE (2-3-5)
Paddy O'Reilly (Athlone Town)
Tom Murphy (St James's Gate)
Jack McCarthy (Bohemians)
John Thomas (Bohemians)
John Joe Dykes (Athlone Town)
Tommy Muldoon (Athlone Town)
Christy Robinson (Bohemians)
Frank Ghent (Athlone Town)
Paddy Duncan (St James's Gate)
Charlie Dowdall (St James's Gate)
Johnny Murray (Bohemians)

MANAGERS: Committee
CAPTAINS: John Joe Dykes

ESTONIA (2-3-5)
Evald Tipner (Sport Tallinn)
Arnold Pihlak (Kalev Tallinn)
Otto Silber (Tallinna JK)
Hugo Vali (Kalev Tallinn)
Bernhard Rein (Sport Tallinn)
Harald Kaarman (Kalev Tallinn)
Alfei Jurgenson (Tallinna JK)
Voldemar Roks (Kalev Tallinn)
Eduard Ellman-Eelma (Kalev Tallinn)
Oskar Upraus (Sport Tallinn)
Ernst Joll (Kalev Tallinn)

Ferenc Konya
Oskar Upraus

Understandably the game was largely ignored by the press corps, which was more interested in the sensational Uruguay team from South America. The few reports covering the Ireland game gave conflicting accounts of the teams and scorers for Ireland but fresh research sheds some light on one of the mysteries that had bugged Irish soccer historians for many a year.

The Irish used the Estonia match to give a run out to the rest of the squad. It was originally thought that Mickey Farrell had scored Ireland's second goal, even though he was not in the side! The third goal had also been credited to Tommy Muldoon but has now been given to Frank Ghent.

This was Estonia's seventh defeat from the twelve internationals they had played. Estonia would continue to play international football until the Soviet Union occupied the three Baltic States in 1940. Estonia, who regained their independence in 1991, would not play Ireland again for another 76 years.

The Free State's first Olympians were back home before the rest of the Irish Olympic team headed out for Paris. There was to be a further treat in store for the FAI when the USA side popped in for a visit before their voyage home across the Atlantic.

Friendly	*Saturday, June 14th, 1924*	*Dublin*
IRISH FREE STATE (2) 3	UNITED STATES (1) 1	
Brooks (3)	Rhody	
Ref: J Kelly (Dublin)	*Dalymount Park*	*5,000*

IRISH FREE STATE (2-3-5)	UNITED STATES (2-3-5)
Frank Collins (Jacobs)	Jimmy Douglas (Newark Skeeters)
Bertie Kerr (Bohemians)	James Mulholland (Paterson Scott)
Tom Murphy (St James's Gate)	Art Rudd (Philadelphia Fleischer Yarn)
John Thomas (Bohemians)	Bill Demko (Philadelphia Fleischer Yarn)
Paddy Duncan (St James's Gate)	Ray Hornberger (Philadelphia Disston)
Tommy Muldoon (Athlone Town)	Fred O'Connor (Lynn Gas & Electric)
Mickey Farrell (St James's Gate)	Irving Davis (Philadelphia Fairhill)
Tony Hunston (Brooklyn)	Herb Wells (Philadelphia Fleischer Yarn)
Ned Brooks (Bohemians)	Andy Stradan (Philadelphia Fleischer Yarn)
Charlie Dowdall (St James's Gate)	Jim Rhody (Kearny Erie)
Johnny Murray (Bohemians)	Ed Hart (St. Louis St Matthew's)

MANAGERS: Committee   George Collins
CAPTAINS: Bertie Kerr   Andy Stradan

Coming, as it did, in the Irish soccer close season, the match against the USA did not attract the big crowd expected for the Free State's first game in Dublin. Given the reception received on their return to Ireland, this is surprising. A crowd of 5,000 turned up on a fine day, paying receipts of £240.

Like Ireland, the USA had been forging contacts in Paris and received two invites. One came from Poland, who they played in Warsaw on the Wednesday, coming away with a 3-2 win. In Dublin their team showed two changes from Warsaw for what would be the Americans' eighth international.

Ireland's team comprised amateurs returned from the Olympics and some who might have been there. Eight of the team had played in Paris, with Collins, Hunston and Brooks added. Of these, perhaps the most unfortunate was Ned Brooks. Having missed most of the season through injury, Brooks had made a comeback in the Shield competition, scoring eleven goals in nine games, including the extra-time winner in the test game with Shels. Work commitments had kept him from going to the Olympics and misfortune would deny him a Free State cap in 1926, but this was to be his finest hour.

Both teams entered the field behind their national flags, Ireland's being carried by Frank Collins. The American side looked physically intimidating but perhaps lacked understanding of the finer points of the game. Ireland, in that regard, were superior throughout. An early mistake by Rudd allowed Brooks to shoot home via a post. An eighteen-yard blaster gave him his second before Rhody pulled one back for the visitors after 43 minutes with a pot shot which Collins saw late and dropped over the line. Five minutes after the break, a corner was cleared out to Brooks, who lobbed the ball in over a cluster of players to become the first man to score a hat-trick for an Irish Free State team. The *Irish Independent* on the Monday lamented the fact that Brooks had not been available in Paris: 'To Brooks fell the honours of the day,' it wrote. 'It seemed a pity that this very resourceful forward was unable to help his country in the Olympic tournament.' The same could be said when he was missing for Ireland's first game, in Italy, in 1926.

A NATION IN THE NATIONAL CONTROL OF FOOTBALL

The stand-off between the IFA and the FAI entered a new phase. The former now proposed a Dublin Football Association under the control of the IFA. A novel approach, certainly, but one which caused more harm then good in terms of a united Ireland association. Writing in the *Irish Independent*, TD Austin Mac Caba summed up the Southern response: '"Northern" Ireland … not being self-governing, or even a geographical unit, has no status in the international sense and it is only because the body governing locally calls itself the IFA that it is recognised even in the "Kingdom" championships.'

Mr Mac Caba described Northern Ireland as 'Northern' Ireland and added that the IFA would 'have to content itself with a very inferior status to that of the FAI'. His solution was that the IFA and FAI should, under other names, be the governing bodies in Northern Ireland and the Free State respectively, and that a new body to be called, for example, the National FA should be created to cater for the whole country and represent Ireland, 'assuming they are open to her under the new conditions in the "Kingdom" competitions.'

It was all empty talk. The split had widened with the Irish Free State joining FIFA. At the close of the 1922-23 season the Irish League reported a loss of £234. Despite hopes of a possible return of 'the Dublin clubs' and Belfast Celtic, after a vote only Larne, Barn and Ards were admitted.

Nevertheless, in June 1923 Free State FA delegates met with the IFA. The proceedings were conducted *in camera* and no reports of what transpired were ever published. It is thought that some Dublin clubs wanted to rejoin the Northern body, and representatives of Bohemians went north for discussions. This was a worrying development for the Free State FA, but a month later the English FA surprisingly agreed to recognise the Irish Free State FA. This freed up the possibility of mutual transfers, although an application for membership of the International Board was refused. International matches with British opponents were therefore still off-limits, though that restriction did not apply to clubs. Free State clubs quickly sought fixtures with English ones.

The English FA's initiative seemed to break the logjam. Scotland and Wales soon followed and recognised the Free State FA. The IFA, too, relented and lifted certain restrictions on the breakaway body. There remained one stumbling block however – international matches. As far as the International Board (England, Scotland, Wales and Ireland) were concerned, there was only one team in Ireland, and the IFA picked it.

On October 18th, 1923, a conference in Liverpool tried to resolve the matter. The two Irish Associations, plus those from England, Scotland and Wales tossed around the arguments and concluded that the problem was purely an Irish affair which could only be settled between the IFA and the Free State FA. As there could only be one Irish team recognised by the International Board, its composition should be decided by the Irish themselves.

In December the two parties met to settle bilaterally the question of the Irish team. The South proposed: 'In order that the whole of Ireland may be represented in international matches with England, Scotland and Wales, the Free State FA is prepared to join with the Northern Association in setting up a Selection Committee, with equal representation from the two Irish associations, to control the games. It will also agree as regards Ireland's home international matches, that they should be played alternately in Northern Ireland and the Irish Free State.'

The IFA's Captain Wilton, in theory an advocate of a united Irish side, saw only obstacles: 'If any agreement were come to regarding the playing of Free State players in International matches, the other countries would ask some time, if not immediately, what right the Irish Football Association had to play players who were not under their control.' There followed a debate about the status of players born in the Irish Free State playing for what was essentially a Northern Ireland team. This argument would continue for many years to come. Of more immediate concern was the fact that the last Irish side (against England, in Belfast, in October 1923) contained three players born in what was now the Free State – Tom Farquharson, 'Bert' Smith, and Billy Gillespie. Considering that all three had played their part in the first win over England since the First World War, and Billy Gillespie was possibly the best Irish player around, it was a difficult to consider leaving them out.

The talks then ventured into realms in which the FAI would become proficient but which the IFA chose to ignore – players born abroad of Irish parents. The IFA's existing policy was to accept them, as shown by the ex-Belfast Celtic player Louis Bookman. Bookman, whose real name was Buckhalter, was born in Lithuania but his family had moved to Ireland when he was young and had started his football career with Shelbourne. His case brought the argument into sharp focus.

Then there was the idea of a future united 'Irish League', although that was a matter for the Irish League and the League of Ireland controlling bodies.

A Joint Anxiety

With most disputes, one side desires a settlement more than the other. But who was the driving force in this one? 'There is a joint anxiety,' was the answer. The clubs might have wanted harmony, but the apparent sticking point – control of Irish international matches – was out of their hands.

In February 1924 Glentoran, six-times Irish League champions, announced themselves on the verge of extinction, whereupon the Irish League granted a loan of £100 to keep them afloat. North and South interpreted this differently. The local explanation was 'unemployment and the unsettled conditions in the city'. Viewed from Dublin, 'the chief reason for the slump is the lack of virile competition due to the absence of Southern clubs.' Faced with such sharp divergence, hopes for a comprehensive agreement appeared slim.

The two parties met on Saturday, March 8th, 1924 at the IFA headquarters in Belfast. The South sought equal representation on a joint Irish executive for Irish international matches. The North took a wider view: discussions should not be confined to 'the question of Internationals, but aim at a larger degree of unity'. In summary, the IFA proposed: (1) The appointment of a committee to control Internationals, the IFA and the Free State FA to be equally represented thereon with the existing chairman of the IFA (Captain Wilton) as chairman. The question of venues shall be decided by this committee; (2) The appointment of a committee with similar equal representation to control all-Ireland senior and junior cup competitions; (3) The formation of an Irish Football Association with representation on a club basis to deal with matters which are outside the jurisdiction of divisional associations.

To the surprise of many, the Free State delegates agreed to everything. All that remained was ratification by the Free State FA, whereupon Ireland would again have a united Irish soccer team. The *Irish Times* crowed: 'There is … little doubt but that a complete healing of the breach will be announced in a very short time.'

The Free State FA convened on Wednesday, March 19th. Robert Murphy, praised for his role in the aborted first meeting in 1923, had been absent from the Belfast talks eleven days earlier. He now insisted that the IFA proposal (1) – permanent IFA chairmanship of an international selection committee – was unacceptable. He preferred alternating chairmanships: 'The present position is that we are reverting to the status of a subordinate divisional association. We have achieved too much to cast that lightly aside.'

This left the chairman of the Belfast delegation, J F Harrison, in an invidious position: 'The proposals should be regarded in the light of the good of the game in the entire country and not from a provincial aspect. I promised the Northern delegates to urge the adoption of the settlement and I would be false to my word if I hesitated to do so.' A show of hands backed Murphy. Peace with the North was torn up. In October, Harrison resigned as Chairman of the Free State FA.

A FOOTBALLING CRUX

When the IFA members waved goodbye to their Southern colleagues they had every reason to expect quick ratification in Dublin. The IFA would regain control of soccer in Ireland and the Free State FA would play its part by controlling the game within its perimeter. The IFA busied itself preparing for an Irish League featuring Linfield and Shelbourne, Glentoran and Bohemians, and Cliftonville and Shamrock Rovers.

Therefore it was with shock and dismay that they received a letter from the Free State FA, refusing to ratify without alternate chairmanship of the selection committee. Wilton would not budge. After all, the March 8th agreement had been all but rubber stamped by both parties. The *Freeman's Journal* was not in conciliatory mood:

'Everyone seems to have lost sight of the fact that the FA of the Irish Free State is a separate legally constituted and internationally recognised body with rights and privileges equal to, and in one respect at least, greater than are possessed by the IFA itself. It fought a long and anxious fight to secure them. Its most aggressive opponent was the IFA. In the face of these facts it passes all understanding how any one could conceive that in its hour of triumph it should obliterate its identity, cast away its hard-won distinctions, step down from its international position and merge itself in another organisation and become an appendage thereto.'

Timing, of course, was at the heart of the whole mess. The soccer split had occurred *before* the political split, which only complicated what was otherwise a simple internal dispute within Irish football circles. When the IFA had first sought to patch matters up, in 1923, the Free State was enjoying its first season. This, coupled with the belief that the Northern body had come cap in hand, had sunk the first conference before it began. This second attempt was as close as the two sides would ever come to unity, but the Irish Free State had been admitted to FIFA, which promised senior internationals. The Olympic Games, although amateur, would provide fixtures with other nations and open the door to top club competition. As things stood, despite being denied fixtures against England, Scotland and Wales, the future looked rosy. So much so, that Belfast were the only serious proponents of a united football Association in Ireland. Consequently, the prevailing attitude from Dublin of 'go it alone' was stronger than ever. This was tacitly admitted by the Free State Council on Thursday, April 20th, 1924: 'I believe that some members of the Council did not want any settlement.'

As for the English FA, in the face of the latest request from the Free State FA for international matches, their reply was terse – pending settlement, England would only play one game a year against Ireland, and that would be under control of the IFA.

By the time of the IFA's next AGM, in May 1925, the dispute merited not a word. The split was permanent. In the meantime, the Free State FA sent out feelers to other associations for international fixtures and the French FA appeared to be on the verge of accepting.

Munster: Season 1924-25

The 1924-25 season began with the visit of South Africa. The President of the South African FA had backed the Free State's bid to join FIFA, and when their team toured Europe in August and September 1924 Dublin was pencilled in. This was what the Irish Free State craved – a full international in Dublin – but it was not to be. The South Africans began their tour in late August. This was too early for the Free State as most of its English-based players were barely back in training. Instead, up stepped Bohemians to take on the tourists, despite being themselves only a week in training. The burly South Africans won 4-2 (Ned Brooks scoring twice for Bohs). A month later they were back in Ireland to play an IFA XI in Belfast (which they also won, 2-1. Frank Rushe, the ex-Shels player, scored for the IFA XI). The South Africans therefore entered the record books as the first international side to play in both Irelands.

The League of Ireland began on September 6th, with Tony Houston of St James's Gate scoring its first goal in a 3-3 draw with Bohs. Shamrock Rovers beat Jacobs 4-1 and were clearly the team to beat. In fact, nobody could beat them and they completed the second League and FAI Cup double since the LOI began. Rovers also won the Shield competition but were denied a chance of adding the Leinster Senior Cup. This was still an important trophy, yet it kicked off in January without the League of Ireland clubs, who had been asked to play in the first round instead of receiving a bye. They stomped out in protest. The April final saw Brideville beat Glasnevin with the only goal. This season was also special for soccer in Cork. Fordsons became the first side from Munster to enter the League of Ireland, the start of a long association between province and league.

Free State League of Ireland final table 1924-25:

	P	W	D	L	F	A	Pts
Shamrock Rovers	18	13	5	0	67	12	31
Bohemians	18	11	6	1	40	11	28
Shelbourne	18	12	3	3	55	20	27
Fordsons	18	10	1	7	35	32	21
Jacobs	18	8	1	9	36	35	17
St James's Gate	18	5	7	6	30	36	17
Athlone Town	18	5	4	9	15	32	14
Brooklyn	18	4	3	11	24	57	11
Bray Unknowns	18	3	3	12	21	44	9
Pioneers	18	2	1	15	21	65	5

1924-25 saw the GAA flex its muscles by banning Joe Stynes for playing 'foreign games'. Stynes had won a Gaelic football All-Ireland medal for Dublin against Kerry in 1923, but he was also a regular for the Bohs' soccer team. One might think the GAA's stance would soften in the wake of Irish independence, but it would persist for over half a century and – unlike the struggle between the Free State FA and the IFA – there would be no negotiations. Not until Kevin Moran played soccer for Ireland in 1980 was the issue of playing both Gaelic and soccer finally laid to rest. In the meantime, many of Ireland's greatest sportsmen were barred from playing a game that, more than most, expressed Irish identity worldwide. The GAA shot themselves in the foot by denying talented soccer players the chance to enhance their sport.

The long-awaited first international never materialised. The French were too busy with internal scandals and their own fixtures to find time for Ireland. However, the return visit of the Welsh League in March proved welcome. Again, the Free State selectors tried out new players. Only two of those who had drawn 3-3 the previous season were included. The team was: Paddy Walsh (Shelbourne), Alec Kirkland (Shamrock Rovers), Paddy Kavanagh (Shelbourne), Ernie McKay (St James's Gate), John Joe Dykes (Athlone Town), Ned Marlowe (Shamrock Rovers), John Joe Flood (Shamrock Rovers), Paddy Kelly (Fordsons), Billy Farrell (Shamrock Rovers), Dave Roberts (Bohemians), Johnny Murray (Bohemians).

The Welsh League won 2-1. The *Irish Times* noted: 'If the Irish Rugby Football Union were to manage the game of Rugby football in this country on lines similar to those which characterise the management of the sister game of Association football, we would not be in the position to-day to chronicle the splendid victory of the Irish XV at Belfast on Saturday [Ireland had beaten Wales 19-3 at Ravenhill the same day]. Instead of applying themselves wholeheartedly to the development of the game over which they have control, as do the IRFU, the governing bodies of Association football are divided into two camps, disputing over such trifles as "alternate chairmen", casting votes, the allocation of funds and so forth, while the standard of Soccer – never on a very high plane in Ireland – is deteriorating all over the country.'

That said, another big crowd turned up at Dalymount Park. Dave Roberts gave the hosts the lead, only for Fred Dent to equalise and William Whitehead to secure the winner, five minutes into the second half. The Welsh then traveled south to play a Munster XI at Victoria Cross, winning 2-0.

In March, both Irish Associations staged their respective Cup finals. On St Patrick's Day, Shamrock Rovers beat Shelbourne in a classic. Four days later, Distillery defeated Glentoran at Solitude, in front of a small crowd that produced receipts of £500. The FAI final had generated £1,250 and was the first occasion the South's returns had outshone those up North. In April, the second Condor Cup match was played between Bohemians and Linfield, which the Dublin club won 2-0.

The FA Cup final, in its third season at Wembley, featured two players born in the Free State, Billy Gillespie for Sheffield United and Tom Farquharson for Cardiff City – the first time since the split that Irish players had featured in the final. To top it all, Gillespie captained his side to a 1-0 win. On the same day, at Richmond Road, Dublin, a young Shamrock Rovers reserve was making waves in the Metropolitan Cup. Jimmy Dunne scored four in Rovers' 6-3 win over Drumcondra and would, in time, become a legend for both Ireland and Sheffield United.

Sixteen: Season 1925-26

By the end of the 1924-25 season the Free State FA felt emboldened to demand from the IFA a share of the gate receipts from international matches. Not suprisingly, this was rebuffed. Neither side was willing to give ground, and this remained the case for many years as both sides strengthened their spheres of influence. One more push would sever ties completely. Article 16 of the Irish Football Association charter was incongruous. It included Leinster and Munster as selectors for the IFA. It was not until May 1925 that they were removed, even though the Article began with the words 'For the government of football in Ireland'.

In 1925-26 the Free State League kicked off in late August with Shamrock Rovers and Fordsons setting the early pace with four wins out of four. In October, the two sides met at St James's Park and a crowd of 18,000 saw Rovers win 3-0, Bob Fullam scoring twice.

Three days later, Fordsons were awarded two points, thanks to the Free State's own Rule 16, when a protest against Bohemians' 2-0 win in Cork was upheld. Shamrock Rovers' 26-game undefeated run in the League was terminated by Shelbourne when a free-kick by 'Boxer' Foley gave the Reds a 3-2 win. Shels then went undefeated for the rest of the season to claim their first League of Ireland title.

Free State League of Ireland final table 1925-26:

	P	W	D	L	F	A	Pts.
Shelbourne	18	14	3	1	65	23	31
Shamrock Rovers	18	13	3	2	62	21	29
Fordsons	18	12	1	5	58	31	*27
Bohemians	18	10	2	6	50	28	*20
Jacobs	18	7	4	7	40	48	18
Brideville	18	6	4	8	36	53	16
Athlone Town	18	7	1	10	46	56	15
St James's Gate	18	4	3	11	33	48	11
Bray Unknowns	18	4	3	11	34	55	11
Pioneers	18	1	0	17	21	82	2

* Fordsons awarded two points from their 0-2 defeat by Bohemians, who were deducted two points.

Saturday, November 7th was memorable for soccer south of the border. The Free State League was in Swansea to play a third match against their Welsh counterparts. Naturally, players from Shelbourne and Shamrock Rovers dominated the line-up: Frank Collins (Jacobs), Sam Russell (Shelbourne), Frank Brady (Fordsons), Ernie McKay (St James's Gate), Val Harris (Shelbourne), Mick Foley (Shelbourne), Paddy Robinson (Shelbourne), John Joe Flood (Shamrock Rovers), Billy Farrell (Shamrock Rovers), Bob Fullam (Shamrock Rovers), Jack Fagan (Shamrock Rovers).

Despite a boggy pitch it was a stirring game. Jock Patterson, a Scot, gave the 'Welsh' the lead, which was cancelled out by Bob Fullam. Patterson again put the home side ahead, but eight minutes from time John Joe Flood raced through to bring the scores level again.

That same day, Dublin hosted the first meeting since the split of representative sides from the Free State and Northern Ireland. The Northern Ireland Intermediate League travelled to Dalymount Park to meet the Leinster Senior League. Both sides represented the reserve Leagues of the IFA and the Free State FA. The teams on this historic occasion were:

Leinster Senior League: J Ronan (St James's Gate), Ballantine (Dundalk), Magill (Chapelizod), J Mulvanny (Edenville), O'Neill (Dundalk), P Maxwell (Drumcondra), Doyle (Shelbourne), C Robinson (Bendigo), Bolton (Chapelizod), Geary (UCD), Butler (Shamrock Rovers).

Northern Ireland Intermediate League: McMinn (Brantwood), Scott (Woodburn), Flack (Crusaders), Coke (Brantwood), Gee (Brantwood), Boyce (Crusaders), Blair (Ballyclare Comrades), Young (Willowfield), Johnston (Woodburn), Croft (Linfield Reserves), McCaw (Brantwood).

The North won 4-0 through two goals from Young, one from Thompson, and an own-goal. The Leinster League side might well have included Jimmy

Dunne, the twenty-year-old Shamrock Rovers forward, but he had signed for Third Division (North) New Brighton two days earlier.

Elsewhere on a busy day, a hat-trick by Newry's Harry McCracken was not enough for Northern Ireland amateurs, who went down 4-6 to England in Maidstone, Kent. Harry Willits of Bohemians saw his penalty saved in Bohs' 2-1 win in Athlone, while Cardiff's Tom Farquharson saved a penalty in his side's 5-2 home win over Leicester.

In December the Irish League requested a match with the Free State. As the *Irish Independent* noted: 'the news [was] hailed with universal satisfaction.' As ever, there were problems. The Irish League proposed February 13th or March 13th, or else the first available Saturday in April. February was out, as it clashed with the Northern Ireland v Wales international, as well the fourth round of the Leinster Senior Cup. The March date was also unsuitable, as the FAI Cup final was scheduled for St Patrick's Day, and April was also hectic. However, as this was an offer hard to turn down, it was decided to risk the March date, despite certain players possibly playing two or three tough games in a week. The Shamrock Rovers trio of 'Kruger' Fagan, John Joe Flood and Bob Fullam would play in all three games, with six others playing in two.

The Inter-League match was first of the three, and it provoked a row over shirts. The Free State League, when confirming the fixture, added that Captain Albert Prince-Cox of England had been approached to referee, and that they intended playing in green with gold shamrocks. The Irish League, when asked to change, replied that they had a stock of green jerseys and nothing else. In the event, the Free State League played in white with a green stripe, while the Irish League turned out in green with a white shamrock.

An 'excursion' train from Belfast bore a large following to Dalymount Park, which was bursting at the seams to squeeze in 20,000 (four days later, 25,000 packed the stadium for the FAI Cup final). In previewing the international, which the *Irish Independent* described as of 'historical significance', the *Irish Times* wrote: 'In circumstances such as these the match is endowed with an interest which has not been associated with a match in Dublin under the "soccer" code for many years now. That Dalymount Park will be taxed to its fullest limits may be taken as a certainty for it is well known that the footballers of the two centres are tired of the impasse and anxious to have a settlement between the two bodies which would be for the good of the game in every part of the country. Such a happy consummation may not be attained to-day, but the match and the friendlier feeling which it will create in the two camps will go a long way in the direction of helping the parties to a better understanding between each other.'

This would be the Irish League's twelfth match since the split and the Free State League's fourth, and both sides had yet to win. The teams for this, a fixture which would not become semi-permanent until after the Second World War, were as follows:

FREE STATE LEAGUE	IRISH LEAGUE
Frank Collins (Jacobs)	Steven Beirne (Cliftonville)
Sam Russell (Shelbourne)	William Brown (Glenavon)
Frank Brady (Fordsons)	Robert Maguire (Cliftonville)
Alec Kirkland (Shamrock Rovers)	William Reid (Glentoran)
Val Harris (Shelbourne)	Robert Magee (Ards)
Mick Foley (Shelbourne)	George Pitt (Newry Town)
John Joe Flood (Shamrock Rovers)	Andy Bothwell (Ards)
Charlie Dowdall (St James's Gate)	Mick McGuire (Ads)
Billy Farrell (Shamrock Rovers)	Sam Curran (Belfast Celtic)
Bob Fullam (Shamrock Rovers)	William Blair (Distillery)
Jack Fagan (Shamrock Rovers)	Jackie Mahood (Belfast Celtic)

Considering the equal merits of both sides, on paper, the match was rather one-sided. Fullam set up Dowdall to volley the opener, which was followed by a first-timer from Dowdall. The visitors pulled one back when Jackie Mahood headed in a cross-cum-shot from McGuire. Late on, Farrell headed in from a Fullam cross to complete a 3-1 victory.

The fifth FAI Cup final four days later included all five Shamrock Rovers representatives from the League side. The Hoops netted inside two minutes against Fordsons when Bill O'Hagan spilled a 'pot shot' from Billy Farrell into his own net. The Cork side levelled within a minute when Dave Roberts headed in a free-kick. 'Kruger' Fagan restored Rovers' lead when he converted a cross from Flood, only for Malachy McKinney set up Paddy Barry for 2-2. Then came the final's defining moment. A penalty for Rovers was taken by Fullam, only for O'Hagan to block. The keeper lunged after the loose ball even though Fullam, known for the fire in his belly, seemed likely to get to it first. Irish soccer folklore insists Fullam would have broken O'Hagan's neck had he connected, but he pulled out and allowed O'Hagan to gather the ball. Fullam's gesture did not go unnoticed by friend or foe and O'Hagan personally thanked him at the final whistle. Fullam's unselfish act probably cost Rovers the Cup, for Paddy Barry scored Fordsons' winner in a goalmouth melee.

The third vital game was on Sunday, March 21st when the Free State played its first ever international, in Turin in Italy. The game posted a further marker on the separation of the two Irelands.

AN INTERNATIONAL IN ITALY

Ever since the split, the Free State FA had been firing off requests, mainly to England, Scotland and Wales, for a fixture, only to be dismissed in favour of the 'real' Irish Football Association. The 1924 Olympics resulted in various offers, one of which was from Italy.

Italy were one of the busier international sides. From 1921 they had played 27 internationals and when the offer was made in 1924 they had already played six internationals that year with a further two scheduled for November, so there was no time for Ireland. The following year was also out, as the Italians were already slated to play six internationals. The first available date was March 1926. The 'March international' was a regular fixture in the Italian soccer calendar and their opponents in 1926 would be the Irish Free State.

The Free State arranged a series of trial games to aid the selectors. The first was at Dalymount Park, between the Probables and Possibles, ending goalless. An inter-provincial match between the Leinster FA and the Munster FA put the spotlight on more candidates. In all, the selectors observed 30 players through February. For the record, the following players featured in trials:

Athlone Town: Brooks, Ghent, Henry, Jim Sweeney; *Barrackton United*: McVeagh; *Bohemians*: Cannon, McCarthy; *Brideville*: Golding; *Clifton*: Kelly; *Cork City*: Lismore; *Drumcondra*: Grace; *Fordsons*: Barry, Baylor, Connolly, Sullivan; *Jacobs*: Collins, Smith; *St James's Gate*: Duncan, Murphy; *Shelbourne*: Daly, Foley, Harris, Watters; *Shamrock Rovers*: Doyle, Fagan, Farrell, Flood, Fullam, Malone, Marlowe.

On Monday, March 1st, the selectors picked the following players to travel to Italy. *Goal*: Harry Cannon (Bohemians); *Backs*: Frank Brady (Fordsons), Jack McCarthy (Bohemians); *Half-Backs:* Mick Foley (Shelbourne, captain), Dinny Doyle (Shamrock Rovers), James Connolly (Fordsons); *Forwards*: John Joe Flood (Shamrock Rovers), Joe Grace (Drumcondra), Ned Brooks (Athlone Town), Bob Fullam (Shamrock Rovers), Jack Fagan (Shamrock Rovers).

Reserves: Alec Kirkland (Shamrock Rovers), Jack Sullivan (Fordsons), Fran Watters (Shelbourne). Mr J L Brennan, Chairman of the Free State Council, was chosen to act as a linesman (in those days, each nation provided one linesman each).

Before setting sail, Jack Sullivan had to withdraw through injury and Ned Brooks on account of the death of his seven-year-old son, who had been hit by a motor car. Fran Watters took his place in the attack, while Ned Marlowe of Shamrock Rovers and Paddy Duncan of St James's Gate were drafted in as reserves.

Only four players were more or less fresh – Harry Cannon, Jack McCarthy, Joe Grace and Fran Watters. Frank Brady had played at left-back in the Inter-League match but would switch flanks in Italy. Mick Foley also changed positions from left-half to right-half. Dinny Doyle had enjoyed a rest since the FAI Cup final, as had 'Sally' Connolly, but forwards John Joe Flood, Bob Fullam and 'Kruger' Fagan would defy fatigue to play their third important game in quick succession.

The players and officials left Dublin on St Patrick's Day for the three-day outward trip and they would return home with a 0-3 defeat. Nevertheless, the Irish Free State had embarked on an international career that would take in many highs and many lows. Over the next thirteen years they would play a total of 30 internationals until the Second World War called a halt.

Ireland's most capped pre-war player was Joe O'Reilly, who played 17 consecutive games for Ireland between 1935 and 1939

The Free State team that played the Italian 'B' side at Lansdowne Road in 1927. Players standing (left to right): Billy Lacey, Frank Collins, Mick O'Brien and Bob Fullam. Seated (left to right): Alec Kirkland, Christopher Martin, Harry Duggan, Frank Brady, Joe Kendrick, "Sacky" Glen and Tommy Muldoon.

Matt O'Mahoney, who made his debut against Czechoslovakia in 1938

The Irish Free State team that played the USA in an amateur international at Dalymount Park in 1924. Players standing (left to right): Johnny Murray, Paddy Duncan, Tommy Muldoon, Frank Collins, Charlie Dowdall and Tony Hunston. Players kneeling (left to right): Mickey Farrell, Ned Brooks, Bertie Kerr, Tom Murphy and John Thomas. On the day the Irish wore blue shirts with a shamrock crest

THE REPUBLIC OF IRELAND SOCCER TEAM 51

Jim Foley is beaten for the fifth time when a shot by Kick Smit (partly hidden by Harry Chatton) gave him no chance. Joe O'Reilly looks on in the background

Tommy Breen, the first Irish goalkeeper to keep two consecutive clean sheets

The great Jimmy Dunne, who began and finished his senior career at Shamrock Rovers

President Douglas Hyde shakes hands with Bill Fallon as captain Jimmy Dunne looks on, prior to the match against Poland in 1938. Both Fallon and Dunne would score in the match, while Hyde would be banned by the GAA for attending the game

The Republic of Ireland Soccer Team

The Shamrock Rovers team (playing in stripes!) of 1922-23 with four players who would play against Italy in 1926. Players standing (left to right): Peter Warren, William O'Kelly, Ned Marlowe and Joe 'Buller' Byrne. Seated (left to right): Willie Egan, John Joe Flood, Bob Fullam, Bob Cowzer and Jack 'Kruger' Fagan. Seated in front are Dinny Doyle (left) and William 'Sacky' Glen. Doyle, Flood, Fullam and Fagan all played in the match in Turin, while Ned Marlowe would be a reserve for Ireland on a number of occasions without being used, and 'Buller' Byrne would later be trainer to the side

Jack McCarthy was capped at amateur level by both the IFA and the FAI

Free Souvenir Programme
International League Match

IRISH FREE STATE v. WALES
At Dalymount Park, Saturday, 9th February, 1924
(KICK OFF 3.15 P.M. SHARP)

IRISH FREE STATE LEAGUE. Colours: Green Jerseys and White Knickers

F. COLLINS
(J. KOBS)

H. KERR   S. BOYNE
(BOHEMIANS)   (J. KOBS)

E. McKAY   J. L. McILROY   M. FOLEY, Capt.
(ST. JAMES'S GATE)   (BOHEMIANS)   (SHELBOURNE)

H. J. HARVEY   C. ROBINSON   D. A. ROBERTS   H. WILLITS   J. FAGAN
(ST. JOHNS)   (BOHEMIANS)   (SHELBOURNE)   (SHAMROCK ROVERS)   (ST. JAMES'S)

o

W. TAYLOR   J. NOCK   R. THOMPSON   J. JONES   A. GOLDIE
(CARDIFF)   (CARDIFF)   (PONTYPRIDD)   (NEWPORT)   (LLANELLY)

G. GROVES   E. RILEY, Capt.   —. FRITH
(NEWPORT)   (LLANELLY)   (MID-RHONDDA)

E. MORLEY   J. MARSHALL
(SWANSEA)   (LLANELLY)

J. KNIPSHAW
(CARDIFF)

WELSH LEAGUE. Colours: Red Jerseys and White Knickers

REFEREE: Mr. T. G. Bryan, who last year Refereed the International between England and Wales at Cardiff.

Music by St. James' Brass and Reed Band

This is the first occasion on which a selected side under the jurisdiction of the Football Association of the Irish Free State will be opposed by the best talent of the League of another country since our Body received International Recognition.

Printed and Presented by Independent Newspapers, Ltd.

Programme for the 1924 Inter-League match between
the Free State League and the Welsh League

THE REPUBLIC OF IRELAND SOCCER TEAM 55

The League of Ireland team that played the Welsh League in 1924. Players standing (left to right): Christy Robinson, Harry Willits, Ernie McKay, Frank Collins, Stephen Boyne and Johnny McIlroy. Players seated (left to right): Jimmy Harvey, Bertie Kerr, Mick 'Boxer' Foley, Dave Roberts and John 'Kruger' Fagan

Reidar Kvammen scored four goals in two games for Norway against Ireland in the World Cup

The Irish team which played a Rhineland XI in Cologne on May 6th, 1936.
Players standing (Left to right): Con Moulson, William 'Sacky' Glen, William Harrington, William O'Neill, Joe O'Reilly and Paddy Gaskins. Players kneeling (left to right): Harry Duggan, Joey Donnelly, Jimmy Dunne, Fred Horlacher and Jimmy Kelly.
The Irish team lost 1-4 with Jimmy Dunne scoring the Irish goal and William Harrington, unusually, credited with an own-goal.

Jim Brennan of Bohemians, who was part of the Free State selection committee and was a member of the delegation which met with the IFA in 1923 to try (unsuccessfully) to heal the Split

ASSOCIATION FOOTBALL

International Match

IRELAND v. ITALY

At LANSDOWNE RD.
On Saturday, April 23, '27

KICK-OFF AT 3.30 P.M.

This match marks a decidedly progressive step in the game in the Saorstat. It is the first time the Free State Football Association play as Ireland, and also is the initial representative game in which they have called on the services of players of Free State birth assisting Cross-Channel Clubs. This is the second match between the Countries, the first, last year at Turin, being won by the Italians by 3 goals to nil

This Souvenir Programme is printed and presented free by Independent Newspapers, Ltd., with the official sanction of the Football Association of the Irish Free State

Programme for the 1927 game between the Irish Free State and Italy 'B' in 1927

Seen as no more then good manners at the time, the Nazi salute given by the Irish players prior to the first international against Germany in 1935 had odious connotations later

Harold Sloan was a legend at Bohemians and their most capped player before the Split. He scored the first ever goal at the future home of Irish soccer, Dalymount Park

Johnny Carey made his debut for Ireland against Norway and did not miss a game until 1950

The Fordsons squad 1925-26. Three players standing at the back are (left to right): Paddy Kelly, Malachy McKinney and Dinny Driscoll. Players standing in the middle row are (left to right): James 'Sally' Connolly, Barney Collins, Bill O'Hagan, Jimmy Carabine, and Jack Baylor. Players seated (left to right): Billy Hannon, Jack Sullivan, Frank Brady, Harry Buckle, Dave Roberts and Paddy Barry.
The FAI would cap Barry, Brady, Connolly and Sullivan at senior level

Billy Gillespie was perhaps the finest Irish player of his generation. He could have played for both Irelands, but was only capped by the IFA

The Republic of Ireland Soccer Team

The Irish team that played the Netherlands in the World Cup in 1934. Players standing (left to right): Billy Jordan, Harry Chatton, Jim 'Fox' Foley, Billy Kennedy and Joe O'Reilly. Kneeling (left to right): Paddy Meehan, Joe Kendrick, Paddy Moore, Paddy Byrne, Johnny Squires and Paddy Gaskins.
Billy Lacey, the team's coach and trainer is standing to the left of the players

Billy Lacey was the most capped player by the IFA and FAI combined

The Irish team that beat Belgium 4-2 in Liege in 1928. Standing (left to right): Billy Lacey, Charlie Dowdall, Harry Cannon, Jack Sullivan and Paddy Barry. Kneeling (left to right): Jimmy White, Joseph 'Lye' Golding, Jack McCarthy, Joe Kinsella, Jeremiah Robinson and Jack Byrne. Although they have all got their caps, only 'Lye' Golding seems happy about it

James 'Sally' Connolly played for Ireland against Italy in 1926

Billy Lacey was capped 20 times by the IFA before the Split and three times after it

Ireland's record pre-war captain, Charlie Turner, shakes hands with Switzerland's Serverino Minelli before the game in Berne in 1937

Irish goalkeeper Jim Foley gathers the ball from Swiss centre-forward Leopold Kielholz, who, as you can see, wore glasses

Charlie Lennon made his international debut against Hungary in 1934

The Irish team in Brussels in 1930. Players (left to right): John Joe Flood, Harry Duggan, Billy Lacey, Tom Farquharson, Joseph 'Lye' Golding, Jimmy Dunne, Fred Horlacher, William 'Sacky' Glen, Mick O'Brien, Frank McLoughlin and Jack McCarthy

Jim 'Fox' Foley kept goal for Ireland for three years

A Record of the Full International Soccer Matches played by the Irish Free State: 1926 to 1939

Note on statistics to follow: The stadium which hosted the match is given with its name at the time. As for the attendance, if there are conflicting figures the lowest attendance is given.

The 2-3-5 outfield formation was standard and was the only one used by both sides for Ireland's 30 pre-war games. It lists the goalkeeper (who wore No 1 when numbers were introduced), the right-back (No 2), the left back (3), the right-half (4), the centre-half (5), the left-half (6), the right-winger or outside-right (7), the inside-right (8), the centre-forward (9), the inside-left (10), and the left-winger or outside-left (11).

The teams appear with Ireland's first, even if they played away. In Ireland's case, players' familiar names are given. For example, Robert Fullam was known as 'Bob' and is given as Bob Fullam. I have also stuck to this method when giving the opposition team whenever possible. Nicknames are not used, except in the match report. 'Sacky' Glen was universally known by that name and not by William, his given name, but is listed as William. Players' clubs are listed as they were then known.

Irish players are also given their appearance (A) and goal count (G). These show the total caps won and goals scored, including the match in question. For goalkeepers, the figures in italics show the number of clean sheets and (/) goals conceded, including the current match.

Ireland had no manager up until the end of the 1960s, as the Selection Committee picked the side. At times, players such as Billy Lacey, Johnny Carey, Noel Cantwell and Charlie Hurley were trainers and coaches to the Irish team but Ireland did not officially have a manager until 1969. The figure after the Irish 'Manager' shows the total number of games in which the selection committee had picked the team.

Match No. 1   *Sunday, 21st March 1926*   *Turin*
ITALY (3) 3   Baloncieri 13, Magnozzi 36, Bernardini 44
REPUBLIC OF IRELAND (0) 0
Ref: P Ruoff (Switzerland)   *Motovelodromo*   *Att: 12,000*

IRELAND (2-3-5)		A-G	ITALY (2-3-5)	
Harry Cannon	Bohemians	1–0/3	Giovanni De Pra	(Genoa)
Frank Brady	Fordsons	1–0	Virginio Rosetta	(Juventus)
Jack McCarthy	Bohemians	1–0	Umberto Caligaris	(Casale)
Mick Foley	Shelbourne	1–0	Antonio Janni	(Torino)
Denis Doyle	Shamrock Rov	1–0	Fulvio Bernardini	(Lazio)
James Connolly	Fordsons	1–0	Carlo Bigatto	(Juventus)
John Joe Flood	Shamrock Rov	1–0	Leopoldo Conti	(Inter)
Joe Grace	Drumcondra	1–0	Adolfo Baloncieri	(Torino)
Fran Watters	Shelbourne	1–0	Giuseppe Della Valle	(Bologna)
Bob Fullam	Shamrock Rov	1–0	Mario Magnozzi	(Livorno)
Jack Fagan	Shamrock Rov	1–0	Mariano Tansini	(Cremonese)
MANAGERS:	Committee (1)		Augusto Rangone	
CAPTAINS:	Mick Foley		Adolfo Baloncieri	

Embarking on a new adventure always instills in the traveller a sense of hope and optimism. None more so than in the players who shipped out from Kingstown (modern-day Dun Laoghaire) for a three-day trip to Italy, hoping to show the home side the best that Ireland had to offer. That our intrepid travellers would return home with a win in this, their first full international under the auspices of the Football Association of the Irish Free State, seemed never in doubt. The foundation of this optimism lay in the fact that the majority of the Irish side had played in the League of Ireland's win over the Irish League just over a week previously. The Inter-League matches were major events, akin to full internationals, so Irish optimism was not misplaced. Italy, it was felt, would present little in the way of threat, even though they were a bit of an unknown quantity and all travellers travel in ignorance.

Italy, however, had not been idle on the footballing front, having played internationals since 1910 – this would be their 55th overall. Not quite the powerful force they were to become in football, Italy in the 1920s were struggling to establish themselves with a mediocre record of 20 wins and 19 defeats in their previous 54 games. The side they put out to face Ireland, however, was an experienced one with over half their players having a cap total in double figures.

Ireland's team comprised players from the top four clubs in the League and one non-leaguer, Drumcondra's Joe Grace. Dubliner Harry Cannon was goalkeeper. A one-club man, Cannon was the first of a number of players who would represent Ireland in different sports. Legend has it that he placed an orange at the back of his goal for good luck.

In front of him was clubmate Jack McCarthy, who had played for Ireland in the 1924 Olympic Games and, like Cannon, would remain an amateur for his entire football career. McCarthy's partner at full-back was Cork-born Frank Brady, the first of his family to be capped by Ireland, with his nephews Ray and Liam winning honours for Ireland in the 1960s and 1970s. Brady, surprisingly, could not make the Fordsons first team but was chosen for Ireland. The oldest and most experienced player was naturally chosen to captain the side. 'Boxer' Foley had been playing football for 17 years, mostly with Shelbourne but had spent six seasons in England with Leeds City. He was part of a half-back line which included Dinny Doyle, who had been part of the Shamrock Rovers success story from the start, and 'Sally' Connolly who had just won the FAI Cup with Fordsons after joining the Cork outfit from Jacobs.

John Joe Flood, Bob Fullam and 'Kruger' Fagan were almost automatic choices in the forward line. Flood and Fullam had gone to Leeds in 1923 but had returned home to become legends at Milltown. Fagan's career was to be cut short by illness but he had four good seasons under him by the time he completed a unique double, along with his captain. Both Foley and Fagan played in the first LOI representative game and now played in Ireland's first international game. Joe Grace was the only non-Leaguer in the squad but was an experienced player having had spells with Belfast Celtic and Olympia. The only surprise in the side was Fran Watters at the expense of Billy Farrell of Shamrock Rovers. Farrell was part of Rovers' feared 'Four F's' forward line which was the strongest in the League. Farrell had not even made the reserves and, in fact, Watters, who had been a reserve, was a late replacement for Ned Brookes whose son had died tragically days before Ned was due to leave.

The Irish were in for a rude introduction to international football. A powerful drive from Baloncieri gave the home side the lead. This was doubled when Watters lost the ball in an Irish attack and the Italians broke quickly for Magnozzi to beat Cannon rather too easily. But Cannon had a good game and almost saved the third goal when he got hands to Bernardini's powerful close-range effort but could not keep it out.

It could only get better for the visitors in the second half and it did, slightly. The Irish had a number of chances but the home side still had most of the play. Flood was starved of the ball. Fagan, on the other wing, had a number of crosses, which Grace tried to feed off. One cross, which almost found Flood, ended in a clash between him and De Pra – both players needed treatment before resuming. Ireland had two good chances to reduce the arrears.

On the way home the Irish played a representative game against French side Cercle Athletique and drew 1-1. Bob Fullam scored Ireland's goal and Ireland's three reserves for the Italy game, Alec Kirkland, Ned Marlowe and Paddy Duncan, all played.

Match No. 2   *Saturday, 23rd April 1927*   *Dublin*

REPUBLIC OF IRELAND (1) 1   Fullam 6
ITALY 'B' (0) 2   Munerati 50, 80
Ref: J Langenus (Belgium)   *Lansdowne Road*   *Att: 20,000*

IRELAND (2-3-5)		A-G	ITALY 'B' (2-3-5)	
Frank Collins	Jacobs	1–0/2	Mario Gianni	(Bologna)
Alec Kirkland	Shamrock Rov	1–0	Mario Zanello	(Pro Vercelli)
Frank Brady	Fordsons	2–0	Delfo Bellini	(Inter)
William Glen	Shamrock Rov	1–0	Pietro Genovesi	(Bologna)
Mick O'Brien	Derby County	1–0	Luigi Burlando	(Genoa)
Tommy Muldoon	Aston Villa	1–0	Alberto Giordani	(Bologna)
Billy Lacey	Shelbourne	1–0	Federico Munerati	(Juventus)
Harry Duggan	Leeds United	1–0	Antonio Vojak	(Juventus)
Chris Martin	Bo'ness	1–0	Pietro Pastore	(Juventus)
Bob Fullam	Shamrock Rov	2–1	Enrico Rivolta	(Inter)
Joe Kendrick	Everton	1–0	Luigi Cevenini	(Inter)
MANAGERS:	Committee (2)		Committee	
CAPTAINS:	Frank Brady		Luigi Cevenini	

Opened in 1872, Lansdowne Road is one of the oldest stadiums in the world. Whereas Dalymount Park was the home of Irish soccer, Lansdowne Road, named after the adjacent road, was the home of Irish rugby. It was also the biggest stadium in Ireland at the time that could host a soccer match. Croke Park in north Dublin, the home of the Gaelic Athletic Association, was bigger but GAA rules forbad 'foreign games'. So it was to Lansdowne Road that the Free State FA looked to host its biggest game to date.

Situated in fashionable Ballsbridge, in south Dublin, it was just a stone's throw away from Ringsend, from where a host of future Shamrock Rovers legends were born. Indeed, a current star at the Milltown club, Bob Fullam was born and worked there, and fittingly it was he who became the first Irish soccer player to score at a venue which would in later years become a surrogate home for the Irish soccer team.

Ireland had been playing rugby internationals at the stadium since 1878 and would shortly host its 50th, with Australia due in November. However, soccer was not unknown at the ground, for in 1900 it hosted the first international soccer match for Ireland in Dublin. On St Patrick's Day Ireland lost 0-2 to England in front of a crowd of 8,000. Sheffield United's Harry Johnson, on his debut, scored the first goal at the stadium, which was quickly followed by another, from another debutant, Bury's Charles Sagar. Portsmouth's Matt 'Ginger' O'Reilly, who was from nearby Donnybrook, became the first Irish player to make his debut at Lansdowne Road when he played in goal.

And now, nearly 50 years after hosting its first Ireland international, there was to be another first for Lansdowne Road when the stadium was chosen as the best venue for the Football Association of the Irish Free State to host its first full international. Or, as the newspapers of the day put it, this was the first visit of a national side since 'the Football Association of the Irish Free State assumed control of its own affairs', and so the Italian team was feted by both football and government dignitaries including the Governor General, Timothy Healy. As such the game was lifted from being just an ordinary friendly.

Unfortunately the Italian FA had committed a *faux pas*, for having slated in a return game with the Irish on April 23rd someone had overlooked the fact that they were already committed to play the French in Paris on the following day. So they sent their 'B' side which, as it turned out, proved just as good.

Italy's 'B' team was made up of ten players from the top six clubs from the two divisions in the Divisione Nazionale and a forward line which had scored over 60 goals in the league — almost double the League total of the Irish forward line. The odd man out was Mario Zanello who had had a good season with unfashionable Pro Vercelli and who would have a memorable first visit to Dublin. This was Italy's second ever 'B' international. They had beaten the Luxembourg 'A' side 5-1 the week before, and most of the team would progress to play for the full Italian side.

Despite the hype, the game itself was a bit of a let-down. The Italian passing game caused problems for the Irish but little in the way of threat. Ireland's forward line lacked pace and height and most of the crosses that came in were gobbled up by the Italian defence. The first real opening fell to Pastore, whose curling shot deceived Collins and hit the bar. Fullam had a header saved and Muldoon a shot wide before the home side scored. Kendrick crossed for Martin, whose shot was blocked. The ball fell nicely for Fullam who blasted into the roof of the net for Ireland's first ever goal. The Italians almost equalised when Collins failed to reach a cross from Rivolta and Pastore's header was headed off the line by Brady.

After the break the Italians were forced to use a substitute when Zanello was knocked unconscious by Fullam's free-kick and took no further part in the game. The Italians brought on a player from the bench, which was something unknown in Ireland and Britain, and surprised almost everybody. As it was so unusual, none of the subsequent Irish match reports mentioned it and the identity of the Italian sub has never been confirmed.

Early in the second half, Martin had a chance to increase the lead but his control failed him. The Italians broke away and, when Munerati saw his shot blocked, a melee developed from which Munerati toe-poked the ball in for the equaliser. Fullam had two further free-kicks that went close before a weak shot from the wing by Munerati, which seemed to be covered by Collins, found its way into the net for the winner. Late on, another piece of poor control denied Martin a chance of an equaliser.

Match No. 3   *Sunday, 12th February 1928*   *Liege*
BELGIUM (2) 2   R Braine 39, Ledent 41
REPUBLIC OF IRELAND (0) 4   White 55, 75, Lacey 57, Sullivan 79 pen
Ref: A Kingscott (England)   *Standard Liege Stadium*   *Att: 25,000*

IRELAND (2-3-5)		A-G	BELGIUM (2-3-5)	
Harry Cannon	Bohemians	2-0/5	Louis Vandenbergh	(Daring)
Jeremiah Robinson	Bohemians	1-0	Armand Swartenbroeks	(Daring)
Jack McCarthy	Bohemians	2-0	Nikolaas Hoydonckx	(Berchem)
Joe Kinsella	Shelbourne	1-0	Henri Van Averbeke	(Beerschot)
Jack Sullivan	Fordsons	1-1	Florimond Vanhalme	(C Bruges)
Paddy Barry	Fordsons	1-0	Gustave Boesman	(Gantoise)
Jack Byrne	Bray Unknowns	1-0	Cornelius Elst	(Beerschot)
Billy Lacey	Shelbourne	2-1	Pierre Braine	(Beerschot)
Jimmy White	Bohemians	1-2	Raymond Braine	(Beerschot)
Charlie Dowdall	Fordsons	1-0	Francois Ledent	(Standard Liege)
Joseph Golding	Shamrock Rov	1-0	Jan Diddens	(Malines)

MANAGERS: Committee (3)   William Maxwell
CAPTAINS: Jack McCarthy   Armand Swartenbroeks

In England, 1927-28 was the season of Everton and Dixie Dean. In Scotland, it was the turn of Glasgow Rangers to do the double for the first time. In Northern Ireland, Belfast Celtic won the League for the third straight time. Down South it was the season of all-conquering Bohemians. The Dalymount residents won the League at a canter and defeated non-Leaguers Drumcondra in the FAI Cup final. The Leinster Senior Cup and the Shield soon followed as the Gypsies cleaned up every trophy available. The season also witnessed the first ever win by the Republic of Ireland on the full international stage.

Given the season Bohs were having, it was only natural that when the selection committee of the Free State FA picked a side to face Belgium for the first time, it would be top-heavy with players from Dalymount Park. Again, with one exception, all the players were from the top four sides in the League, with 'Squib' Byrne, from next-to-bottom Bray Unknowns, slotting in at right-wing. Strangely enough, Byrne was the only one of the forwards to finish top League scorer for his club.

The man chosen to lead the line was Jimmy White. White was never to top score for Bohemians in the eight seasons he was with the Gypsies and, for this special season for the north Dublin club, he was constantly in the shadow of Englishman Billy Dennis. White's eleven League goals were one short of those of Dennis, but he managed fourteen in the Cups, including one in every round of Bohs' successful FAI Cup run. White was notoriously short-sighted and was known in some parts as 'Blind' White. However, it was to this 28-year-old amateur that the honours of scoring Ireland's first brace in Ireland's first victory fell.

White was only in his second season of League of Ireland football, but the rest of the squad was experienced. The three other Bohs players had played between five and ten seasons at top level, as had most of the rest of the Irish side. 'Barney' Kinsella, an exception, was in his first season with Shels, while compatriot Billy Lacey was nearing the end of a 22-season career. Lacey, at 38, was the oldest player on the side but would create his own little bit of history by becoming the first man to score for both the Irelands.

This was Belgium's 96th match of a long international record, which started in 1905. Their highlight was winning the 1920 Olympic Games, which was akin to winning the World Cup then. They failed to retain their title in 1924, when hammered by Sweden in the first round, and were now preparing for the Amsterdam Olympics with a number of friendly games, including this one against Ireland. This Belgium side would be one of the most experienced Ireland would face for a long time, bringing a cap count of 145 and one player (Swartenbroeks) who had been playing international football since before the Great War. Ireland's Billy Lacey was also a pre-World War One veteran who had played in the green before the split.

Both sides' defences were to the fore at the start, and scoring chances were at a premium. When an opening did arise it resulted in a goal for Raymond Braine. Belgium had lost their previous six internationals, but this was the first time they had taken the lead, and it was doubled shortly before the break when Francois Ledent scored his second goal in two games.

During the half-time break, a violent thunderstorm turned into sleet, which kept the players indoors until it had abated. When they returned it was to a boggy pitch which suited the Irish better then their hosts. Ireland drew level just before the hour when, first, White scored and then Lacey planted a shot from seventeen yards into the back of the net. Belgium tried to recover but ran into a strong defence while, up front, the forward line – and White in particular – tried to take advantage of the conditions. White notched his second goal after 73 minutes, and four minutes later Ireland got a penalty when Hoydonckx handled the ball in the box. Before the kick could be taken, the Belgian goalkeeper, Vandenbergh, had to go off injured. Van Averbeke took over in goal but could do nothing about Sullivan's penalty. The Irish continued to press against ten-man Belgium and could have increased their lead. When the whistle blew for full time they were again on the attack.

In August 1929, the four Bohemian players would return to Liege with their club for a tournament and come away with the Acieries d'Angleur trophy, following victories over Royal Tilleur and Standard Liege. In 1966 the Irish team returned to the city in the midst of a poor run and won 3-2, this time without any Bohs players. Liege, however, was to prove to be a lucky city for Ireland.

Match No. 4
REPUBLIC OF IRELAND (1) 4
BELGIUM (0) 0
Ref: M Westwood (England)

Saturday, 20th April 1929   *Dublin*
Flood 43, 80, 89, D. Byrne 73

Dalymount Park   *Att: 15,000*

IRELAND (2-3-5)		A-G	BELGIUM (2-3-5)	
Tom Farquharson	Cardiff City	1–1/0	Louis Somers	(Royal Antwerp)
Jim Maguire	Shamrock Rov	1–0	Theodoor Nouwens	(Maines)
John Burke	Shamrock Rov	1–0	Nikolaas Hoydonckx	(Exelsior)
William Glen	Shamrock Rov	2–0	Henri Van Averbeke	(Beerschot)
Mick O'Brien	Walsall	2–0	Florimond Vanhalme	(C Bruges)
Paddy Barry	Fordsons	2–0	Gustave Boesman	(Gantoise)
Jimmy Bermingham	Bohemians	1–0	Pierre Braine	(Beerschot)
John Joe Flood	Shamrock Rov	2–3	Michel Vanderbauwhede	(Cercle Bruges)
David Byrne	Shelbourne	1–1	Raymond Braine	(Beerschot)
Charlie Dowdall	Barnsley	2–0	Jacques Moeschal	(Racing)
Robert Egan	Dundalk	1–0	Jan Diddens	(Malines)
MANAGERS:	Committee (4)		Viktor Lowenfeld	
CAPTAINS:	John Burke		Florimond Vanhalme	

Had things turned out differently Ireland's first game at the home of Bohs could have been at 'Pisser Dignam's Field' and the tenants there would have been Dublin Rovers. Thankfully things did not work out that way.

Formed in 1890, a new Dublin soccer club decided by a casting vote to call themselves 'Bohemians' instead of the other option, which was 'Rovers'. At the time they played in Phoenix Park, which was to remain a hotbed of soccer activity for many years. Bohs decided to move to a pitch on Jones's Road a while later, but stayed there only for a short time. As the site now forms part of Croke Park it could be argued that soccer was indeed played on the GAA's hallowed turf well before Ireland's first match there in 2007. The club planned a further move north when they took up residence in Whitehall, later to become the base for Home Farm. At the time, Whitehall in Drumcondra was just a bit too far for soccer fans who lacked decent transportation, so the club looked for a nearer ground.

The story goes that a property developer was building a row of houses on the North Circular Road in Phibsborough. One house was bought by a friend of the then Bohemians Treasurer, Mr W J Sanderson, who was invited around for a cup of tea. When Sanderson was shown the back garden he found a large, partly overgrown vegetable plot called 'Pisser's Dignam's Field'. He decided this was a perfect home for Bohemians and rented the site. A name-change was called for and, as the developer had called the row of houses 'Dalymount', it was decided to call the plot of land 'Dalymount Park'.

The development of what was to become the home of Irish soccer began immediately and progress was such that it soon became one of the major stadia of north Dublin. In 1901 Bohemians opened the stadium with a friendly against Shelbourne and Bohs Harold Sloan had the honour of scoring the first goal there. Two years later, the stadium hosted its first IFA Cup final when Bohs were beaten 1-3 by Distillery. On March 26th, 1904, Dalymount hosted Ireland's second match in Dublin. Robert Hamilton of Glasgow Rangers and Scotland scored the first ever international goal there, with Paddy Sheridan from Everton becoming the first to score there for Ireland. Dalymount would host four more games, all defeats, before the split, with Jimmy Quinn of Glasgow Celtic and Scotland being the first to record a hat-trick in an international (in fact, he notched four in the 5-0 win over Ireland in 1908). Ireland's last game at Dalymount was in 1913 — a 1-2 loss to Scotland.

It was not Bohemians but Shelbourne which was top club in 1928-29, but it was to runners-up Bohemians and third-placed Shamrock Rovers that the selectors looked for players for the return match with Belgium. With the season also over in England, a number of other Irish players were available. Tom Farquharson was capped by Northern Ireland seven times between 1923 and 1925 and was one of the top goalkeepers in Division One. Charlie Dowdall had played in Ireland's 1924 Olympic side and was enjoying a short stay with Division Two Barnsley. Mick O'Brien had ten caps for Northern Ireland and one for the Free State but was now in the Third Division (South) with Walsall.

John Joe Flood had returned to Ireland after a brief spell with Crystal Palace. This was his first representative game since rejoining Rovers. He was one of the famous 'Four F' forward line and was top scorer in the Rovers team that won the FAI Cup for the second time, a fortnight earlier. Flood had topped Rovers' scoring charts, as well as grabbing two of Rovers' three goals in the Cup final victory over Bohs. It was to Flood that the honour of scoring Ireland's first-ever hat-trick now fell.

Since the first meeting, Belgium had played eight games, winning three and scoring sixteen goals. Their forward line had accumulated 86 caps between them and 20 goals. Centre-forward Raymond Braine had 14 goals in 27 games. Fine scoring stats, certainly, so it is all the more surprising that it was their forwards who let the visitors down. The Belgians were on top for most of the game and created openings but, as one newspaper put it, 'they had not a forward who possessed the slightest notion of how goals are scored.'

For all their pressure, Belgium only forced Farquharson into one save in the opening half and the home side went ahead with a fortuitous goal. The Belgians should have cleared before the diving Flood put away Byrne's cross.

In the second half the Belgians tired and Farquharson's long punt upfield was latched onto by Byrne to shoot past the static goalkeeper. Belgium were still the better side and Flood's late strikes put an unfair reflection on the overall play. Ireland would have to wait seven years for their next home win.

Match No. 5 *Sunday, 11th May 1930* *Brussels*
BELGIUM (1) 1 Bastin 20
REPUBLIC OF IRELAND (1) 3 Dunne 32, 57, Flood 77
Ref: R Melcon (Spain) *Parc Astrid* Att: 15,000

IRELAND (2-3-5)		A-G	BELGIUM (2-3-5)	
Tom Farquharson	Cardiff City	2–1/1	Arnold Badjou	(Daring)
Billy Lacey	Shelbourne	3–1	Theodoor Nouwens	(Malines)
Jack McCarthy	Bohemians	3–0	Nikolaas Hoydonckx	(Exelsior)
William Glen	Shamrock Rov	3–0	Pierre Braine	(Beerschot)
Mick O'Brien	Norwich City	3–0	August Hellemans	(Malinois)
Frank McLoughlin	Fordsons	1–0	Jean De Clercq	(Royal Antwerp)
Harry Duggan	Leeds United	2–0	Louis Versyp	(Royal Bruges)
John Joe Flood	Shamrock Rov	3–4	Ferdinand Adams	(Anderlecht)
Jimmy Dunne	Sheffield Utd	1–2	Michel Vanderbauwhede	(Cercle Bruges)
Fred Horlacher	Bohemians	1–0	Jacques Moeschal	(Racing)
Joseph Golding	Shamrock Rov	2–0	Desire Bastin	(Antwerp)

MANAGERS: Committee (5) Hector Goetinck
CAPTAINS: Mick O'Brien Pierre Braine

Unbeaten under new coach Hector Goetinck, Belgium were in good form as they prepared to take the long boat trip to Uruguay for the first World Cup. The Jules Rimet Trophy was a FIFA initiative open to all members, including the Irish Free State. The thought of a two-month excursion to South America put off all but four European nations, but Rodolf William Seeldrayers happened to be the Belgian Vice-President of FIFA. Ireland, only nine years in existence, declined the invitation as they had their own worries.

Ireland were deterred partly by the poor form of the League of Ireland side (three heavy defeats in their last three games) and sown the seeds of doubt in those who believed Ireland had a strong pool of domestic players to compete on the big stage. A look across the Irish Sea also showed few pickings. Farquharson was still in goal for a Cardiff City in decline, Duggan was in and out of Division One side Leeds, and Mick O'Brien was in the lower regions of Division Three (South) with Norwich.

There was one bright light which might have illuminated what was to become the world's biggest sporting contest. Jimmy Dunne had spent three seasons at Sheffield United and broken into the first team the previous season with two goals in two games. He started 1929-30 with a hat-trick and finished with 36 goals to keep relegation at bay. The impact Dunne would have had in Uruguay can only be imagined. He already had one cap for Northern Ireland.

The ninth League of Ireland Championship was won by Bohemians, who equalled the three titles held by Shamrock Rovers. Instrumental in Bohs' run was a 20-year-old of German extraction: Alfred Horlacher, commonly known as Fred. A powerfully built butcher from Dun Laoghaire, he had just broken into the first team and would become a legend at the club where he would remain an amateur for his entire career. Horlacher was picked at inside-left, the start of an on-off international career that would see him banned by the Free State for three months the following season when he, along with club mates Jimmy Bermingham and Alex Morton, turned out for Northern Ireland amateurs against England.

In fact four Bohemians players were picked for the side that beat England 3-1 but Johnny McMahon was born in Derry so he was not banned. McMahon would later win a full cap for Northern Ireland when playing for Bohs in 1933 and would be the first and only League of Ireland player capped by Northern Ireland until Derry's Liam Coyle against Chile in 1989.

Horlacher would for a time be the preferred option at inside-left until Joey Donnelly arrived on the scene. Horlacher would leave his mark on Irish soccer history by becoming Ireland's first substitute. He made his debut along with Jimmy Dunne in the forward line and, like Dunne, would die early, after international soccer was suspended by the Second World War.

The bad weather deteriorated as the game progressed. The main danger to Ireland was inside-right Ferdinand Adams, who had not played for Belgium since January 1928 but had returned with two goals in two games. He now had nine goals in 18 appearances and was expected to shine in the forthcoming World Cup. But he never got a sniff against Ireland, frozen out by their third debutant, Frank McLoughlin, one of several no-nonsense Cork defenders. While headlines focused on the two other debutants, McLoughlin's part in Ireland's second away win should not be overlooked. The experienced Glen and O'Brien also blunted the Belgian attack, especially Vanderbauwhede (six goals in nine games).

The Belgians opened the scoring when veteran Bastin, 30, tore past 41-year-old Billy Lacey to hook in Versyp's cross. Lacey was earning his last cap of a distinguished career which began 21 years earlier. As one international career ended another began when Dunne equalised for Ireland after being put through by Horlacher. In the second half Farquharson in the Irish goal continued to have a quiet game. The Irish defence could take some credit by blunting an attacking line that had scored 16 goals in their last five games. But the game's outstanding personality was Dunne, who scored yet again. Flood, Ireland's top scorer, added another to bring his tally to four overall.

In Uruguay, Belgium lost both their games with much the same team as that beaten by Ireland. The tournament was largely ignored by Europe, which had other concerns following the Wall Street crash. With hindsight it was a missed opportunity for Ireland. Travel costs would largely have been met by the hosts, even though many players could never have taken two months off work. Next opponents Spain didn't travel either.

Match No. 6
SPAIN (1) 1
REPUBLIC OF IRELAND (1) 1
Ref: S Rosmaninho (Portugal)

Sunday, 26th April 1931   *Barcelona*
Arocha 38
Moore 35
Montjuich Stadium   *Att: 35,000*

IRELAND (2-3-5)		A-G	SPAIN (2-3-5)	
Tom Farquharson	Cardiff City	3–1/2	Ricardo Zamora	(Real Madrid)
George Lennox	Dolphin	1–0	Ciriaco	(Real Madrid)
Paddy Byrne	Shelbourne	1–0	Jacinto Quincoces	(R Madrid)
Jeremiah Robinson	Dolphin	2–0	Cristobal Marti	(Barcelona)
Harry Chatton	Shelbourne	1–0	Pedro Sole	(Alcoyano)
Sean Byrne	Bohemians	1–0	Jose Castillo	(Atletico Madrid)
John Joe Flood	Shamrock Rov	4–4	Vicente Piera	(Barcelona)
Charlie Dowdall	Cork	3–0	Severino Goiburu	(Valencia)
Paddy Moore	Shamrock Rov	1–1	Jose Samitier	(Barcelona)
Charlie Reid	Brideville	1–0	Angel Arocha	(Atletico Madrid)
Peter Kavanagh	Glasgow Celtic	1–0	Guillermo Gorostiza	(Bilbao)
MANAGERS:	Committee (6)		Jose Maria Mateos	
CAPTAINS:	John Joe Flood		Ricardo Zamora	

At the start of 1931 Spain was the top nation in international soccer. They had beaten everyone, including a strong England side, 4-3 in 1929. It was a notable scalp but by no means their only one. Italy, Hungary and Austria had all been put to the sword and only three teams – Italy, Belgium and Czechoslovakia – had beaten Spain since they started playing international football in 1920. A formidable record of 27 wins in 38 games with only six losses was indeed something to trouble the Irish, whose only wins were against the part-timers of Belgium. Worse, in fifteen home games, the Spanish had never lost and only Italy had escaped with a draw. In fact, Spain had started the year's internationals the week before with a scoreless draw against the Italians.

The Irish arrived having played, and beaten, Belgium three times but lost heavily to Italy, who were fast becoming a powerhouse in Europe. The League of Ireland representative side, on which much of the team was based, had had a wretched time, losing their last three games by heavy margins. Harry Chatton (3), Tom Farquharson (7), and Peter Kavanagh (1) had all been capped by Northern Ireland, so when the Free State lined out in Barcelona it showed a total of 19 international caps (Spain had 95).

The FAI Cup final between Shamrock Rovers and Dundalk had ended in a draw. The date for the replay had yet to be decided. The League had been wrapped up by Shelbourne, and of the side that lined up in Barcelona only three players came from the top three clubs and none from Dundalk, runners-up in League and Cup. Jimmy Dunne, who had made such a good impression on his debut, was not released by Sheffield United, and 21-year-old Paddy Moore who had recently returned from a move to Cardiff City took his place at centre-forward. Moore and Dunne were, perhaps, the greatest Irish players of their generation and both would leave their mark.

The Irish were not expected to put up much of a fight against Spain. Pre-match optimism was much in evidence in the Spanish press but very limited in their Irish counterparts. Both were in for a shock. In summing up the match the leading Spanish daily *La Hoja de Lunes* reported that 'The Match was a fight between two entirely different techniques. Ours, Latin, was based on pure enthusiasm for the sport; that of the Irishmen was cold and calculating'. Be that as it may, it was one of the first of many memorable games played by the Irish team.

The match started 40 minutes late as a host of dignitaries arrived one-by-one to be greeted by cheering crowds. Last to arrive was the President, Aleala Zamora – no relation to the greatest Spanish player of the time, goalkeeper and captain Ricardo Zamora. There were also exhibitions of athletics and rugby before the 'main event' started.

The Spanish tore into the Irish and pegged the visitors in their own half. Farquharson was beaten early on but the shot hit a post and was cleared. Piera later cut inside from the wing and hit the bar. The Irish attack never really got going but after 30 minutes they forced a fruitless corner. Five minutes later, the Irish broke away again up the right wing. Flood's cross found Moore in the center in space. Moore took it on and as Zamora came out to meet him he lifted the ball over his head and into the empty net. Ireland's lead lasted three minutes. A scramble in front of goal saw the ball run free to Piera, whose cross was headed home by Arocha – like Moore, making his debut. Late in the half, the Irish could have scored again but were denied by a fine interception from Ciriaco.

The clouds had gathered over the stadium before the start and a light rain was falling when the second half kicked off. In contrast to the Spanish domination of the opening half, the play was now fairly even. Both sides had chances. Moore had two, the first of which, from a pass by Byrne, saw Zamora save easily. Other chances fell to Dowdall and Reid before the match exploded with ten minutes to go. Arocha had a shot gathered by Farquharson but Samitier charged in. The Irish goalkeeper stood his ground, offering his shoulder to the Spaniard. In those times, the rules allowed for a forward to knock the goalkeeper into the net and the goal would stand. Ireland themselves would benefit from that rule in due course but for now Farquharson stood firm and Samitier bounced off him poleaxed. The Portuguese referee, who until that moment, had been given the bird by the Spanish crowd, awarded a penalty. Irish protests were long and voluble but to no avail. Goiburu, the leading scorer on the team, took the kick but placed it too near Farquharson, who fisted it away and earned Ireland a famous result.

Match No. 7 *Sunday, 13th December 1931* *Dublin*
REPUBLIC OF IRELAND (0) 0
SPAIN (3) 5
Ref: J Langenus (Belgium) Regueiro 6, 34, Arocha 40, 80, Vantolra 88
Dalymount Park *Att: 35,000*

IRELAND (2-3-5)		A-G	SPAIN (2-3-5)	
Tom Farquharson	Cardiff City	4–1/7	Gregorio Blasco	(Bilbao)
George Lennox	Shelbourne	2–0	Ciriaco	(Real Madrid)
Larry Doyle	Dolphin	1–0	Ramon Zabalo	(Barcelona)
William Glen	Shamrock Rov	4–0	Leoncito	(Real Madrid)
Harry Chatton	Dumbarton	2–0	Francisco Gamborena	(Irun)
Frank McLoughlin	Cork	2–0	Roberto	(Bilbao)
John Joe Flood	Shamrock Rov	5–4	Martin Vantolra	(Seville)
Patsy Gallagher	Falkirk	1–0	Luis Regueiro	(Real Madrid)
David Byrne	Shamrock Rov	2–1	Jose Samitier	(Barcelona)
Fred Horlacher	Bohemians	2–0	Angel Arocha	(Atletico Madrid)
Peter Kavanagh	Glasgow Celtic	2–0	Guillermo Gorostiza	(Bilbao)

MANAGERS: Committee (7) Jose Maria Mateos
CAPTAINS: Harry Chatton Jose Samitier

Spain arrived in Dublin feeling shell-shocked. On Wednesday they had played a return match against England and were thrashed 1-7, equalling their worst ever defeat. Of the side that played at Highbury, five were dropped, including their star Zamora who, by all accounts, had a stinker. In came Blasco, Ciriaco, Leoncito, Regueiro and Arocha, who had scored for Spain against Ireland in Barcelona. Spain's away record had been impressive – only four defeats in eight years – but they had only managed three wins in their last nine away games, which included two 1-7 defeats. Spain now called on two players, Gamborena and Samitier, who each had more caps then the entire Irish team.

The Irish team was a mixed bag. Jimmy Dunne and Mick O'Brien were not released by their clubs, and though Harry Duggan was, he chose to stay in Leeds where he was enjoying a run in the first team. Paddy Moore was injured and there were recalls for 'Sacky' Glen, 'Babby' Byrne and Fred Horlacher. For all but four of the team it was to be their last cap, including the two debutants – Larry Doyle and Patsy Gallagher. For Gallagher it was one last highlight of a career which had seen him play at the top level with Celtic (over 400 League appearances). He was now 37, but such was his fame that many of the crowd came to see him play once again in Ireland. He had been capped eleven times by Northern Ireland before being called on by the Free State.

Season 1931-32 was a busy one for Irish soccer. The Free State had arranged two senior internationals – a trip to Holland in May would follow – as well as the Inter-League game against the Welsh. On top of that there was a domestic programme with many clubs importing players from across the water. Waterford and Cork benefited from their spending to vie for the lead with six games to go. In fact, Cork had started the League campaign with only one player born in the Free State. However, the title did not go to Munster as Shamrock Rovers, with fewer imports, came up on the rails to pip both for the title. Rovers had a splendid season, winning the FAI Cup and Shield. Dolphin, beaten finalists in the FAI Cup, picked up the Leinster Senior Cup when they beat Shelbourne 3-0 in the final. Despite finishing third, in only their second season in the League, Waterford resigned at its conclusion, citing 'lack of support'. Waterford were not the only ones feeling the pinch, and most clubs felt that importing 'big name' players from across the water was the answer. It was not and neither was the Free State selectors' decision to play an aging star from a lowly Scottish club.

As in Barcelona, the Spanish tore into the Irish from the off. Their first-time passing and speed overwhelmed the hosts and contributed largely to a record home defeat. The Irish goal survived intact for the first five minutes of unrelenting attack before Gamborena sent Vantolra away up the right. The beret-wearing winger beat McLoughlin and Doyle for pace and sent over a cross that was met on the volley by Samitier. Farquharson fisted out to Regueiro who shot into the empty net. From the restart Gallagher was fouled just outside the box. Lennox took the free-kick, which tested Blasco.

However, the half belonged to Spain and Farquharson had to save headers from Arocha and Samitier before Ireland's best chances fell to Horlacher and Byrne. A cross from Flood was nodded down by Byrne to Horlacher whose shot hit the bar and went over. Then Byrne headed a cross from Horlacher, with the ball appearing to cross the line before Blasco scrambled it away. There were strong Irish appeals for a goal but John Langenus was unmoved. That was about as good as it got for Ireland as Spain forced the pace. Leoncito and Gamborena combined to put Regueiro in to beat Farquharson with a right-footed drive. Five minutes before the break, Gamborena, who was involved in all the goals, then sent Vantolra away and when his accurate cross came over Arocha shot home the third.

Spanish domination continued in the second half but whereas the right wing was prominent in the opening period it was the left that was to the fore after the break. Gorostiza was fed by Roberto and tricked his way past Glen and Lennox before crossing to Samitier, whose header was brilliantly saved by Farquharson. Arocha's pot-shot only just went over, and a header was saved by Farquharson. The busy Irish keeper also denied Gorostiza, but eventually the Spanish pressure told when, from the right, Arocha converted Vantolra's cross for the fourth. Right-winger Vantolra got the visitors' fifth near the end when he cut inside and shot low past Farquharson. Spain had turned in a brilliant performance and Ireland had been thought a football lesson, just as Spain had been on the Wednesday in London.

Match No. 8   *Sunday, 8th May 1932*   *Amsterdam*
NETHERLANDS (0) 0
REPUBLIC OF IRELAND (1) 2   O'Reilly 20, Moore 48
Ref: J. Langenus (Belgium)   Olympic Stadium   Att: 30,000

IRELAND (2-3-5)		A-G	NETHERLANDS (2-3-5)	
Mick McCarthy	Shamrock Rov	1–1/0	Gejus van der Meulen	(Haarlem)
Jimmy Daly	Shamrock Rov	1–0	Mauk Weber	(ADO)
Paddy Byrne	Shelbourne	2–0	Sjef van Run	(PSV)
Joe O'Reilly	Brideville	1–1	Bas Paauwe	(Feyenoord)
Mick O'Brien	Watford	4–0	Wim Anderiesen	(Ajax)
Owen Kinsella	Shamrock Rov	1–0	Puck van Heel	(Feyenoord)
Billy Kennedy	St James's Gate	1–0	Frank Wels	(Unitas)
Alex Stevenson	Dolphin	1–0	Wim Volkers	(Ajax)
Paddy Moore	Shamrock Rov	2–2	Wim Lagendaal	(Xerxes)
Fred Horlacher	Bohemians	3–0	Jaap Mol	(KFC)
Jimmy Kelly	Derry City	1–0	Joop van Nellen	(DHC)

MANAGERS: Committee (8)   Bob Glendenning
CAPTAINS: Mick O'Brien   Gejus van der Meulen

It had been another successful season for Shamrock Rovers. Despite bucking the trend and not signing players wholesale from England, Rovers had captured the double as well as the Shield. Rovers' team that defeated Dolphin in last month's FAI Cup final in front of a record crowd contained two Scots and a former England international but also eight Freestaters. 'Tipp' Burke, 'Sacky' Glen, 'Babby' Byrne, John Joe Flood and Paddy Moore had already been capped by Ireland, and they were now joined by the three others – Jimmy Daly, Mick McCarthy and Owen Kinsella. In February, only Moore was chosen from Rovers to play in Llanelly for the League of Ireland against the Welsh League. The League of Ireland won 4-2, with Paddy Moore scoring twice. Moore had had a wonderful season with the Hoops, scoring eighteen goals in the League and in every round of the FAI Cup, including the headed winner in the final against Dolphin. Such was his form that a number of scouts from England and Scotland kept tabs, but it was Aberdeen's shrewd manager Paddy Travers who swooped to sign Moore alongside teammate Jimmy Daly and Brideville's Joe O'Reilly. Daly would soon return home but Moore and O'Reilly would carve out decent careers in their three years away. However, talk of transfers and big money moves were far from the minds of all three players as they headed for the Grosvenor Hotel to meet up with the rest of the players and officials for the trip to Holland.

In those days the trip to Holland was not such an easy task as it is today. The party departed from Westland Row railway station to Dun Laoghaire, where the boat would carry them to Holyhead – which was even more remote in the 1930s then it is today. The train to London took another eight hours. In London they picked up Mick O'Brien and stayed overnight before catching the morning sailing from Dover to the Hook of Holland. An arduous trip, but for this young squad it was something of an adventure.

The Dutch, like the Belgians, still fostered an amateur ethos which was fast becoming outdated as professionalism became the norm in international football. Belgium, to an extent, still prospered with its non-professional side but the Dutch had become one of the whipping boys of Europe, despite coming into this game with four straight wins. They had won only four of the previous 25, even though they had scored in all but two of them. The Dutch believed in attacking football.

Only Fred Horlacher survived from the Spanish game. Although Shamrock Rovers had been the team of the season, Cork and Waterford had started strongly and there was dismay in both camps when no players from either club were picked. Instead, the selectors plumped for players from the lower placed Dublin sides, as well Watford's Mick O'Brien and their first player from the Irish League, Jimmy Kelly. Kelly was from Ballybofey in Donegal and had been capped twice by Northern Ireland, scoring three goals. Derry had finished runners-up to Linfield with Kelly scoring 13 goals. In fact, Ireland's forward line had topped 50 League goals between them.

The Irish and the Dutch had met once before, in the 1924 Olympic soccer tournament's quarter-final. The Dutch had prevailed in extra time and had one survivor from that encounter – goalkeeper Gejus van der Meulen. All the Dutch were amateur, as could possibly be said for most of the Irish. The only 'true' amateur on the Irish side was Fred Horlacher and the only 'true' professional was Mick O'Brien. In the end, it was the fitness of the Irish semi-pros that was to be the telling factor.

Both sides played a short-passing game with the Dutch showing a neat attacking style. Their leading goalscorer, Lagendaal (twelve goals in nine appearances), had the first chance when he shot against a post. That was about the only chance he had, as he was marked out of the game by O'Brien. Ireland's centre-forward, Moore, on the other hand, caused the Dutch all sorts of problems, but when a goal arrived it came from an unusual source. Right-half Joe O'Reilly gathered the ball in midfield and unleashed a swerver which beat van der Meulen all ends up. O'Reilly thus became the first defender to score for Ireland from open play.

Ireland's best player was Jimmy Kelly and it was another of his scintillating runs that set up Ireland's second. Combining with Horlacher, Kelly broke away and found Kennedy, whose cross was belted in by Moore from outside the box. The Irish then eased off, but Mick McCarthy was equal to anything that was thrown at him. Ireland were now unbeaten in their last four away games but would not have another fixture until the 1933-34 season.

Match No. 9 (World Cup)   *Sunday, 25th February 1934*   *Dublin*
REPUBLIC OF IRELAND (1) 4   Moore 27, 48, 56, 75
BELGIUM (2) 4   Capelle 13, Vanden Eynde 26, Vanden Eynden 47, 63
Ref: T Crew (England)   *Dalymount Park*   *Att: 28,000*

IRELAND (2-3-5)		A–G	BELGIUM (2-3-5)	
Jim Foley	Cork	1–0/4	Andre Vandewyer	(Union St Gilloise)
Miah Lynch	Cork Bohs	1–0	Jules Pappaert	(Union St Gilloise)
Tom Burke	Cork	1–0	Philibert Smellinckx	(Union St Gilloise)
Paddy Gaskins	Shamrock Rov	1–0	Joseph Van Ingelgem	(Daring)
Joe O'Reilly	Aberdeen	2–1	Felix Welkenhuysen	(Union St Gilloise)
Joe Kendrick	Dolphin	2–0	Desire Bourgois	(Malinois)
Billy Kennedy	St James's Gate	2–0	Louis Versyp	(Royal Bruges)
David Byrne	Coleraine	3–1	Jean Brichaut	(Standard Liege)
Paddy Moore	Aberdeen	3–6	Jean Capelle	(Standard Liege)
Tim O'Keeffe	Cork	1–0	Andre Saeys	(Cercle Bruges)
Jimmy Kelly	Derry City	2–0	Stanley Vanden Eynde	(Beerschot)
			Sub: Francois Vanden Eynden	(Union St Gilloise)
			for Stanley Vanden Eynde (37 mins)	

MANAGERS: Committee (9)   Hector Goetinck
CAPTAINS: Paddy Gaskins   Jules Pappaert

It is not often that Ireland went into a World Cup qualifying competition hopeful of making the finals. For the 1934 World Cup, Ireland were placed in a group with Belgium and Holland, and, having a 100 per cent record against both sides, expectations were high. The fact that two of the three nations would qualify strengthened that conviction. The teams would play each other just once. All Ireland required was a home win and an away draw.

Since they last played Ireland, Belgium had won just one in three internationals. They had been one of the few European teams to travel to Uruguay in 1930 but came home having lost both their games without scoring a goal. Belgium had scored in all but one of their games since then, but had still lost 18 of the 33 played. This season they had played three games and won none. In fact, they had suffered their heaviest defeat under Hector Goetinck in October when Germany – no great shakes themselves – beat them 8-1. This was Belgium's third World Cup match.

Ireland had gone through 1932-33 without an international and had, in fact, not played for a year and nine months – a long time to go without international experience (Belgium had played 13 games in the same period). There was always the Inter-League games (but only one) and the players picked for the North (Jimmy Kelly four times, Jimmy Dunne two, Paddy Moore, Harry

Duggan two, Alex Stevenson three) but, of these, by the time the World Cup came around only Kelly and Moore would be available.

A series of trial games were held, from which an unusual line-up resulted. This was the outcome of some last-minute changes. 'Sacky' Glen was injured and his place at right-half was taken by Paddy Gaskins. Gaskins was originally chosen at right-back, and so Miah Lynch took his spot. Of the players chosen, only Moore and Byrne had more then one cap, while nearly half the rest were making their debuts. Jim 'Fox' Foley was in his second season with Cork, as were Tom Burke and Tim O'Keeffe. Miah Lynch was basically a one-club man, aside from a brief spell at Cork.

Paddy Gaskins from the Hoops would captain the side, but it was an ex-Shamrock Rover who was to make all the headlines. Paddy Moore was in his second season at Aberdeen and came into this match having scored seven goals in his last eleven games for the Dons. He was already a household name in Ireland having been one of the stars of Rovers' FAI Cup wins in the early 1930s. He had top-scored for the Milltown club when they won the title in 1931-32 and had already scored in his first two appearances for Ireland. Moore was one of the most gifted players of his generation but humble with it. The story goes that Moore indulged in a kickaround with kids near his home before he turned up at Dalymount Park for his date with history.

As the players trotted out from under the main stand at Dalymount Park, few probably knew that this was the 27th World Cup game, and of the previous 26 there had only been three hat-tricks. Patenaude of the USA recorded the first in 40 minutes, Stabile of Argentina followed with another in 72 minutes, and Cea the last when he netted three against Yugoslavia in 54 minutes. Paddy Moore would score his hat-trick in 32 minutes, making it the quickest in the brief history of the World Cup. He also became the first player to score four goals in a World Cup-tie.

It was a match Ireland should have won. As the *Irish Press* pointed out, 'Belgium were presented with their four goals while a chance or two … was thrown away by O'Keeffe.' For O'Keeffe it was a day to forget because after the match he was accused of stealing the wallet of the Belgian goalkeeper during the after-match banquet. Whatever did happen (and it is not all that clear), O'Keeffe did not play again for Ireland for four more years.

Taking the match as a whole, it represented the best and worst of the team. Four goals were conceded but Ireland managed to haul themselves back into the game through sheer determination. It is curious to note the difference between this, Ireland's first competitive match, and the friendlies that preceded it.

Whereas in Ireland's eight previous games their opponents had indulged in exhibition stuff, for this game (and that in Amsterdam to follow) there was nothing fancy. Both teams played kick-and-rush (or a British style, if you want). It may not have been pretty but it was exciting. Before kick-off there were two minutes' silence for the late King Albert of Belgium. The St James's Band played *The Last Post* and the sombre air seemed to affect everyone because there was a quiet opening to the game. Both Irish full-backs were clearly out of their depth and when Burke was dispossessed by the experienced Versyp his cross found Capelle who scored Belgium's first ever World Cup goal. Then Kelly presented O'Keeffe with the first of those 'chances' but he failed badly. Versyp volleyed over and Kennedy came close with a header before Belgium scored again. Another cross by Versyp was not dealt with. Foley came out to punch but was stranded as Stanley Vanden Eynde coolly lobbed the ball over him into the net.

A minute later Moore scored Ireland's first World Cup goal. Kelly broke up the left wing and crossed. Pappaert and Welkenhuysen moved in, but Moore got to the ball a fraction earlier and shot past Vandewyer as he was toppled by the backs. Kelly and O'Keeffe switched places on the left to revitalise the Irish attack.

The Belgian front line was also forced into a change when, in what was described as a brutal tackle, Stanley Vanden Eynde broke his leg and was replaced by Francois Vanden Eynden. Substitutes were not condoned by FIFA at this time, but Belgium were not the only ones to use them in the World Cup so a blind eye was turned. Vanden Eynden came on at inside-left while Saeys moved out to the left wing. Yet the home side edged the rest of the half. Moore was put through, but the advancing Vandewyer got a hand to the shot, which slowed enough for Smellinckx to clear. O'Keeffe had his second 'chance' but with the goal at his mercy shot tamely wide.

Gaskins had been uncomfortable in the unusual position of right-half and for the second period exchanged places with O'Reilly, which benefited both. However, within two minutes of the turnaround Ireland were again two goals adrift. A hard, low cross from Van Ingelgem flashed past four defenders to Saeys on the left wing. He cut inside and squared for Vanden Eynden to score from close range. Within seconds Kennedy burst up the right and crossed for Moore, who somehow got to the ball ahead of the goalkeeper and knocked it past him.

Ireland soon drew level at 3-3. O'Reilly found Kelly at inside-left, whose pass through the center enabled Moore to flick the ball into the net. Belgium appeared shell-shocked and Ireland pressed for a winner, only to be caught on the break. A long ball found Brichaut on the right and he committed Burke to a tackle as he slipped the ball to Vanden Eynden. The substitute beat Lynch and the advancing Foley to put the visitors 4-3 ahead.

Belgium's lead lasted just twelve minutes. A corner-kick from Kelly was cleared out to Kennedy who lobbed the ball back into the box. Moore was only small (barely 5ft 6ins) but he could jump like a gazelle. He once again surprised the Belgian defence by leaping highest to head home Ireland's second equaliser.

There were still fifteen minutes left to play, enough time for either side to nick a winner. Both sides tried their best but neither could manage it. In the final analysis, this dropped point was to cost Ireland qualification for the World Cup.

Match No. 10 (World Cup) *Sunday, 8th April 1934* *Amsterdam*
NETHERLANDS (1) 5 Smit 40, 85, Bakhuys 67, 78, Vente 83
REPUBLIC OF IRELAND (1) 2 Squires 42, Moore 57
Ref: O Ohlsen (Sweden) *Olympic Stadium* Att: 38,000

IRELAND (2-3-5)		A-G	NETHERLANDS (2-3-5)	
Jim Foley	Cork	2–0/9	Adri van Male	(Feyenoord)
Paddy Gaskins	Shamrock Rov	2–0	Mauk Weber	(ADO Den Haag)
Paddy Byrne	Drumcondra	3–0	Sjef van Run	(PSV)
Joe O'Reilly	Aberdeen	3–1	Henk Pellikaan	(Longa Tilburg)
Harry Chatton	Cork	3–0	Wim Anderiesen	(Ajax)
Joe Kendrick	Dolphin	3–0	Puck van Heel	(Feyenoord)
Billy Kennedy	St James's Gate	3–0	Frank Wels	(Unitas)
Johnny Squires	Shelbourne	1–1	Leen Vente	(Neptunus)
Paddy Moore	Aberdeen	4–7	Beb Bakhuys	(ZAC)
Billy Jordan	Bohemians	1–0	Kick Smit	(Haarlem)
Paddy Meehan	Drumcondra	1–0	Kees Mijnders	(DFC)
Sub: Fred Horlacher	Bohemians	4–0		
for Jordan (40 mins)				

MANAGERS:	Committee (10)	Bob Glendenning
CAPTAINS:	Paddy Gaskins	Puck van Heel

Another long trip to Amsterdam for the Irish players but they arrived in good spirits. After all, Ireland had gone to the Dutch capital two years earlier and won 2-0, and there seemed little to suggest that they could not repeat it. There were five changes from the side that drew with Belgium and an overall team reshuffle. Gaskins returned to his more familiar right-back role and was partnered by the experienced Paddy Byrne on the left. The half-back line looked stronger with Harry Chatton back at centre. Of the forwards, only Billy Kennedy and Paddy Moore retained their places. Tim O'Keeffe was 'suspended', and 'Babby' Byrne and Jimmy Kelly were needed by their clubs and not released. In came Johnny Squires, who had a surprisingly good game, Billy Jordan – a left-winger who played at inside-left – and Paddy Meehan, in his first full season for Drums. As one of the travelling officials noted after the match: 'It was one of the best teams which ever represented the Free State, but it was also the unluckiest.'

If Ireland needed any boost beforehand, then it came a month earlier when an almost identical Belgium side which had drawn with Ireland was trounced 3-9 by the rampant Dutch. Should Ireland lose in Amsterdam, it would hardly be by such a margin, and it seemed a distinct possibility that whatever margin the Dutch might beat the Irish by, the Dutch would possibly surpass that against their neighbours.

Since losing to Ireland, the Dutch had played eight games, winning three but losing the rest, including to Belgium in Amsterdam. Their 9-3 win was their biggest since 1924 and all nine goals were shared by three players: Leen Vente (five), Kick Smit (two) and Bekhuys (two). Of the team that now lined out against Ireland these were the only players ever to have scored for Holland.

FIFA's 20th World Cup qualifying match kicked off on a hot day with little wind in front of a record Amsterdam crowd. The Irish, as one report stated, 'played rings around Holland' and only a well-marshalled defence kept the Dutch afloat. Ireland were playing so well it seemed only a matter of time before they would score. However, after 40 minutes the impressive Jordan took a knock and could not continue. Ireland capitalised on the 'Continental rule' to send on a substitute. Nowadays this is commonplace, but back then it was akin to picking somebody out of the crowd and telling them to get togged out. Fred Horlacher was the one chosen from the three reserves. He quickly donned the green and took up his position at inside-left, his usual club position. Up to that point Ireland were running the game but the Dutch scored almost immediately. Wels delivered a cross which was put away by Smit for the Netherlands' first ever World Cup goal. The Irish equalised shortly with the 95th away goal scored in the World Cup. Moore set it up, jinking into the box and laying the chance on a plate for Squires. It was the only goal Squires would score all season for club or country. At half-time it was all-square, which suited the Irish as it meant they would qualify, providing the Dutch and Belgians did not contest a high-scoring draw.

The Irish had the better start to the second half and scored early. Hefty challenges on goalkeepers went unpunished in those days, so when van Male plucked the ball out of the air and was slow in clearing, Moore charged in and bundled man and ball over the line. The goal was allowed and Ireland led 2-1. If that score held they would be on their way to the finals in Italy, but the Dutch levelled when Mijnders broke from halfway and crossed for Bakhuys to score off a post. Soon afterwards, Moore should have restored Ireland's lead, but his lob went over van Male and the crossbar. This miss would prove very costly.

Reprieved by Moore's miss, the Dutch took heart and in seven devastating minutes the match was over, leaving one Irish correspondent to lament 'to be beaten by a goal margin would have been bad enough, but by three ...' Bakhuys headed the Dutch in front, after which Vente and Smit scored in quick succession. It was noted that a more experienced goalkeeper then Foley might have saved two of the five goals, but he could do nothing about the fifth, a drive from Smit which flew past him.

For Ireland to qualify they needed the Dutch to beat Belgium by four clear goals. In fact, the Dutch went a goal down but came back with three before Belgium pulled another goal back. In the end, the Dutch won 4-2. Both they and Belgium, with better goal figures than Ireland, went through to the finals.

Match No. 11   *Sunday, 16th December 1934*   *Dublin*
REPUBLIC OF IRELAND (1) 2
HUNGARY (2) 4
Ref: J Langenus (Belgium)

J Donnelly 35, P Bermingham 62 pen
Avar 18, 83, Vincze 28, Markos 85
Dalymount Park   *Att: 25,000*

IRELAND (2-3-5)		A-G	HUNGARY (2-3-5)	
Jim Foley	Glasgow Celtic	3–0/13	Jozsef Hada	(Ferencvaros)
Paddy Gaskins	Shamrock Rov	3–0	Jozsef Vago	(Bocskai)
Paddy Bermingham	St James's Gate	1–1	Laszlo Sternberg	(Ujpest)
Paddy O'Kane	Bohemians	1–0	Gyula Seres	(Bocskai)
Charlie Lennon	St James's Gate	1–0	Gyorgy Szucs	(Ujpest)
Fred Horlacher	Bohemians	5–0	Antal Szalay	(Ujpest)
Bob Griffiths	Walsall	1–0	Imre Markos	(Bocskai)
Joey Donnelly	Dundalk	1–1	Jeno Vincze	(Bocskai)
Alf Rigby	St James's Gate	1–0	Istvan Avar	(Ujpest)
Paddy Moore	Aberdeen	5–7	Laszlo Cseh	(Hungaria)
Bill Fallon	Notts County	1–0	Pal Titkos	(Hungaria)
			Subs: Antal Szabo	(Hungaria)
			for Hada (half-time)	
			Jozsef Gyori	(III Kerulet)
			for Seres (half-time)	

MANAGERS: Committee (11)   Dr Karoly Dietz
CAPTAINS: Paddy Gaskins   Laszlo Sternberg

The visit of famed Hungary was a big pre-Christmas attraction. Hungary had been favourites to win the World Cup in Italy that summer. As in most European nations, Hungarian football was changing from amateur to professional, and was reaping the rewards. Hungary was an early pioneer of international football and, with their neighbours Austria, slogged it out for the bragging rights of Europe's best. Italy's emergence meant these three kingpins sought domination of the Continent. So by the time of the World Cup it was basically these three (and whoever turned up from South America) who could expect to lift the Jules Rimet trophy. Hungary got past Egypt but then ran into the Austria 'Wunderteam' in the quarter-finals. An 'over competitive' match, saw Hungary knocked out. Most of that defeated team were picked for the match in Dublin, Hungary's 180th international.

    December was an unusual time for Ireland to play as the League was in full swing, and this weekend saw almost a full league programme. Consequently, the Irish team was a mixed bag of veterans and debutants. Paddy Moore was out of favour at Aberdeen and had not played since the start of the season, but he was named at inside-left to accommodate the long-awaited debut of Alf Rigby. Rigby had top-scored for Gate since signing from Bray Unknowns and had it not been for Moore he would have led Ireland's attack in the World Cup. 'Fox' Foley retained his place. He, too, wasn't getting games in Scotland and needed a game, any game. Rovers and Bohs were in action the day before Hungary but had released Gaskins, O'Kane and Horlacher to play, while the Gate and Dundalk had a free weekend. Bob Griffiths had joined Walsall from Southport. He would see a lot of the ball but perform poorly. Bill Fallon was enjoying a good season at Notts County but saw little of the ball on his international debut. Joey Donnelly was called up when Everton refused to release Alex Stevenson. Donnelly capitalised on his opportunity while Stevenson was left in the wilderness until after World War Two.

Despite the scoreline, Hungary did not live up to their reputation. One criticism of the recent World Cup was that football was sacrificed for the sake of winning. This was certainly true for Hungary, who relished the rough stuff.

Ireland lacked pace but, in the words of one of the Hungarian delegation, were 'equal to the standard of any of the central European teams'. Considering that over half the Irish team were making their debuts, this was a compliment, indeed. Ireland had the majority of the opening play and forced four corners in the first 15 minutes, yet the visitors opened the scoring. Paddy O'Kane won a tackle on Cseh, fair and square, but the referee awarded a free-kick to Hungary. As the Irish protested, the ball was quickly played out to Titkos, whose cross was turned in by Avar. The visitors then forced two corners, the second of which resulted in an unusual goal. As with Moore's goal in Holland, it stemmed from a challenge on the goalkeeper. As Foley came out to punch away, Vincze barged into him, forcing Foley to fist the ball into the roof of the net. Again, Irish protests fell on deaf ears. Rigby headed wide and Griffiths missed a sitter before Ireland reduced the arrears. Rigby put Fallon away up the left and his low cross was tucked away by Donnelly. Just on half-time a Rigby header was turned around the post by Hada.

Hungary tried to bring on three subs for the second half, but Irish captain Gaskins protested, as the general custom was that only an injured player could be replaced, and only before half-time. Goalkeepers were exempt from this custom, so John Langenus allowed only the goalkeeper and one other. Mihaly Solti, the third sub, returned to the stand and Avar rejoined the attack.

Moore headed on for Rigby, only for Sternberg to knock the ball away with his arm for a penalty. Paddy Bermingham, one of the more experienced players on the side, took it and gave sub goalie Szabo no chance. At 2-2, the turning point came after an hour. Moore, despite being unfit, had played well until slowed by a knock. Gaskins, in stopping an attack up the Irish right, was also crocked. The captain had no option and had to play on but was basically just a passenger. It was only when Ireland were reduced to nine fit men that Hungary settled the match. Donnelly, dropping back to cover, conceded a free and from it Avar shot home Hungary's third. Two minutes later Markos wriggled free to chip the ball over the advancing Foley.

Match No. 12   *Sunday, 5th May 1935*   *Basle*
SWITZERLAND (0) 1   Weiler 62 pen
REPUBLIC OF IRELAND (0) 0
Ref: A Beranek (Austria)   *Wankhof Stadium*   *Att: 23,000*

IRELAND (2-3-5)		A–G	SWITZERLAND (2-3-5)	
Jim Foley	Glasgow Celtic	4–0/14	Renato Bizzozero	(Lugano)
Paddy Gaskins	Shamrock Rov	4–0	Severino Minelli	(Grasshoppers)
Leo Dunne	Manchester C	1–0	Louis Gobet	(Bern)
Paddy O'Kane	Bohemians	2–0	Francis Defago	(Grasshoppers)
Charlie Lennon	St James's Gate	2–0	Walter Weiler	(Grasshoppers)
Freddie Hutchinson	Drumcondra	1–0	Eduard Muller	(Young Fellows)
Jimmy Daly	Shamrock Rov	2–0	Lauro Amado	(Lugano)
Plev Ellis	Bohemians	1–0	Aldo Poretti	(Lugano)
Alf Rigby	St James's Gate	2–0	Leopold Kielholz	(Servette)
Joey Donnelly	Dundalk	2–1	Engelbert Bosch	(Bern)
Paddy Monahan	Sligo Rovers	1–0	Alfred Jaeck	(Basel)

MANAGERS: Committee (12)   Henry Muller
CAPTAINS: Paddy Gaskins   Severino Minelli

Since the foundation of the League of Ireland, only five clubs had won the championship. Dublin's three kingpins Shamrock Rovers (four), Bohemians (four) and Shelbourne (three) had been joined by St James's Gate and the first non-Dublin team, Dundalk. The 1934-35 title was won by a sixth club and perhaps the most surprising. Dolphin was formed by butchers in 1921. They had only been members of the League of Ireland for five years but had walked off with the domestic scene's biggest trophy with Bohs and Rovers trailing in their wake. This was to be the south Dublin's club only trophy in their brief League of Ireland career (they resigned two years later) and in their short life they had five players capped but none on this first tour of the Continent.

The 1934-35 season had also seen the debut of Connacht's first senior club, Sligo Rovers. Sligo played 40 games this season and their record against Shamrock Rovers showed two wins and two draws. Outstanding for Sligo was Winger 'Monty' Monahan, who was chosen in the League of Ireland XI and then for the full side for this European tour. Sligo Rovers would later enjoy better things, but Monahan would be their only player capped by Ireland.

However, the biggest news was the row between Shelbourne and the Free State League of Ireland. Shels were miffed that the previous season the Free State had arranged an international at the same time as a Shelbourne home game, and sought compensation for loss of revenue. When the Free State FA shrugged their shoulders, Shels resigned from the League. In a twist reminiscent of the problems that had preceded the split, Shelbourne applied to join the Irish League, only to be rebuffed. They sought to return to the League of Ireland, only to be fined and suspended for a year. In Shelbourne's absence, a new club, Reds United was admitted to the League of Ireland. Most Shels players turned out for the new club, while Shels played in the AUL League.

Switzerland returned from the World Cup in Italy with their reputation enhanced. They had qualified for the finals without winning a game, but were awarded two points by FIFA when Romania fielded an illegal player in a 2-2 draw in Berne. In the first round they beat Ireland's conquerors, Holland, and then lost to future losing finalists Czechoslovakia in the quarter-finals. For the Swiss it was another high point of an international record that stretched back to the early years of the century. They had made the final of the 1924 Olympic Games, when beaten 0-3 by Uruguay. A run of only three wins in their last 18 internationals hinted at regression, but just the month before entertaining the Irish they recorded a 6-2 win over Hungary.

End-of-season tours had become the norm for most British clubs, and the English and Free State national teams decided to follow suit. Unfortunately, Ireland met with refusal when they sought from the English FA the release of players. Only Leo Dunne, transfer listed at Manchester City, was released. Fourteen players were chosen to travel, including Paddy Moore, on his way out of Aberdeen. Moore was picked against Switzerland, only for Joey Donnelly to take his place when Moore failed to arrive on time. This left a vacancy on the right wing, and full-back Jimmy Daly filled it.

A frantic opening saw both goals visited in turn. The Swiss showed the more skilful play but could not compete in the air. Ireland's best chance came when Daly's cross saw Hutchinson and Monahan collide. They ended up on the deck and the ball cleared. The Swiss came close when Kielholz hit the crossbar and the ball flew over. Rigby and Donnelly came close with headers, only to be denied by good saves from Bizzozero.

The Swiss dominated most of the second half. Gaskins had his hands full trying to contain Bosch and Jaeck, despite being assisted by Dunne, who proved to be one of the successes of the tour. Early on Monahan took a knock and even though he played on he never quite shook it off. Then Hutchinson went down injured and had to be taken off to receive treatment. He was gone some time. When he returned, Gaskins hurt his leg in a tackle and he too had to go off. He came back at right-wing, with Daly dropping back to right-back. Just after an hour's play, Amado broke up the right flank and crossed for Kielholz, who was miles offside. The Swiss centre-forward obviously thought so, for he hesitated and Dunne, assuming his hesitation was an admittance of guilt, bent down to pick up the ball. Referee Alois Beranek, to the amazement of the Irish players, immediately blew for a penalty that was tucked away by Weiler. In the last minute, Dunne and O'Kane sent Ellis free up the right. His low cross shaved an upright, with Donnelly only just failing to get a touch to the ball.

Match No. 13   *Wednesday, 8th May 1935*   *Dortmund*
GERMANY (1) 3   Damminger 31, 49, Lehner 86
REPUBLIC OF IRELAND (1) 1   Ellis 19
Ref: A Krist (Czechoslovakia)   *Kampfbahn Rote Erde*   *Att: 35,000*

IRELAND (2-3-5)		A-G	GERMANY (2-3-5)	
Jim Foley	Glasgow Celtic	5–0/17	Fritz Buchloh	(VfB Speldorf)
Paddy Gaskins	Shamrock Rov	5–0	Paul Janes	(Fortuna Dusseldorf)
Leo Dunne	Manchester C	2–0	Willi Tiefel	(Eintracht)
Paddy O'Kane	Bohemians	3–0	Paul Zielinski	(Union Hamborn)
Charlie Lennon	St James's Gate	3–0	Ludwig Goldbrunner	(Bayern)
Freddie Hutchinson	Drumcondra	2–0	Jakob Bender	(Fort' Dusseldorf)
Plev Ellis	Bohemians	2–1	Ernst Lehner	(Augsburg)
Paddy Moore	Aberdeen	6–7	Otto Siffling	(SV Waldhof)
Alf Rigby	St James's Gate	3–0	August Lenz	(Borussia Dortmund)
Joey Donnelly	Dundalk	3–1	Ludwig Damminger	(Karlsruhe)
Paddy Monahan	Sligo Rovers	2–0	Josef Fath	(Wormatia Worms)

MANAGERS: Committee (13)   Dr Otto Nerz
CAPTAINS: Paddy Gaskins   Fritz Buchloh

Ireland made the short hop to Germany for the second match of their tour. The injuries to Gaskins, Hutchinson and Monahan had healed and they resumed their allotted positions. Paddy Moore was also available, and Jimmy Daly – who had done sterling work at right-wing and right-back against the Swiss – was dropped and the attack reshuffled. For the first time there were no debutants in the Irish team. So far, the selectors had used 72 players in 13 matches (almost six new players per game) but there were signs that things were settling down. Only 28 new players were picked for the remaining 17 internationals before the Second World War.

1935 was to be a busy year for Germany. The game against Ireland was the first of two internationals within five days and overall they were to play a record 17 that year, losing only three. Adolf Hitler's Germany demanded every effort to promote national superiority, in team sports as well as individual events. Germany's record in international football had been modest until he came to power in 1933, but in 18 games since then Germany had won 14, including seven successive wins before this game, Germany's 50th home international and their first in Dortmund.

The Germans had returned from their first World Cup as heroes. They had qualified by beating Luxembourg 9-1 and had faced Ireland's betters, Belgium, in the first round. The Belgians led 2-1 at the break but a second-half goal-spree saw the Germans easy winners. In the quarter-finals they beat Sweden but in the semis met the Czechs, who beat them 3-1. Germany finished third when they beat Austria in the consolation final. They had won all six games since the World Cup by convincing margins. Ireland's task to stop them registering a record eighth successive victory seemed daunting.

Before kick-off both sides gave the Nazi salute, as did most sides visiting Germany during this time. It was seen as a 'friendly gesture' towards their hosts but its odious connotations left a bitter taste in the mouths of players. Ireland would play Nazi Germany twice more before the outbreak of war but on neither occasion was that salute given. The story goes that in 1936 at Dalymount Park a German press photographer tried to get spectators at the 'school end' to give the salute, once the Irish team had refused, but got a different type of 'salute'. Then in 1939, Jimmy Dunne, who had never abandoned his nationalist principles, told his charges in no uncertain terms that they were not to salute but 'to remember Aughrim. Remember 1916'. In 1935, however, there was some sympathy for a country that was well on its way to recovery after the devastating effects of the First World War.

The match kicked off in brilliant sunshine. The first chance fell to the hosts but Lenz shot wide. Damminger then headed over before, in a surprise move, Ireland took the lead. A free-kick was awarded on the halfway line and Gaskins sent a high ball into the area. The German goalkeeper and Tiefel both went for it, as did Ellis. The ball came off the heads of the two outfield players and past the stranded Buchloh. Minutes later Moore powered in a shot which Buchloh turned around the post for a corner.

Hutchinson was injured and had to leave the field, so Ireland played with ten men for much of the remainder of the half. Ernst Lehner, the German player of the year, was giving Dunne a torrid time and when he got around him once again the full-back pulled him down 25 yards from goal. Lehner took the free-kick, which Foley turned onto the crossbar, only for Damminger to bang in the loose ball. Foley made another magnificent save but, in doing so was injured. He played out the rest of the half in pain.

During the break it was discovered that Foley, Hutchinson and O'Kane were all walking wounded so the Irish team was reshuffled. O'Kane went to the right wing and Ellis dropped back to right-half. Ellis was a versatile player but not suited to the half-back role. O'Kane was a fine back but again unsuitable for the wing. But Ireland had little option. Foley, too, had little choice but to soldier on between the sticks.

The Irish opened the second period strongly, with Rigby forcing a splendid save by Buchloh. A good run and cross by Lehner set up the second German goal, which was put away by Damminger. From then on it was all Germany and Ireland did well to hold them to a single-goal deficit until four minutes from the end when the splendid Lehner broke away and unleashed a shot which found the roof of the net. Late on, a break by Monahan resulted in a cross which was headed past the advancing Buchloh by Moore but the ball hit the bar and went over.

Match No. 14   *Sunday, 8th December 1935*   *Dublin*
REPUBLIC OF IRELAND (3) 3   Ellis 13, Horlacher 32, 35
NETHERLANDS (2) 5   Bakhuys 1, van Nellen 15, 48, Drok 67, Smit 87
Ref: P Bauwens (Germany)   *Dalymount Park*   *Att: 22,000*

IRELAND (2-3-5)		A-G	NETHERLANDS (2-3-5)	
William Harrington	Cork	1–0/5	Leo Halle	(Go Ahead)
William O'Neill	Dundalk	1–0	Mauk Weber	(AGOVV)
Bill McGuire	Bohemians	1–0	Bertus Caldenhove	(DWS)
William Glen	Shamrock Rov	5–0	Bas Paauwe	(Feyenoord)
Paddy Andrews	Bohemians	1–0	Wim Anderiesen	(Ajax)
Joe O'Reilly	Brideville	4–1	Puck van Heel	(Feyenoord)
Plev Ellis	Bohemians	3–2	Frank Wels	(Unitas)
Joey Donnelly	Dundalk	4–1	Daaf Drok	(RFC)
Paddy Moore	Shamrock Rov	7–7	Beb Bakhuys	(HBS)
Fred Horlacher	Bohemians	6–2	Kick Smit	(Haarlem)
Joe Kendrick	Dolphin	4–0	Joop van Nellen	(DHC)

MANAGERS: Committee (14)   Bob Glendenning
CAPTAINS: William Glen   Puck van Heel

The 1935-36 season in Ireland began with the Free State Shield, won by St James's Gate. Alf Rigby showed fine form for the brewery side and could well have lined out for Ireland had it not been for the equally fine form shown by Paddy Moore. Moore had returned home from Aberdeen in the summer after 'problems' – alcoholism was little understood at the time. He returned to Rovers and seemed to rediscover his form. The selectors thought so and picked him as centre-forward for this third game against the Dutch.

This was the third time the selectors had to pick an all-League of Ireland team, as this was a busy month for the domestic game in both Britain and Ireland. This gave the selectors a chance to reward some Irish players who had shown superb form during 1934-35 and early in 1935-36. One such was Dolphin's Joe Kendrick. Kendrick, who had last played for Ireland against the Dutch a year earlier, had given fine displays for Dolphin during their title-winning season. He was joined in the front line by Plev Ellis and Fred Horlacher – who would spearhead Bohemians' charge to their fifth title this season – and Joey Donnelly, playing his fourth successive game for Ireland.

Joe O'Reilly and 'Sacky' Glen were the only players with previous international experience in defence, as four others made their debuts. William Harrington was emerging as one of the best goalkeepers in Cork since 'Fox' Foley, and some said he was even better than old favourite Mick McCarthy, who was now at Shamrock Rovers. William O'Neill would, in time, nail down the right-back spot and in doing so would become Dundalk's most capped player. He was still a teenager when he debuted against the Dutch and would be one of those players whose international career would be interrupted by the Second World War. Bill McGuire, a right-back, was picked to play at left-back. A former Tailteann handballer, he had been banned by the GAA for playing a 'foreign game'. Paddy Andrews was captain at Bohemians but had shown his sporting prowess at Gaelic football and hurling as well as the shot-put and discus. He too was banned by the GAA.

For some seasons the League of Ireland clubs had been using players from Britain, and as a consequence the LOI representative side had seen a fair few British players in their side. Now came a long-overdue opportunity for an all-Irish team to showcase what the League had to offer, albeit on the international stage.

Since beating Ireland in the World Cup, things had gone well for the Dutch and especially centre-forward Beb Bakhuys. The Dutch had played nine games, won five and Bakhuys had scored twelve of their 25 goals (with the two other scorers against Ireland, Kick Smit and Leen Vente adding another ten). Ireland, by contrast, had lost every game since defeat in Amsterdam and had gone five games without a win.

Despite the unavailability of British-based players, this was probably the strongest team the Free State had yet put out, with a total of 26 caps. The Free State FA had tried out 27 players in various trials, from which 15 were chosen (including four reserves). The Dutch cap total was over 170!

On a heavy pitch, Smit was instantly brought down by Glen. From the free-kick Wels crossed for Bakhuys to head the first goal. The home side levelled when Horlacher found Moore, whose header looped over Halle and Ellis smashed the ball in before the keeper could recover. The Dutch regained the lead in their next attack. Van Nellen unleashed a 40-yarder that flew across Harrington into the far corner.

Moore had penalty appeals turned down before Ireland drew level again. Moore headed on a cross and Horlacher volleyed in off the bar from 25 yards. Then Donnelly put Ellis clear on the right and his cross found Horlacher who headed in. Ireland were 3-2 up and heading for an overdue win.

Early in the second half, van Nellen made it 3-3 when he met Wels' corner with an overhead kick. Then, when Glen burst into the box and was fouled, O'Reilly drove the penalty too near Halle, who saved it at the second attempt. More chances came Ireland's way. They could have been 6-3 up with 25 minutes to play but ended up conceding another two goals. Drok received a pass from Bakhuys on the run and powered a shot past Harrington to give the visitors the lead for the third time. Late on, Harrington parried a shot from Drok and from the rebound the Dutch worked the ball out to Wels, whose cross was met with a downward header from Smit. Andrews appeared to stop the ball on the goal-line, which was by now non-existent in the mud, but the referee ruled it had crossed the 'line'.

Match No. 15   *Tuesday, 17th March 1936*   *Dublin*
REPUBLIC OF IRELAND (1) 1   Dunne 34
SWITZERLAND (0) 0
Ref: J Langenus (Belgium)   *Dalymount Park*   *Att: 32,000*

IRELAND (2-3-5)		A-G	SWITZERLAND (2-3-5)	
William Harrington	Cork	2–1/5	Gustav Schlegel	(Young Fellows)
William O'Neill	Dundalk	2–0	Severino Minelli	(Grasshoppers)
Bill Gorman	Bury	1–0	Walter Weiler	(GC)
William Glen	Shamrock Rov	6–0	Francis Defago	(Bern)
Charlie Turner	Southend Utd	1–0	Fernand Jaccard	(Basel)
Joe O'Reilly	Brideville	5–1	Eduard Muller	(Young Fellows)
Plev Ellis	Bohemians	4–2	Eugen Diebold	(Young Fellows)
Joey Donnelly	Dundalk	5–1	Leopold Kielholz	(Bern)
Jimmy Dunne	Arsenal	2–3	Alessandro Frigerio	(Young Fellows)
Fred Horlacher	Bohemians	7–2	Jacques Spagnoli	(Lausanne)
Jimmy Kelly	Derry City	3–0	Georges Aeby	(Servette)

MANAGERS: Committee (15)   Henry Muller
CAPTAINS: William Glen   Severino Minelli

Switzerland arrived in Dublin on the back of six straight away defeats and with a side that showed six changes from the one that beat Ireland nearly a year previously. The Irish team also had changes; nine in all, from the side that had narrowly lost in Basle, but also contained a number of players who would enjoy a long run in the side. Particularly outstanding were the two debutants, Gorman and Turner, who would retain their places for some time to come. There was also a second cap for Jimmy Dunne, a goalscoring sensation in England with Sheffield United, and who had recently joined Arsenal. Another Jimmy – Kelly – also returned to the side and again proved to be an excellent player. If the Swiss hoped to put an end to their run of just seven wins in their last 24 internationals, then they would have to overcome possibly the strongest side Ireland had yet put out.

    The Swiss defence showed two changes from the one that coped reasonably well with the Irish attack in Basle. One of those changes, Schlegel in goal, played particularly well. He was in action early on, producing a full-length diving save to keep out a shot from Donnelly. He then produced a similar save to deny Horlacher. Then Ellis had a chance but pulled his shot wide of the post. The Swiss forward line was noticeably weak but still forced Harrington into action to deal with headers from Diebold and Spagnoli. The visitors' defence was tough. A noticeable feature of nearly all the matches Ireland had played was what was called 'obstructive tactics' employed by European defenders, which was legal according to the rules.

The Swiss, however, went a step further and used their elbows whenever an Irish player received the ball. These tactics were not something the Irish were used to, and they took some of the sting out of their attack. Kelly and Ellis still prospered on the wings, however, and produced headed chances for O'Reilly and Dunne, which were saved. Dunne slowly got the measure of the Swiss defence and came more into the game. He worked an opening and shot just too high, and then got on the end of a Kelly cross, only to be denied by a superb save by the goalkeeper.

Irish pressure finally had its reward when Ellis put Dunne clear to round Schlegel, only to see his shot cleared off the line by Minelli. The ball flew out to Horlacher, who passed across to the waiting Dunne, who tapped home. Soon afterwards Aeby had the best chance for the visitors but Glen cleared his close-range shot off the line.

Ireland were on top for the rest of the half and could have added another two goals. The left-wing partnership of Horlacher and Kelly was causing all sorts of problems and when Kelly found Dunne once more, the centre-forward's shot was again brilliantly kept out by Schlegel.

A minute later, another Kelly cross was headed goalwards by Dunne. Schlegel caught the ball but dropped it and as Dunne went to prod the loose ball into the net he was hauled back by a Swiss defender. Amazingly no penalty was awarded.

In a effort to enliven their attack in the second half, Kielholz and Frigerio – both centre-forwards for their clubs – switched positions but to little effect. Schlegel seemed to have a case of the 'wobblies' as, soon after the turnaround, he dropped another shot from Donnelly but cleared the danger before there could be any follow-up.

Kielholz, a bespectacled star for Switzerland in the last World Cup, managed to put in a first-time effort from a cross by Diebold but Harrington made a tremendous save. Harrington was on his way to becoming only the third Irish goalkeeper ever to keep a clean sheet.

The left flank of the Irish attack, and Kelly in particular, continued to cause problems, and Kelly sent in a swerving shot which just went wide. Dunne then tricked two opponents to squeeze in a shot, which also went just the wrong side of the upright. Ellis became the next Irish player to be denied by Schlegel, who turned his shot out for a corner. From the corner, Dunne had a header punched out by Schlegel to Donnelly, whose return header was again punched out by the agile goalkeeper. When the ball fell to O'Reilly a goal seemed certain but, again, the Swiss custodian thwarted the attempt, this time catching the ball.

Schlegel was kept busy until the end of the game, which nearly produced an equaliser for the Swiss. A Diebold cross gave Frigerio a great chance but in lashing out at the ball he missed it completely and it went harmlessly wide of the post.

Match No. 16   *Sunday, 3rd May 1936*   *Budapest*
HUNGARY (1) 3   Sarosi 7, 48 pen, Sas 75
REPUBLIC OF IRELAND (2) 3   Dunne 11, 68, O'Reilly 19
Ref: J Brull (Czechoslovakia)   *Hungaria uti Stadium*   Att: 20,000

IRELAND (2-3-5)		A-G	HUNGARY (2-3-5)	
William Harrington	Cork	3–1/8	Antal Szabo	(Hungaria)
William O'Neill	Dundalk	3–0	Gyula Futo	(Ujpest)
Bill Gorman	Bury	2–0	Karoly Deri	(Kispest)
William Glen	Shamrock Rov	7–0	Istvan Bela Magda	(Budai)
Con Moulson	Lincoln City	1–0	Jozsef Turay	(Hungaria)
Joe O'Reilly	Brideville	6–2	Janos Dudas	(Hungaria)
Harry Duggan	Leeds Utd	3–0	Ferenc Sas	(Hungaria)
Joey Donnelly	Dundalk	6–1	Jeno Vincze	(Ujpest)
Jimmy Dunne	Arsenal	3–5	Gyorgy Sarosi	(Ferencvaros)
Owen Madden	Cork	1–0	Laszlo Cseh	(Hungaria)
Bill Fallon	Notts Co	2–0	Tibor Kemeny	(Ferencvaros)
			Sub: Jozsef Hada for Szabo (half-time)	(Ferencvaros)

MANAGERS: Committee (16)   Dr Karoly Dietz
CAPTAINS: William Glen   Gyorgy Sarosi

Ireland's second European tour began in sunny Budapest with their sternest test to date. Hungary were virtually unbeatable in their capital, having won their last seven games on the banks of the Danube in convincing manner. In fact, since the Great War, Hungary had won 40 of their 57 games in Budapest and only Austria, England, Spain, Italy and Czechoslovakia had ever returned home with a win. Hungary's overall record in Budapest read: played 92, won 62, lost 14 and drew 16. Since their last meeting, Ireland had played four matches, losing three. Hungary had played nine, winning five and losing two. Of the 29 goals they had scored in that time their forward line for this match accounted for 18. It would constitute a formidable task for Ireland to emerge from Budapest with anything other then a defeat.

'Ireland hold Hungary' ran the headline in the following day's match reports. If understated and to the point, the headline was still sensational and captured the shock and pride of one of Ireland's greatest ever results since the draw with Spain five years earlier. If truth be told, the typesetter could have been using 'beat' instead of 'hold'.

There was an interesting clash of tactics in a game that was played, as was noted, on the only pitch in Hungary that was completely covered in grass. Hungary, as was the norm for most European sides, used the short-passing game and relied more on teamwork. Ireland, relied on the long-ball game and individual skills. The tactics used by both sides were the standard ones employed since Ireland came on the scene.

The rainy clouds that had hung round Budapest in the days preceding the match gave way to a clear sky, which suited both sides and contributed to an entertaining game. The Irish defence, in which Gorman and Harrington were outstanding, were put under pressure straight away. In the first five minutes, the home side launched attack after attack. The Hungarian wingers, especially, flourished in those opening minutes and both Sas and Kemeny had shots saved well by the Irish goalkeeper before Sas got away up the right and his low cross from near the corner flag was slammed past Harrington by Sarosi. It was his eleventh goals in his last nine internationals.

Surprisingly, the Irish settled down well after this, and Moulson had Sarosi in his pocket for the rest of the game. With the threat of their centre-forward nullified, Hungary's attacks were sporadic and Ireland capitalised. Dunne collected a long ball from O'Reilly and ran on a few yards before unleashing a scorcher that bamboozled Szabo.

Eight minutes later the Irish caught the Hungarians sleeping again. The Irish won a free-kick 30 yards from goal and O'Reilly placed the ball as if to shoot. The Hungarians stood off, as it was so far out but, to the surprise of nearly everybody O'Reilly ran up to blast the ball past the startled Szabo to give Ireland the lead. Two quick pieces of individual brilliance had undone the home side. The Hungarians came back strongly but ran into a defence now playing at top form. The Irish forward line was not finished yet and launched a series of attacks late in the half until an injury to Madden took the wind out of their sails. At the break, however, Ireland held their one-goal lead.

The Hungarians came out for the second half determined to turn things around. Within minutes they were awarded a penalty when Moulson handled a cross, leaving Sarosi, free of his shackles, to equalise from the spot. Despite Madden's injury, the Irish forward line still posed danger and Dunne proved to be an elusive opponent for the home backs. Dunne, Duggan and Donnelly, who also took the eye, had chances to score before the Irish reclaimed the lead. Another long ball found Dunne in space just outside the penalty box and his snap shot beat the half-time substitute goalkeeper, Hada, and flew into the net.

Following this, there was a heavy shower which made the ball and pitch slippery. The conditions should have suited the visitors but it was the Hungarians who seemed to make the better of them. The home side equalised, unluckily as far as Ireland were concerned. Sas got the ball on the right wing, cut inside and shot. Harrington had the effort covered but the ball hit O'Reilly and wrong-footed the goalkeeper. The last fifteen minutes were played out with Ireland on the back foot, and a thrilling game ended in a draw. The following day, Jimmy Dunne learnt that he had been put on the transfer list by Arsenal.

Match No. 17   *Saturday, 9th May 1936*   *Luxembourg*
LUXEMBOURG (0) 1   Mart 59 pen
REPUBLIC OF IRELAND (1) 5   Dunne 9, 86, J. Donnelly 65, Kelly 71, 87
Ref: P Bauwens (Germany)   *Municipal Stadium*   *Att: 8,000*

IRELAND (2-3-5)		A-G	LUXEMBOURG (2-3-5)	
William Harrington	Cork	4–1/9	Jean-Pierre Hoscheid	(Jeunesse d'Esch)
William O'Neill	Dundalk	4–0	Jean-Pierre Frisch	(The National)
Bill Gorman	Bury	3–0	Victor Majerus	(Jeunesse d'Esch)
William Glen	Shamrock Rov	8–0	Jean Schmit	(Stade Dudelange)
Con Moulson	Lincoln City	2–0	Alfred Kieffer	(Red Boys)
Joe O'Reilly	Brideville	7–2	Joseph Fischer	(The National)
Plev Ellis	Bohemians	5–2	Oscar Stamet	(Spora Luxembourg)
Harry Duggan	Leeds Utd	4–0	Andre Schmit	(Fola Esch)
Jimmy Dunne	Arsenal	4–7	Leon Mart	(Fola Esch)
Joey Donnelly	Dundalk	7–2	Robert Geib	(Spora Luxembourg)
Jimmy Kelly	Derry City	4–2	Theophile Speicher	(Spora Luxembourg)

MANAGERS:	Committee (17)	Committee
CAPTAINS:	William Glen	Joseph Fischer

In midweek Ireland had crossed into Germany to play a Rhineland XI and were beaten 1-4. The selectors used that match to rest Fallon and the injured Madden and bring in Horlacher and Kelly. The ubiquitous Jimmy Dunne scored the Irish goal. Then it was on to Luxembourg, where Madden and Fallon were unable to play, so Ellis and Kelly were brought in. Kelly, who had scored 32 goals for Derry this season, was a straight swap for Fallon, but Ellis came in at right-wing, with Duggan moving in to inside-right and Donnelly to partner Kelly on the left. 'Sacky' Glen again took his place at right-half to become Ireland's most capped player with eight caps.

Being so centrally located in Europe, and therefore so geographically accessible, Luxembourg had proved a useful venue for nations to test up and coming players against the amateurs of the Grand Duchy. In consequence, Luxembourg's international record is littered with games against 'B' selections as well as other amateur sides. They commenced international football in 1911 with a 1-4 defeat by France, and defeats became the norm for the next 25 years. By the time Ireland came to town, Luxembourg had lost 43 of their 67 internationals and all but one of their 13 wins were against 'B' or Amateur sides.

A curious connection between the two competing nations was that both had faced the Italian 'B' side in 1927 and these matches still form part of both's international records. Now, in 1936, Luxembourg were preparing for the Olympic Games in Berlin, due to take place in August. In February they played the Belgium 'B' side and drew 5-5, with Leon Mart grabbing a hat-trick. Defeats by Switzerland 'B' and Belgium 'B' followed. This was to be their final warm-up before heading for Germany. The Luxembourg squad for this, their first encounter with a team from the British Isles, was experienced in terms of caps – 105 as compared to Ireland's 41 – but the majority of these were earned against the lesser sides of most nations.

The teams and officials were presented to the Prince of Luxembourg prior to kick-off and a sizeable crowd (by Luxembourg standards) watched the game, which was played on a rough pitch in sunny weather. The Irish began well and forced a few corners early on. After nine minutes the Irish were awarded a free-kick, which was taken by O'Reilly. The ball was knocked high into the box and Dunne, losing his marker, headed the ball past Hoscheid. It now meant that all six goals scored by English League players for Ireland had been scored by Dunne. Soon afterwards Ellis had a great chance for a second goal but his effort was just off target. The home side put together some nice moves but ran into a strong Irish defence and got nowhere. A long ball from Glen put Dunne away and he slipped it to Duggan who would have scored had it not been for a fine save from Hoscheid. Glen then worked his way into the box. Just as he was about to shoot, Dunne, with a 'what the hell are you doing' tackle, took the ball off his toe and shot inches wide. Late on, Stamet had a wild fling at a ball and missed one of the few opportunities the home side had created.

In the second half the Irish again pressed and for a good ten minutes bombarded the Luxembourg goal with shot after shot. On a rare breakaway, Stamet broke into the Irish box and was hauled down by Moulson. A penalty was awarded and Mart sent Harrington the wrong way with his spot-kick to notch his seventh goal in six international appearances. Taking heart from this equaliser and with the backing of the crowd, the home side began to press but made little headway against a firm defence.

Ireland regained the lead within six minutes when a free-kick by Gorman was knocked down by Dunne for Donnelly to sweep the ball home from just outside the box. In another six minutes Ireland were 3-1 ahead, when Dunne put Kelly in for a screamer of a shot which swerved away from Hoscheid. O'Reilly had an effort clip the bar before the visitors sealed the outcome with two goals in a minute against a tiring Luxembourg. Dunne shot home a fine fourth to become joint top scorer for Ireland, along with Paddy Moore. Kelly finished things off with another excellent shot. For the second match in a row, Ireland had been involved in a six-goal feast which included a penalty to the opposition. This was also Ireland's record win, which would remain until they beat Cyprus 6-0 in 1980.

The Luxembourgers' involvement in the German Olympics ended in the first round when they were thrashed 0-9 by the host nation. Eight of the players who had played against Ireland were in the defeated side.

Match No. 18   *Saturday, 17th October 1936*   *Dublin*
REPUBLIC OF IRELAND (2) 5   J Donnelly 25, 69, Davis 35 pen, 76, Geoghegan 59
GERMANY (2) 2   Kobierski 26, Szepan 32
Ref: W Webb (Scotland)   *Dalymount Park*   *Att: 27,109*

IRELAND (2-3-5)		A–G	GERMANY (2-3-5)	
Jim Foley	Glasgow Celtic	6–0/19	Hans Jakob	(Jahn Ragensburg)
William O'Neill	Dundalk	5–0	Reinhold Muenzenberg	(Aleman' Aachen)
Bill Gorman	Bury	4–0	Andreas Munkert	(1 FC Nurmberg)
Joe O'Reilly	St James's Gate	8–2	Josef Rodzinski	(Hamborn 07)
Charlie Turner	Southend Utd	2–0	Ludwig Goldbrunner	(Bayern Munich)
Hugh Connolly	Cork	1–0	Albin Kitzinger	(Schweinfurt 05)
Plev Ellis	Bohemians	6–2	Ernst Lehner	(Schwaben Augsburg)
Joey Donnelly	Dundalk	8–4	Otto Siffling	(SV Waldhof)
Tom Davis	Oldham Athletic	1–2	Karl Hohmann	(VfL Benrath)
Paddy Moore	Shamrock Rov	8–7	Fritz Szepan	(Schalke 04)
Matty Geoghegan	St James's Gate	1–1	Stanislaus Kobierski	(Fortuna Dusseldorf)

MANAGERS: Committee (18)   Dr Otto Nerz
CAPTAINS: Charlie Turner   Fritz Szepan

In terms of caps, this German side was one of the most experienced Ireland had yet faced. Nearly all the players were in double figures, and between them they had accumulated 178 caps. Ireland, by comparison, could only muster a quarter of that total. The Germans arrived in Dublin on the heels of a 0-2 defeat by Scotland on the Wednesday, and were in the process of changing managers. Dr Nerz was nearing the end of his long association with the German team and his successor, Josef Herberger, was being groomed as his heir. Both were in the German party that arrived in Dublin in a bad mood. The German press had not been kind to the team and intimated that they had forgotten how to score.

The German side that lined up at Dalymount Park showed four changes from the team beaten by Scotland, three of them in the forward line. In came Rodzinski – the least capped member of the squad – Hohmann, Kobierski and Lehner. Lehner was one of three survivors of the 1935 meeting between the two nations and the man of the match from that game in Dortmund. The Germans had played 21 games since then, winning over half and losing only six. Away from home, too, the German record was worthy of note, showing they had lost only four of their last 15 games. For the record, Ireland were about to inflict on Germany their 50th defeat overall.

This was the first ever game played by Ireland in the month of October. The League of Ireland Championship had yet to commence. The Shield was in full swing but its importance in the 1930s could be gauged by the fact that most of the LOI players who played against Germany turned out for their clubs the following day. The one advantage of playing in October was that it tied in with the international fixture list across the water, so it was a bit easier to gain player release. Harry Duggan was to have captained the side, but a week earlier he had transferred to Newport County who needed him for a League game. The always-reliable Plev Ellis took his place. Jimmy Dunne was also denied permission to play by his club, Southampton, for much the same reason, so in came Tom Davis, the former Shels and Cork forward, who had been banging in the goals for Oldham.

There was also a recall for Paddy Moore, who despite being only a year older than Davis was now described as a veteran. Moore had galvanised Rovers since his return from Scotland just over a year earlier. They won the FAI Cup for the first time in three seasons and were enjoying a good run in the Shield, with Moore not showing visible ill-effects of the alcohol problems that would end his startling career so early. Moore's form in the Shield prompted the selectors to try him in the problematic inside-left berth. Moore would flourish.

It would be years before the expression 'put them under pressure' would become commonplace and associated with Jack Charlton. However, the type of play practised in the early years of the Charlton era, namely denying the opposition the time and space to play their type of football, was something which was used well before the arrival of the Englishman. One of its earlier uses was in this game against Germany. Ireland's team may have been picked by a selection committee but those responsible for team fitness and tactics were the team's trainer. Val Harris and Billy Lacey, two of Ireland's most experienced ex-players, had been trainers to the team on a number of occasions, and for this match the wily Lacey was the one responsible.

All the trainer could do was get the players fit, but he might also work on a few tactics. Lacey, having experienced the short-passing style of play adopted by most visiting teams, decided that the best way to combat this was to get at them early on and deny them the chance to dwell on the ball. These tactics worked to perfection and the Germans were never allowed the time to settle and dictate the course of the game as, say, the Spanish had done five years earlier. The German manager was left to rue: 'It was not a good game. It was not good football [but] it was a good fight. The Irish side deserved to win.'

It was, nevertheless, the Germans who applied the early pressure and Siffling had a diving header saved by Foley. A mistake by Muenzenberg let in Davis for a shot that was well held by Jakob, who despite the scoreline, had a good game. At the other end, Foley, due to lack of match fitness, had a few nervous moments but emerged as one of Ireland's better players on the day. He intercepted a cross from Kobierski but the ball spun out of his hands to Hohmann. As the German centre-forward steadied himself, Gorman arrived from nowhere to kick the ball clear. Hohmann would not get another chance as Turner marked him out of the rest of the match. Foley redeemed himself a few minutes later when he saved a close-range shot from Lehner. Donnelly put Geoghegan away but Jakob showed good anticipation by saving at the winger's feet.

That preceded a four-goal burst in four minutes. First, Donnelly got on the end of a cross from Geoghegan, appeared to lose the ball, but regained possession and from six yards swivelled and shot low past Jakob. From the restart, the Germans broke up the right with Lehner's short cross catching the Irish out of position and Kobierski shot home from close range. Foley then saved a shot from Kobierski, Moore – who was beginning to control the game – shot against the post, and Hohmann shook off the attentions of Turner to have a speedy shot saved by the goalkeeper. In the visitors' next attack, Kobierski broke up the left and his cross-shot found Siffling who set up the inrushing Szepan to drive past Foley and into the net.

The German lead lasted a minute. Davis took down a high ball by O'Reilly but in the act of shooting was taken down by Goldbrunner. Davis, described as a rough player by the German press, had been giving Goldbrunner the runaround all match and the centre-half's 'tackle' was pure frustration. Davis, who was his club's penalty-taker, converted the spot-kick himself. Ireland's next attack should have yielded another penalty but Muenzenberg's impetuous tackle on Geoghegan went unpunished. This tackle incapacitated the winger and slowed him for the rest of the game. Just before the break, Kobierski got clean through and tried to chip the advancing Foley but the Irish goalkeeper made a good save seem simple.

Early in the second half the Germans almost regained the lead. Foley failed to hold another cross and the ball fell to Szepan whose shot was kicked off the line by Gorman. Ten minutes later Kobierski struck a post. From these escapes Ireland went on to dominate the half. A corner from Geoghegan found the leaping Moore but Jakob took the ball off the Irishman's head. Then a cross by Moore was headed out to Ellis, whose return header to the far post went in off the chest of Geoghegan.

If this seemed lucky, it should be noted that the former Belfast Celtic man had thrown himself forward to make the connection. The Germans might have equalised but for a super save by Foley. Kobierski was again put through but the Irish goalkeeper narrowed the angle, turning the ball out for a corner. However, it was Jakob who was to be the busier goalkeeper. Davis was denied another goal when Jakob, who had only conceded eleven goals in his last ten internationals, made a brilliant save. Geoghegan should have put Ireland further in front but sent an unmarked header wide of the target from six yards. Ireland were not to be kept out, though, and it was Moore who set up Ireland's fourth.

From a throw-in, Moore sent over an accurate cross. Ellis headed down for Donnelly, whose shot went in off Muenzenberg. Even though the defender's foot caused a major deflection it was, as the *Irish Independent*'s 'Pivot' insisted, Donnelly's goal.

Ellis and Davis had further chances to put the game to bed but were denied by Jakob. Germany's heaviest defeat since 1931 was completed when Moore dribbled forward and unleashed a 25-yard shot, which Jakob parried on the line. Davis rushed in to make sure and prodded the ball home.

Germany would not lose another game for two years.

Match No. 19   *Sunday, 6th December 1936*   *Dublin*
REPUBLIC OF IRELAND   (1) 2   Fallon 20, Davis 72 pen
HUNGARY   (2) 3   Titkos 36, Vincze 37, Toldi 48
Ref: H Nattrass (England)   *Dalymount Park*   *Att: 27,000*

IRELAND (2-3-5)		A-G	HUNGARY (2-3-5)	
Jim Foley	Glasgow Celtic	7–0/22	Jozsef Palinkas	(Szeged)
William O'Neill	Dundalk	6–0	Gyula Polgar	(Ferencvaros)
Bill Gorman	Bury	5–0	Jozsef Vago	(Bocskai)
Joe O'Reilly	St James's Gate	9–2	Jozsef Turay	(Hungaria)
Charlie Turner	Southend Utd	3–0	Gyorgy Szucs	(Ujpest)
Con Moulson	Notts Co	3–0	Janos Dudas	(Hungaria)
Plev Ellis	Bohemians	7–2	Laszlo Cseh	(Hungaria)
Joey Donnelly	Dundalk	9–4	Jeno Vincze	(Ujpest)
Tom Davis	Oldham Athletic	2–3	Gyorgy Sarosi	(Ferencvaros)
Paddy Moore	Shamrock Rov	9–7	Geza Toldi	(Ferencvaros)
Bill Fallon	Notts Co	3–1	Pal Titkos	(Hungaria)
			Sub: Antal Szabo	(Hungaria)
			for Palinkas (66 mins)	

MANAGERS: Committee (19)   Dr Karoly Dietz
CAPTAINS: Charlie Turner   Dr Gyorgy Sarosi

The Irish selectors had a wealth of options for the return game with Hungary. The win over Germany eased their task as they picked all but two of that side. Hugh Connolly had looked slow against the Germans and Matty Geoghegan was injured. Con Moulson, who had done well in his first two games, and Bill Fallon – the former Dolphin player in his third season with promotion-chasing Notts County – took their places. The settled Irish team meant it was the first time at home that no player was making his debut. Davis again led the forward line, having recently turned out for Northern Ireland against England and scored in a 1-3 defeat. Paddy Moore was also included.

On the Wednesday the Hungarians had lost 2-6 to England at Highbury. Their team in Dublin showed five changes, and also featured five players – Szucs, Cseh, Vago, Titkos and Vincze – who had played at Dalymount two years previously. Despite a recent slump in form (three defeats in five games since that draw with Ireland), Hungary still had a formidable record, winning nearly half of more than 190 internationals.

December was not a good month for Ireland, who had lost all three previous internationals played in that month. However, they were on a run of four games without defeat and the win over Germany had given everyone a boost. An expectant crowd witnessed the most exciting game since Continental sides started visiting these shores, according to the newspapers of the day.

Ellis quickly sent over a cross. The ball was held by Palinkas but Davis charged in and almost forced him and it over the line. There were appeals for a goal but the referee waved play on. Mr Nattrass was to have a busy game and described it as 'one of the hardest games I have ever refereed' Ireland then forced three quick corners from which Fallon and Davis had shots saved.

Fallon worked his way into a position to blast in a shot which swerved away from Palinkas and into the back of the net. Moore then had to leave the field for attention to an eye injury. Despite being down to ten men, Ireland still forced the pace, but suddenly found themselves 1-2 down as their goal fell twice. Titkos cut in from the left and placed a low shot towards the far corner. Foley pushed the ball out but Titkos, following up, fired in the loose ball. A minute later, a harmless looking cross from Dudas sailed over Moulson and Gorman and fell to Vincze, who netted easily. Near the break, another strong Hungarian attack resulted in Toldi being presented with an easy chance but, somehow, the inside-left missed with the goal yawning.

Ireland were back to full strength for the second half and came out fighting. However, they were surprised by an early Hungarian attack. Cseh broke away up the right and crossed for Toldi, who skipped over O'Neill's tackle. Foley came out but Toldi placed his shot past the advancing goalkeeper and into the net. It was the 25th goal Ireland had conceded at home.

Shortly afterwards Vincze – who had scored at Dalymount two years earlier – could have made it 4-1 but his shot flew inches wide. Following this Ireland had all the play and should have been on at least equal terms. Palinkas, who was getting a rare run-out in place of Szabo, was proving to be an excellent shot-stopper. Davis and Moulson tested the keeper during a sustained bout of Irish pressure which ended with Moore, Donnelly and Ellis all having efforts stopped by the young Hungarian.

Palinkas, who like Sarosi, was a medical doctor, was injured in saving from Davis's effort and had to be replaced. Szabo, who had endured a torrid time in London on the Wednesday, ran on to take his place in goal, only to be sent back to the dressing room by Mr Nattrass to change his green shirt for a white one. Szabo, who was Hungary's first-choice custodian, was more flamboyant then Palinkas and his acrobatics to deny Ireland provided the crowd with even more entertainment. Ireland pulled one goal back when a cross by Ellis was handled by Szucs. Davis blasted the spot-kick home to become the first Irish player to score in two consecutive home games. Ireland could have had another penalty when Donnelly was fouled in the box. The referee seemed about to blow for the foul but saw that Donnelly was in a good position so played an advantage. Donnelly, playing his ninth straight game for Ireland, missed.

Afterwards the President of the Hungarian FA, Mr Fischer, complimented the Irish Free State FA on ten years of international football: 'Your country is definitely on the high road of football. It is a great achievement that you are able to place international teams of such high quality in the field.'

Match No. 20   Monday, 17th May 1937   *Berne*
SWITZERLAND   (0) 0
REPUBLIC OF IRELAND   (1) 1   Dunne 30
Ref: W Lewington (England)   *Wankdorf Stadium*   *Att: 15,000*

IRELAND (2-3-5)		A–G	SWITZERLAND (2-3-5)	
Tommy Breen	Manchester Utd	1–1/0	Renato Bizzozero	(Lugano)
William O'Neill	Dundalk	7–0	Severino Minelli	(Grasshoppers)
Johnny Feenan	Sunderland	1–0	Gusti Lehmann	(Lausanne)
Joe O'Reilly	St James's Gate	10–2	Hans Liniger	(Young Boys)
Charlie Turner	Southend Utd	4–0	Sirio Vernati	(Grasshoppers)
Con Moulson	Notts Co	4–0	Ernest Lortscher	(Servette)
Johnny Brown	Coventry City	1–0	Fredi Bickel	(GC)
Davy Jordan	Wolverhampton	1–0	Paul Aebi	(Young Boys)
Jimmy Dunne	Southampton	5–8	Eugen Rupf	(GC)
Paddy Farrell	Hibernian	1–0	Willy Karcher	(Luzern)
Bill Fallon	Notts Co	4–1	Georges Aeby	(Servette)

MANAGERS: Committee (20)   Henry Muller
CAPTAINS: Charlie Turner   Serverino Minelli

By the time Ireland arrived in Berne on their two-match tour of Europe, their away record was better than at home. Ireland had four wins, two draws and four defeats from ten away games, as opposed to three wins, one draw and five defeats from nine at home. Ireland's two wins on this short tour meant a record three in a row away from home, a record not equalled until 1993.

The Irish squad had a cosmopolitan look. Gone were the days of an all-Dublin XI, and for the first time ever no Shamrock Rover made the starting line-up. Of the team that started in Berne, three were born in Dublin, five from the provinces, and three from outside the Free State. Johnny Feenan, Davy Jordan and Jackie Brown were born in Northern Ireland but only Brown (five caps, one goal) had been capped by the North. Brown would eventually double his caps, but neither Feenan nor Brown would play for the North

In 1923 in Liverpool, the British International Board had laid down guidelines under which the IFA and the FAI could coexist. The IFA could choose players for their national side born within their controlling area, while the Free State could do the same. The grey area concerned the definition of 'their controlling area'. The IFA, which clung to the belief that it was the controlling body for all Ireland, picked players from North and South who were mainly based in Britain. So, Dubliners like Jimmy Dunne and Tom Davis were picked for Northern Ireland. The IFA stopped short of picking League of Ireland players until the 1930s when, first, they picked four Bohemians players for an Amateur international, even though three were born in the Free State. In 1933,

Derry-born Johnny McMahon of Bohs was picked for the North against Scotland, the first and only League of Ireland player to play for Northern Ireland until the late 1980s.

Prior to 1937 the Free State FA had stuck with players from within its own boundaries for international matches but – capitalising on lax enforcement of the rules – picked players born outside the Free State. There was little objection from the IFA at the time and this *ad hoc* relationship continued. With time it might have resulted in two teams representing Ireland from two different Associations, with the same team playing one week for the IFA and the FAI the next. This nearly happened in 1946.

With the wealth of talent now available, there were fewer spaces available to League of Ireland players. In fact, for the first time ever, there was only one representative from the League in the squad, Gate's Joe O'Reilly. The absence of Shamrock Rovers players reflected the Milltown club's recent poor League season. Rovers were the country's most popular club and would supply players for all but three of Ireland's first 50 internationals. The team that garnered most Irish support in England, Manchester United, would also supply many players, the first of whom – Tommy Breen – made his debut in this game. Joe O'Reilly played his seventh successive international and became the first player to win ten caps for Ireland.

Switzerland had played 150 international fixtures, but its overall record was poor – just one win in every four games. Ireland's record was about one win in every three. With Switzerland winning just one of their last 14 internationals, hopes were high of an Irish win.

The Swiss did most of the attacking but Breen, a late replacement for the injured 'Fox' Foley, kept them at bay. Ireland's first attack resulted in a chance for Dunne from an O'Reilly pass but the centre-forward fluffed it. A sustained period of Irish pressure resulted in the only goal of the game. Ireland attacked down the middle with Jordan. The inside-right found Dunne who took the ball on to the edge of the box before placing a low shot past the Swiss goalkeeper. It was Dunne's eighth goal in five internationals, and he was now Ireland's record goalscorer. The Swiss tried hard for an equaliser but relied too much on Rupf, who was marked out of the game by Turner.

The second half saw a change in emphasis in the Swiss attack. With Rupf nullified, the focus of the Swiss attacks fell on Bickel. Dunne had two goals from his previous three away Ireland games, but was to be denied another in this match. The Swiss, on the other hand, came close to equalising three times. First, Bickel got away and should have scored but O'Neill recovered to make a saving tackle. Then a shot from Paul Aebi beat Breen but hit the bar. Breen deserved his clean sheet but might have been denied it in the last minute when Bickel shot low against the butt of the upright and went wide.

Ireland had been lucky for sure. All three games with the Swiss had now been settled by a single goal.

Match No. 21 *Sunday, 23rd May 1937* *Paris*
FRANCE (0) 0
REPUBLIC OF IRELAND (0) 2
Ref: G Krist (Czechoslovakia) Jordan 52, Brown 58
 Colombes Stadium *Att: 16, 688*

IRELAND (2-3-5)		A-G	FRANCE (2-3-5)	
Tommy Breen	Manchester Utd	2–2/0	Laurent Di Lorto	(Sochaux)
William O'Neill	Dundalk	8–0	Abdelkader Ben Bouali	(Olym' Marseille)
Johnny Feenan	Sunderland	2–0	Raoul Diagne	(Racing)
Joe O'Reilly	St. James's Gate	11–2	Francois Bourbotte	(SC Fivois)
Charlie Turner	Southend Utd	5–0	Georges Meuris	(Red Star Olymp')
Con Moulson	Notts Co	5–0	Edmond Delfour	(Racing)
Johnny Brown	Coventry City	2–1	Michel Lauri	(Sochaux)
Davy Jordan	Wolverhampton	2–1	Ignace	(Olympique Marseille)
Jimmy Dunne	Southampton	6–8	Roger Courtois	(Sochaux)
Paddy Farrell	Hibernian	2–0	Michel Frutuoso	(RC Roubaix)
Bill Fallon	Notts Co	5–1	Alfred Aston	(Red Star Olympique)

MANAGERS: Committee (21) Committee
CAPTAINS: Charlie Turner Edmond Delfour

The second match of the European tour was Ireland's first against France, and for the first time the selectors named an unchanged line-up. Ireland's travelling reserves, goalkeeper Mick McCarthy and centre-half Terry Fullerton, were the unfortunate ones to lose out. McCarthy, the only Shamrock Rover on the tour, already possessed one cap, but Waterford's Fullerton would never play for Ireland.

France would host the third World Cup in 1938 and their warm-up games had not been going well. This season they had played four games and lost all but one. In fact, since their early exit from the last World Cup, France had played 15 games, losing nine, but they were rebuilding. The French team that faced Ireland had four players making their only appearance, while just three had a cap-count in double figures. One of these, Edmond Delfour, had played in both the 1930 and 1934 World Cup finals and was aiming for a third. Surprisingly, for such an inexperienced team, the average age was a high 26.5. (Ireland's average was nearly two years younger).

Given that in later years the Irish team would be top-heavy with non-Irish born players, it is notable that only five of the French team were actually born in France. Two were born in Algeria and one in Guyana – French colonies. The other three were born in Switzerland, Poland and Argentina. Lauri, in fact, had been capped 13 times by Argentina and was now making his French debut. Abdelkader Ben Bouali, one of the Algerians, and brilliant Guyanese full-back Raoul Diagne were the first coloured players Ireland had faced.

The match kicked off in searing heat and Turner soon had to intercept Frutuoso's shot, at the expense of a corner. The first real opening saw Lauri break free on the right and hone in on goal. Out came Breen to meet him and when the Argentine-born winger shot the young keeper saved well. Lauri was a shining light in a poor French team but it was Breen who earned the plaudits with a string of saves. In fact, Joe 'Buller' Byrne, the trainer, not given to lavish praise, described Breen as 'the best goalkeeper in the World' after this performance. He even saved a penalty after twelve minutes, after Moulson handled Aston's cross. Ireland's record with penalties was pretty good. Five had been awarded against them, all away from home, and two had been saved. It was the third penalty awarded against Moulson.

It took Ireland 20 minutes to settle, launching raids which saw Feenan and Moulson set up Fallon for a shot which Di Lorto saved. Farrell broke into the box, only for the French goalkeeper to save, as he then did from Brown. Not to be outshone, Breen was in action when Lauri bore down on him. The shot struck the underside of the bar and bounced down into play. Breen raced after the ball but Ignace, who was from Poland, got to it first and fired a shot which grazed the crossbar. The French then threw themselves into the attack coming up to the break and Breen brought off two more saves to keep the scoreline even.

The respective centre-forwards, Roger Courtois and Jimmy Dunne – of which much was expected, given their scoring records – were invisible during the opening half. Turner was having a storming game and never gave the Swiss-born forward a chance. Dunne, on the other hand, prospered after the half-time cup of tea and a positional change with Jordan. Dunne soon got away and was only stopped when Diagne cleared for a corner.

Brown broke up the right wing and found Moulson cutting in from the left. The left-half sent the ball forward to Jordan who fired into the back of the French net. The ex-Ards man became the 20th different player to score for Ireland.

Courtois got his only chance soon after. Clever play by Frutuoso and Aston gave the centre-forward the chance to clear Turner's shackles, but he too was foiled by Breen who saved at his feet. Ireland went two up when Dunne, at inside-right, found Jordan in the centre who lobbed over Meuris. Brown met the falling ball on the volley and gave Di Lorto no chance.

Before long, Dunne got on the end of another move but Di Lorto turned his shot for a corner. The French fought hard to get a goal back but each time they got clear of the Irish defence Breen was there to save. His two clean sheets set a pre-war record that would not be beaten. Breen would play nine games for Northern Ireland before the war but none again for the Republic until 1946. For Jimmy Dunne, victory celebrations were tinged with regret as he had failed to score for Ireland for the first time. It was the first of only five matches that Dunne would fail to be on the scoresheet for his country.

Match No. 22 (World Cup)   *Sunday, 10th October 1937*   *Oslo*
NORWAY (1) 3   Kvammen 30, 64, Martinsen 78
REPUBLIC OF IRELAND (1) 2   Geoghegan 37, Dunne 49
Ref: P Bauwens (Germany)   *Ullevaal Stadium*   *Att: 19,000*

IRELAND (2-3-5)		A–G	NORWAY (2-3-5)	
George McKenzie	Southend Utd	1–0/3	Tom Blohm	(Hugin)
Joe Williams	Shamrock Rov	1–0	Rolf Johannesen	(FFK)
Mick Hoy	Dundalk	1–0	Oyvind Holmsen	(Lyn)
Joe O'Reilly	St James's Gate	12–2	Frithjof Ulleberg	(Lyn)
Charlie Turner	Southend Utd	6–0	Nils Eriksen	(Odd)
Owen Kinsella	Shamrock Rov	2–0	Rolf Holmberg	(Odd)
Tom Donnelly	Drumcondra	1–0	Odd Frantzen	(Hardy)
Joey Donnelly	Dundalk	10–4	Reidar Kvammen	(Viking)
Jimmy Dunne	Shamrock Rov	7–9	Alf Martinsen	(Lillestrom)
Billy Jordan	Bohemians	2–0	Magnar Isaksen	(Lyn)
Matty Geoghegan	St James's Gate	2–2	Arne Brustad	(Lyn)

MANAGERS: Committee (22)   Asbjorn Halvorsen
CAPTAINS: Charlie Turner   Nils Eriksen

The 1938 World Cup would have two fewer entrants than for the previous one, but also four new names – the Dutch East Indies, Finland, Latvia and Norway. Of these, Finland and Latvia had already been knocked out, while the Dutch East Indies had qualified for France by the time Norway made their World Cup debut against Ireland. Norway and Ireland were placed in qualifying Group Two, along with Poland and Yugoslavia. The 'group' was sub-divided, with Yugoslavia playing Poland, and Norway playing Ireland in two-leg ties; the winners on aggregate going through to the finals.

Norway were amateurs and had been playing international football since 1908, without much success. In fact, it took them ten years to claim their first win. In 1925 football in Norway had split in two when the Norwegian Labour movement established its own sports association, the AIF. The Norwegian FA – the NFF – was part of the National Association of Sports. Both the AIF and the NFF organised internationals. The split remained in place until the Norwegian Sports Association united the two parties after World War Two. It was the NFF that first took part in the World Cup and one of the AIF players, Alf Martinsen, played in the side.

The split in Norwegian football followed similar lines to that which had hit Irish football 16 years earlier. The Norwegian dispute is forgotten now and in other circumstances the same might well have happened in Ireland had it occurred, say, ten years before it did. Instead, the Irish dispute erupted when great changes were afoot, provoking a situation where a Free State XI instead of an all-Ireland team went to Norway to play a World Cup-tie. Then again, the British Associations were still cold-shouldering the competition so, perhaps, Ireland's participation could be viewed as one benefit of the split.

Strangely, given the insular nature of British football, this was not the first visit of an Irish team to Norway. Shortly after the split, the IFA accepted an invite from the Norwegian FA to play in Bergen. A squad of twelve players was assembled by the IFA. However, as Norwegian football was strictly amateur it was assumed that the IFA would send an amateur side. The game went ahead anyway on Thursday, May 25th, 1922, and Norway won 2-1. The IFA treated it as a full international but not Norway, who annulled the result even though both sides awarded caps (the Norwegians awarded amateur caps while the IFA awarded full caps). The game has never appeared in either nation's records. Three days later, a further match took place when Northern Ireland beat a Norwegian 'B' side 3-1.

In 1936, a Norwegian team shocked the footballing world by reaching the semi-finals of the Olympic Games. They almost made the final but a strong Italian side beat them 2-1 after extra-time. The Norwegians went on to claim the bronze medal by beating Poland, but since then results had deteriorated, and coming into their first World Cup game they had only won two of their last eight games.

Ireland were on a good run of one defeat in their last seven games. Their their defence and forwards were all playing well. In attack, Dunne, who at 32 had returned to Ireland to play for Rovers, was still in fine scoring form. He had played 13 games for the two Irelands and scored twelve goals and he still wasn't finished. In defence, Turner, the centre-half and captain, had played five games for Ireland and in each one had dominated the opposition's centre-forward. In fact, no centre-forward had scored against him. For his first World Cup match Turner would be up against Alf Martinsen, who had six international goals but none of them in Oslo.

A circular by the Free State FA to clubs in Britain enquiring about available and eligible players had yielded some interesting results. Southend United had recommended goalkeeper George McKenzie with a note from their manager saying: 'You were pleased with Turner and you will be delighted with McKenzie'. Norwich City's Peter Burke was another who had come to the attention of the selectors, even though he was born in Liverpool and had played for England schoolboys. The Irish selectors had never seen either of them play but picked both to face Norway, alongside Mick Hoy, Tom Donnelly and Jimmy Buchanan (Bray Unknowns). Unfortunately, both Burke and Buchanan were injured and unable to play and, in fact, never got a chance again.

The team also lost William O'Neill of Dundalk to injury, so Joe Williams was introduced for his debut. There were also recalls for Owen Kinsella, after five years, and Billy Jordan, who had made his debut in Ireland's last World

Cup match. The FIFA representative in Oslo objected to the inclusion of Jimmy Dunne, as he had also played for Northern Ireland who were not members of FIFA. His objection was noted but Dunne played!

On a warm and sunny day, with the King and Prince of Norway watching, the Norwegians kicked off and dominated the early play. In the first 15 minutes the Irish goal led a charmed life and the only shot of note from the Irishmen in that period was from Tom Donnelly, which was saved by Blohm.

After this opening onslaught, which was nothing new to the Irishmen on their travels, the Irish settled down and play swung from end to end. The best chance of the opening half-hour was presented to Martinsen when McKenzie slipped but the centre-forward rushed his shot and the ball flew wide. Norway's two wide men gave the Irish backs plenty of problems and from one raid Brustad forced a corner off Williams. The left-winger took the kick himself, found Kvammen in the box, and he shot home past McKenzie.

Ireland responded to this set-back with some strong attacking play, which saw an effort from Dunne saved by Blohm. Then O'Reilly passed out to Geoghegan who rushed into the box and shot low past the Norwegian goalkeeper for the equaliser. It was Geoghegan's second goal for Ireland in two appearances and Ireland's 25th away goal overall.

The Norwegians upped the tempo and should have taken a commanding lead at the break. Isaksen got clear of the defence and should really have scored but, with only McKenzie to beat, shot badly wide. Then Martinsen had another chance but his finishing was equally poor. McKenzie produced three great saves in quick succession before Martinsen was fouled by Turner and Herr Bauwens – who had awarded penalties against Ireland on both previous occasions he had taken charge of them – awarded another. Rolf Holmberg took the kick but shot against a post and the ball went out. It was the second penalty miss against Ireland in successive matches.

It had taken the Ireland party four days to reach Oslo and, with Norway's players being amateur, fatigue played its part in the second period. The game was played at a slower pace and both teams had chances early on. Dunne, who until recently had been playing full-time football, became more influential, despite his age. When Billy Jordan found Dunne in the box the Shamrock Rovers captain shot low past Blohm for his first World Cup goal to put his team 2-1 up. Shortly afterwards Dunne could have stretched the lead when he got his head to a Tom Donnelly cross but the ball went over the bar. Isaksen was then presented with another 'sitter' but somehow shot wide with only the goalkeeper to beat.

As with Ireland's last World Cup-tie, they let a lead slip when they should have increased it. Brustad, a hat-trick hero in the 1936 Olympics, received the ball out on the left and dribbled to the bye-line before crossing for Kvammen to give McKenzie no chance. Both sides carved out chances for a winner. Geoghegan was put clean through but shot over. Dunne had another chance but shot wide. Then, after another fine movement, Geoghegan was again set free but, with only the goalkeeper left to beat, he shot too close to Blohm who parried.

Norway had some equally telling chances but the one that counted came with twelve minutes to go. Isaksen played the ball up to Martinsen and the centre-forward held off Turner to beat McKenzie from close range. Norway merited their win but would have to wait 20 years for their next in the World Cup.

Match No. 23 (World Cup)   *Sunday, 7th November 1937*   *Dublin*
REPUBLIC OF IRELAND (1) 3   Dunne 10, K. O'Flanagan 62, Duggan 88
NORWAY (2) 3   Kvammen 16, 33, Martinsen 49
Ref: T Gibbs (England)   *Dalymount Park*   *Att: 27,000*

IRELAND (2-3-5)		A-G	NORWAY (2-3-5)	
George McKenzie	Southend Utd	2–0/6	Sverre Nordby	(Mjondalen)
William O'Neill	Dundalk	9–0	Rolf Johannesen	(FFK)
Bill Gorman	Bury	6–0	Oyvind Holmsen	(Lyn)
Joe O'Reilly	St James's Gate	13–2	Kristian Henriksen	(Frigg)
Charlie Turner	Southend Utd	7–0	Nils Eriksen	(Odd)
Tom Arrigan	Waterford	1–0	Rolf Holmberg	(Odd)
Kevin O'Flanagan	Bohemians	1–1	Kjell Eeg	(Djerv Bergen)
Harry Duggan	Newport Co	5–1	Reidar Kvammen	(Viking)
Jimmy Dunne	Shamrock Rov	8–10	Alf Martinsen	(Lillestrom)
Johnny Carey	Manchester Utd	1–0	Odd Frantzen	(Hardy Bergen)
Tommy Foy	Shamrock Rov	1–0	Jorgen Hval	(Mjondalen)
MANAGERS:	Committee (23)		Asbjorn Halvorsen	
CAPTAINS:	Charlie Turner		Nils Eriksen	

Ireland were in with a shout of making it to the finals of the World Cup for the first time. All they had to do was win by two clear goals, or a single goal to force a play-off (the away-goals rule did not yet apply). Nowadays, the two-leg aggregate format is commonplace, as is the understanding of what is needed for either team to qualify. However, in the 1930s the two-legged tie was just an experiment, the World Cup just another competition, and a match like this was viewed as just another game. In another time, Ireland would have come away from Oslo with high expectations and with a reasonable idea of what was required at Dalymount Park to get through to the finals. As it was, the format and the competition were somewhat to the back of the minds, as not one of the Irish post-match comments expressed any disappointment with the loss of a finals berth.

    What was clear was that the game was being played for the game's sake but also that it was developing. The last shackles of amateurism were slowly fading (although in Norway's case it would take another 30 years), and new ideas were coming to the fore. One, introduced this season, was to paint an arc outside the penalty box to keep all players at least ten yards from a penalty-kick. Another was the introduction of numbered shirts which both Ireland and Norway donned for the first time in this match.

    Ireland's line-up showed seven changes from the first leg. Gone were all the forwards, bar Dunne, and three of the backs. The selectors had, in fact, made eight changes, with Tommy Breen starting in goal again. Breen had obtained permission to play for Ireland from his club, but elected to play for Northern Ireland against Scotland the following Wednesday. As a consequence, he was suspended by the Free State FA and McKenzie donned the No 1 jersey. Despite the changes, Ireland's side had a settled look. O'Neill and Gorman were possibly the best backs available, and Turner and O'Reilly had been rocks in the Irish defence. In at left-half, or No 6, came the experienced Tom Arrigan who had played for both Irelands. However, the most exciting changes were in the forward line. Teenagers Kevin O'Flanagan and Johnny (or Jackie) Carey had recently broken into their respective club sides and much was expected from them. Harry Duggan had first represented Ireland nearly ten years earlier, and at 34 was coming to the end of an international career that had earned him twelve caps between the two Irelands. The forward line was completed by Tommy Foy, who had recently returned to Ireland from a three-year stint in England, and, of course, 'Snowy' Dunne.

Norway had taken on Germany before coming to Dublin, losing to an Otto Siffling hat-trick with virtually an identical side to that introduced to the Lord Mayor shortly before kick-off. The Norwegian side showed four changes from that in Oslo. Blohm, who had had a poor game, and Brustad, who had been outstanding, were amongst those who were not awarded a number.

A big crowd turned up on the Sunday afternoon expecting Ireland to win, even though they had never won at home on football's traditional day in Ireland. Ireland did everything they could in a fruitless effort but the majority went home happy anyway, thanks to one of the most exciting games seen at Dalymount in some time or, as one commentator put it, having seen six goals for a shilling. The Irish began with their standard tactics and never varied them. Norway came to defend their one-goal advantage, but when that fell apart after ten minutes they switched their tactics and the outcome.

Ireland had much of the early play but the Norwegian defence coped pretty easily. In fact the first real opening fell to the visitors with Holmberg getting on the end of a free-kick to send an effort wide. Ireland needed a goal and almost got one when a pass by Carey was shot home by O'Flanagan but was ruled offside.

It took Ireland ten minutes to level the aggregate scores. Foy broke up the left and his cross was nodded on by Duggan for Dunne to head in, becoming the first Irish player to reach double goal figures. Gorman went on a galloping run up the left to set up Duggan, but the shot was saved by Nordby. The Irish pressure was so intense that at one stage every outfield player was in the visitors' half. Relief for the hard-pressed Norwegians came from their forwards, and especially the tricky Martinsen, who was giving Turner a tough time. The Southend United centre-half had never let Ireland down, but Martinsen now dragged him all over the pitch and thus left gaps for his inside partner Kvammen. Turner, as was his wont, stuck to his man like glue but after 14 minutes the Norwegian slipped past him and should have scored had McKenzie not produced a one-handed save to keep the ball out. Eeg then skipped past Gorman to have his shot saved.

Norway's next attack made it 1-1 on the day. Gorman was lax in clearing a ball, which gave Holmberg the chance to set up Kvammen, who blasted in off the underside of the crossbar. Ireland's response was to take the game to the Norwegians. Carey twice had chances to score but both times his efforts were off target as the tall Norwegians, and Eriksen in particular, began to dominate in the air.

Again the Norwegians found an outlet in their forwards and when they got a chance they proved deadly. Martinsen was cropping up all over the place with poor Turner in tow, but when he turned up on the right wing, the captain left the responsibility of marking him to Gorman, who was unable to cope with the Norwegian's speed and ball control. The Norwegian sidestepped Gorman before drawing McKenzie and shooting towards the open goal. O'Neill, covering his keeper, hacked the ball off the line but only to Kvammen, who dribbled past desperately retreating defenders to put Norway 5-3 ahead on aggregate. Back came Ireland with Duggan's shot seeming goalbound until Nordby, diving full length, diverted the ball for a corner. Foy snatched at a chance minutes later and blazed over. Before the break Kvammen almost completed his hat-trick but shot wide.

Ireland now needed three goals to qualify and they set about trying to get them after changing ends. However, four minutes in, their hopes were dashed when more defensive lapses allowed Martinsen to dash on to a pass from Frantzen. The centre-forward again drew McKenzie before shooting in off a post. Norway were all but home and dry.

A common criticism of the football exhibited in the previous World Cup, and the forthcoming one for that matter, was that it had become too competitive. A 'must win at all costs' ethos had replaced entertainment. So, it is a tribute to both sides in this match that neither gave up trying to score more goals or display their skills. Kvammen and Martinsen continued to lead the Irish defence a merry dance, while youngsters Carey and O'Flanagan played with all the energy and vigour of youth. They combined with Carey heading just wide from an O'Flanagan corner.

Just after an hour's play, a cross from Foy was back-headed by Dunne for O'Flanagan, stealing in at the far post, to score Ireland's 50th international goal. The Bohs man almost earned himself another, but Nordby was out early to save at his feet. Then it was Matinsen's turn to shine. He beat both Turner and McKenzie to a long ball but fired across the goalmouth and wide. A few minutes later Kvammen was denied by McKenzie, who then hustled Martinsen into shooting wildly. McKenzie, who later made a diving save at Hval's feet, was having a fine game and was named Ireland's man of the match.

Ireland eventually leveled the scores when Duggan hammered a cross from Carey into the net. There were only two minutes left and the home side never got another sight of the Norwegian goal becausea the visitors, to their credit, attacked to the final whistele. In the end, it needed a good save from McKenzie to deny Norway a victory and Kvammen his hat-trick.

Match No. 24   *Wednesday, 18th May 1938*   *Prague*
CZECHOSLOVAKIA (1) 2   Nejedly 3 pen, 46
REPUBLIC OF IRELAND (1) 2   Davis 42, Dunne 89
Ref: R Barlassina (Italy)   *AC Sparta Stadium*   *Att: 17,000*

IRELAND (2-3-5)		A–G	CZECHOSLOVAKIA (2-3-5)	
George McKenzie	Southend Utd	3–0/8	Frantisek Planicka	(Slavia)
Paddy Gaskins	St James's Gate	6–0	Jaroslav Burgr	(Sparta)
Bill Gorman	Bury	7–0	Ferdinand Daucik	(Slavia)
Joe O'Reilly	St James's Gate	14–2	Josef Kostalek	(Sparta)
Matt O'Mahoney	Bristol Rov	1–0	Jaroslav Boucek	(Sparta)
Charlie Turner	West Ham	8–0	Vlastimil Kopecky	(Slavia)
Kevin O'Flanagan	Bohemians	2–1	Jan Riha	(Sparta)
Jimmy Dunne	Shamrock Rov	9–11	Ladislav Simunek	(Slavia)
Tom Davis	Tranmere Rov	3–4	Vojtech Bradac	(Slavia)
Johnny Carey	Manchester Utd	2–0	Josef Ludl	(Viktoria Zizkov)
Tim O'Keeffe	Waterford	2–0	Oldrich Nejedly	(Sparta)

MANAGERS: Committee (24)   Josef Meissner
CAPTAINS: Charlie Turner   Frantisek Planicka

The Europe that Ireland toured in 1938 was in turmoil. Nazi Germany had swallowed up Austria and coveted Czechoslovakia and Poland. The Czechs would soon be abandoned by British Prime Minister Chamberlain's policy of appeasing Hitler. The British might not have known much about this faraway country, to paraphrase Chamberlain, but Czech football was world-renowned.

    Czechoslovakia had entered international football with a bang. In the 1920 Olympics, in Belgium, they reached the final against the hosts but at 0-2 down stormed off after 40 minutes in protest at one of their players being sent off. They also got to the final of the 1934 World Cup, again losing to the hosts, and had twice given the powerful England side a run for its money. This was their final match before the 1938 World Cup in France.

    This Czech side was by far the most experienced Ireland faced before the Second World War. The players – all bar one from Slavia or Sparta – had amassed 250 caps and 41 goals. Ireland's paltry total was 46 caps and 16 goals. But the Czechs were slipping. Since finishing runners-up to Italy in the last World Cup they had only won eleven of their 28 games and only one of their last five. Yet the Czechs were outstanding in Prague, losing only five times in 52 games, although three of these losses were in the past two years.

    Since being eliminated by Norway, Ireland had undergone a name change. Previously known as the 'Free State of Ireland', the Constitution of Ireland had changed the name to 'Eire'. That name was now used by the FAI to distinguish it from their neighbours up North. Article 2 of the Constitution granted citizenship to anyone born on the island of Ireland, and in that spirit the FAI chose three players for this tour who were born in the North – Johnny Brown of Coventry City, who had two caps, Billy McMillan from double winners Belfast Celtic, and Harry Baird, the ex-Linfield player now at Manchester United. However, the English FA telegraphed the three players and told them to decline their selection. So the selectors called upon a tried and trusted squad which saw recalls for Paddy Gaskins, Tim O'Keeffe and William Harrington and a first selection for Tipperary's Matt O'Mahoney, who had been doing the rounds in England for three years.

For the first time, Eire could field two useful strikers in the same side. Tom Davis, once at Oldham, was now scoring freely for Tranmere (whom he joined in February). He lined up at centre-forward, with incumbent Jimmy Dunne, who recently passed 180 League goals, moving to inside-right. Between them they had scored 13 goals in ten games for Ireland.

Ireland got off to a bad start. Gorman handled in the box and Nejedly gave the home side the lead with his 25th international goal. Davis got in a shot for Ireland but Planicka, rated one of the best goalkeepers in Europe, easily handled his effort. Planicka was nearing the end of his career whereas McKenzie was just starting his and needed to be on his toes. Simunek, who had scored a hat-trick on his debut, sent a high, dipping shot past the goalkeeper and against an upright.

As with most of their away games, Ireland had been under the cosh early on but then settled down and forced a few openings themselves. O'Keeffe and Carey began to turn the game in Ireland's favour. Three minutes before the break, O'Keeffe passed to the unmarked Davis, who dashed between Kostalek and Boucek to score past the advancing Planicka.

The Czechs kicked off the second half. Nejedly jinked past O'Reilly, cut inside Gaskins, beat O'Mahoney and shot past the advancing McKenzie for a fantastic goal. Ireland recovered well. Planicka denied Davis and Dunne in quick succession. Nejedly sprinted after a long ball but pulled up with a hamstring injury. There was just under a month to the World Cup finals and, not wishing to take any chances, he left the field, limping, and did not return. The Czechs could quite easily have used a sub but as it was against the rules they didn't, even if others would have. Even down to ten men the Czechs had most of the play and Riha's long-range shot thumped off the crossbar.

Boucek and O'Reilly then clattered into each other. O'Reilly was able to play on but Boucek was off for ten minutes getting treatment. He returned at right wing, limping badly, with Kopecky taking over his old position. The home side were never the same and Ireland took advantage to launch a series of raids. A pass from Gaskins found Dunne in space midway in the Czech half. Dunne, seeing Planicka out of position, fired in a long-range shot which flew in. It was a tremendous strike from Ireland's record goalscorer and the 30th goal scored by League of Ireland players for Ireland.

Match No. 25
POLAND (3) 6

Sunday, 22nd May 1938 *Warsaw*
Wasiewicz 12, Wodarz 21, 78, Piontek 43, 50, Wilimowski 58

REPUBLIC OF IRELAND (0) 0

Ref: F Majorszky (Hungary) *Legia Stadium* *Att: 25,000*

IRELAND (2-3-5)		A–G	POLAND (2-3-5)	
George McKenzie	Southend Utd	4–0/13	Edward Madejski	(Wisla Krakow)
Paddy Gaskins	St James's Gate	7–0	Wladyslaw Szczepaniak	(Polonia)
Bill Gorman	Bury	8–0	Antoni Galecki	(Lodz KS)
Joe O'Reilly	St James's Gate	15–2	Wilhelm Gora	(Cracovia)
Matt O'Mahoney	Bristol Rov	2–0	Jan Wasiewicz	(Pogon Lwow)
Charlie Turner	West Ham	9–0	Edward Dytko	(Dab Katowice)
Kevin O'Flanagan	Bohemians	3–1	Ryszard Piec	(Naprzod Lipiny)
Jimmy Dunne	Shamrock Rov	10–11	Leonard Piontek	(AKS Chorzow)
Tom Davis	Tranmere Rov	4–4	Fryderyk Scherfke	(Warta Poznan)
Johnny Carey	Manchester Utd	3–0	Ernest Wilimowski	(Ruch Chorzow)
Tim O'Keeffe	Waterford	3–0	Gerard Wodarz	(Ruch Chorzow)
Sub:				
William Harrington	Cork	5–1/10		
for McKenzie (69 mins)				

MANAGERS:	Committee (25)	Marian Spoida
CAPTAINS:	Charlie Turner	Wladyslaw Szczepaniak

The trip from Prague to Warsaw was not arduous – no more then a return trip from Cork to Belfast. Over the years the journey to Poland would become a well-trodden route for Irish teams, but none would return as chastened as the one that arrived there in May 1938. Ireland's away record was pretty decent up to that point, only five defeats out of 14, and only Italy and Switzerland had kept clean sheets in those games. Everything seemed in place for another good performance. The team was unchanged, the defence playing well, the forwards scoring freely, and with the boost of a good result from the game in Prague. The only uncertainty was Poland.

Poland's record in international football was nothing special. This was their 85th game since 1921 with a record of 32 wins, 14 draws and 38 defeats. Their best performance to date was a semi-final place in the 1936 Olympics and they were on a roll of one defeat in their last six games. They were heading to France for their first World Cup, having knocked out the fancied Yugoslavs. As with the Czechs, this was their last game before heading for France.

Poland's biggest home crowd since the visit of Germany two years earlier turned up to see their first ever visitors from the British Isles. Poland had usually confined themselves to playing their near neighbours, the exception being two visits from the United States. Ireland's exploits on the Continent had not gone unnoticed and the chance to see a 'quality' side was not to be missed for the Poles. The visitors did not disappoint early on, and forced a succession of chances. Joe O'Reilly, Ireland's most capped player, shot just the wrong side of the post. Ireland's rising star, Carey, had the next chance and sent in a stinging shot which Madejski did well to save. The best chance was made by O'Keeffe who set up Carey, but the teenager badly miscued.

After ten minutes the Poles forced their first corner which produced a shot by Wilimowski saved by McKenzie. Two minutes later, Ireland were behind. Another corner by Wodarz was met by centre-half Wasiewicz who fired a low shot past McKenzie into the far corner. It was the Pole's first goal in 14 appearances. As ever, Ireland fought back and Davis headed wide after another O'Keeffe cross. Carey had yet another chance but scraped over the bar.

Wodarz, who had bagged a hat-trick against Great Britain in the 1936 Olympics, got in a rasper of a shot which brought the best out of McKenzie. But Wodarz was not to be denied and finally beat the Irish goalkeeper with a fine low shot for his twelfth goal in 24 appearances. Again the Irish came back, this time with skipper Jimmy Dunne's shot well held by Madejski. Ireland's record goalscorer had only once failed to score for his country and should have netted with a header a few minutes later but the ball went over. From the resulting goal-kick, Madejski sent the ball out to his captain, Szczepaniak, who in turn found Piec racing up the right wing. The winger cleared the Irish defence and crossed in for Piontek to make it 3-0. McKenzie produced another brilliant save to deny the Poles a fourth before half-tme.

Ireland had not been three goals down at the break since 1931 and complained that the ball was too soft. As excuses go, the 'ball was too soft' was as good as any to present to their hosts at half-time, and the obliging Poles replaced it with another, which still did not stop them scoring another three in the second half.

Number four saw Piontek shooting home from a Piec pass. Poland went further ahead when Wilimowski waltzed through the Irish cover and gave McKenzie no chance. The Irish goalkeeper was playing well despite the scoreline and showed his bravery when he came out to save at the feet of Scherfke but was injured in doing so. The rules did allow for the use of a substitute keeper so when McKenzie departed he was replaced by William Harrington, whose last cap was two years earleir. Harrington had to strip out of his suit and don McKenzie's jersey, gloves and hat. The substitute goalkeeper did not have much to do until Wodarz broke up the left. Harrington moved to cover his near post and when the winger's cross-cum-shot came in the Corkman left it, thinking it was off target. Unfortunately the ball dipped under the crossbar and found the far corner. This knocked the stuffing out of the Irish who never threatened again. At the final whistle the crowd invaded the pitch and carried their players off shoulder-high.

Match No. 26　　　　　　　　　　　*Sunday, 18th September 1938*　　*Dublin*
REPUBLIC OF IRELAND　　(3) 4　　Bradshaw 1, 20, Dunne 8, T. Donnelly 72
SWITZERLAND　　　　　　(0) 0
Ref: R Mortimer (England)　　　　*Dalymount Park*　　　　*Att: 31,000*

IRELAND (2-3-5)		A–G	SWITZERLAND (2-3-5)	
George McKenzie	Southend Utd	5–1/13	Willy Huber	(Grasshoppers)
Bill Gorman	Bury	9–0	Severino Minelli	(Grasshoppers)
Mick Hoy	Dundalk	2–0	Gusti Lehmann	(Grasshoppers)
Joe O'Reilly	St James's Gate	16–2	Hermann Springer	(G'hoppers)
Matt O'Mahoney	Bristol Rov	3–0	Sirio Vernati	(Grasshoppers)
Dick Lunn	Dundalk	1–0	Ernest Lortscher	(Servette)
Tom Donnelly	Shamrock Rov	2–1	Ferdi Bickel	(Grasshoppers)
Jimmy Dunne	Shamrock Rov	11–12	Trello Abegglen	(Servette)
Paddy Bradshaw	St James's Gate	1–2	Lauro Amado	(Lugano)
Johnny Carey	Manchester Utd	4–0	Eugene Walaschek	(Servette)
Bill Fallon	Sheffield Wed	6–1	Georges Aeby	(Servette)
MANAGERS:	Committee (26)		Henry Muller	
CAPTAINS:	Jimmy Dunne		Severino Minelli	

The Swiss had returned from the World Cup in France with a higher profile, having been the last nation to qualify. The finals were on a knockout basis and saw a few upsets. The Swiss caused one of them by beating the fancied Germans before losing 0-2 to the powerful Hungarians in the next round. Their first match after the finals was in Dublin. They brought a squad of players from the World Cup but not their manager. Karl Rappan had resigned, to be replaced by Henry Muller – his second spell in charge. This was Muller's fourth game in charge against Ireland – a pre-war record.

The Irish had not played at home for close on a year. They had lost only one of their last four games at Dalymount, and their forwards had scored 20 goals in the last seven home games. Free-scoring Jimmy Dunne and Tom Davis led the way, but others like 'Babby' Byrne, Joey Donnelly and Tim O'Keeffe – 21 goals last season – were still hitting the onion sack.

The selectors picked Paddy Bradshaw to lead the line. At 25 he had only made his Gate debut a month earlier in the Dublin City Cup. Bradshaw would establish himself as one of the League's top marksman despite only playing six seasons in Ireland's top flight. The selectors also gave a first cap to the 'Mighty Atom' from Portadown, Dick Lunn who was only 5ft 4ins. He formed part of a side subsequently viewed as the best Ireland had fielded to date.

For Switzerland, still basking in the glory of France, the stakes were higher. Their preferred style was obstruction. This is a misnomer. 'Obstruction' meant roughhouse tactics which involved physically taking a player out by any means possible, including elbows and bodies. This 'rule' had been outlawed the previous season, but the Swiss were adamant that unless they could defend their goal in a manner they saw fit then they would not take the field. Severino Minelli, the Swiss captain, had a ten-minute argument with English referee Reg Mortimer before Jimmy Dunne stepped in and agreed to play under the rule. Mortimer thanked Dunne for his level-headedness but described the subsequent game as the most difficult he had refereed and that he 'went on the field practically without a pea in my whistle'. Unfortunately for the Swiss, the Irish were used to putting it about themselves, so that after the match the Swiss captain had as many, if not more, bruises then the Irish forwards.

After 20 minutes the Swiss protests were all but forgotten as the Irish had scored three times. The rout began after 20 seconds with a debut goal for Bradshaw, who blocked Huber's drop-kick and the ball flew into the net for the quickest if not flukiest goal Ireland had ever scored. Fallon then forced Huber to save his shot at the expense of a corner, which Dunne headed in for his third goal in as many games against the Swiss. Dunne's cross was then headed in by Bradshaw for Ireland's third. The Swiss had identified Dunne as the danger-man and neglected Bradshaw, who then received some rough Swiss marking, while freeing Dunne who might have had a personal hat-trick coming up to the break. The Irish captain first had another header saved by Huber, before meeting a cross from the outstanding Carey with the outside of his foot. Huber turned the ball around the post.

Ireland continued to have the better of things after the interval, as the Swiss defending became more desperate and rougher. In fact they even managed to 'tackle' Mr Mortimer off the ball when the Yorkshireman was in the process of playing a hop ball! Carey headed wide from a Donnelly cross before Donnelly missed a sitter by heading Fallon's cross over an open goal. Bradshaw had another header saved by Huber who soon flung himself to save a spectacular effort for the increasingly influential Carey.

Ireland were carving plenty of openings with the high ball but it was a low cross which brought them their fourth goal. Bradshaw sent Fallon away up the left. This time the winger elected to send a low ball across the face of the goal. Donnelly met it at the far post and knocked in his first goal in his second international. Following this, the Swiss had their two best chances of the game. Walaschek – who only got his Swiss passport in the summer even though he had been playing for Switzerland for a year – got in a shot which McKenzie saved. Then Aeby's effort hit a post and the rebound was fisted away by the Irish goalkeeper. The Irish captain summed up the game: 'The Swiss played some stylish football, but they lacked the "punch" that we displayed.'

After the match the Swiss blamed the long sea trip for their poor performance, an excuse that the Irish had often used themselves. There was also another that made for an interesting comparison to Ireland's game in Poland. The Swiss complained that the ball was 'too hard'.

Match No. 27   *Sunday, 13th November 1938*   *Dublin*
REPUBLIC OF IRELAND (2) 3   Fallon 10, Carey 12, Dunne 68
POLAND (1) 2   Wilimowski 15, Piontek 75
Ref: P Bauwens (Germany)   *Dalymount Park*   *Att: 34,295*

IRELAND (2-3-5)		A-G	POLAND (2-3-5)	
George McKenzie	Southend Utd	6–1/15	Edward Madejski	(unattached)
Bill Gorman	Bury	10–0	Wladyslaw Szczepaniak	(KKS Polonia)
Mick Hoy	Dundalk	3–0	Antoni Galecki	(LKS Lodz)
Joe O'Reilly	St James's Gate	17–2	Wilhelm Gora	(KS Cracovia Krakow)
Matt O'Mahoney	Bristol Rov	4–0	Edward Nyc	(KKS Polonia)
Dick Lunn	Dundalk	2–0	Edward Dytko	(GKS Dab Katowice)
Kevin O'Flanagan	Bohemians	4–1	Ryszard Piec	(Naprzod Lipiny)
Jimmy Dunne	Shamrock Rov	12–13	Leonard Piontek	(AKS Chorzow)
Paddy Bradshaw	St James's Gate	2–2	Jerzy Wostal	(AKS Chorzow)
Johnny Carey	Manchester Utd	5–1	Ernest Wilimowski	(KS R Wielk' Hajduki)
Bill Fallon	Sheffield Wed	7–2	Gerard Wodarz	(KS Ruch Wielkie Hajduki)

Sub: Roman Mrugala (AKS Chorzow) for Madejski (14 mins). Madejski returned after 48 mins for Mrugala

MANAGERS: Committee (27)   Jozef Kaluza and Marian Spojda
CAPTAINS: Jimmy Dunne   Wladyslaw Szczepaniak

Relations between the Gaelic Athletic Association (GAA) and the sports they referred to as 'foreign games' were always tetchy, but they boiled over following this clash with Poland. The GAA had imposed a ban on their members playing or even attending soccer, cricket or rugby, so when the newly elected President of Ireland was seen at the match (and apparently actually enjoying it!), the GAA found themselves in a bit of a dilemma. As President of Eire, Dr Douglas Hyde had turned up at a damp Dalymount Park along with An Taoiseach, Eamonn De Valera as representatives of the Government for this prestigious international.

This was the first occasion that such dignitaries had attended (or at least had been observed to attend) a soccer game in Ireland, and their presence raised the ire of the GAA. Their dilemma, however, was that Hyde was a founder of the Gaelic League and a patron of the GAA. The Gaelic League had witnessed a revival in the Gaelic language and culture and might conceivably even be responsible for the lofty position the GAA held in Irish society. But rules are rules and in December the GAA announced that Hyde would no longer be part of their organisation on account of his attendance at this soccer match.

Hyde and Dev were part of a big crowd that packed into the home of Irish soccer on a wet day in Dublin. The crowd was buoyed by another Irish revival, a soccer revival. Ireland had never known such a time. Crowds were up and half the teams in the League of Ireland were from outside Dublin. The Irish team was also doing well and boasted an undefeated home record stretching back almost two years. They had not played many games at home but, like the CIE buses, you wait for one for a long time and three come in quick succession (Hungary were due in March).

The Irish team that was introduced to its new President shortly before kick-off was possibly the strongest pre-war that Ireland possessed. George McKenzie's statistics of only one clean sheet and 13 goals conceded in five internationals hid the fact that his performances for Ireland had been consistently good. Bill Gorman, winning his tenth cap, was now Ireland's most capped full-back. Billy Hayes of Huddersfield Town should have partnered him but he elected to play for Northern Ireland against England, and so Mick Hoy was drafted in. Joe O'Reilly was playing his 14th consecutive international and was Ireland's most capped player, despite a dip in form.

Ireland were blessed with fine centre-halves and Matt O'Mahoney, aged 25, again got the nod over the more experienced Charlie Turner. The left-half berth was always a problem and the latest incumbent, Dick Lunn, was the 15th player tried out, all but two of whom never featured more then twice. As it turned out, the match was won and lost by the wing-backs. Gora and Dytko never got to grips with the conditions for Poland, whereas Lunn and O'Reilly excelled. Ireland's forward line contained two teenagers destined for greater things, Kevin O'Flanagan and Johnny Carey. All the forwards were from Dublin and all were exceptional, including the 'Old Man' Jimmy Dunne who was player-manager at his club Shamrock Rovers.

The powerful Polish team had nearly upset Brazil at the 1938 World Cup finals. In one of the most memorable games of that tournament the Poles had recovered from 1-4 down to draw 4-4, only to lose 5-6 in extra-time. That performance was one of the highlights for a Poland team enduring a dismal run. Since beating Ireland 6-0 in May, they had played five games and won none. However, they had scored plenty of goals and Ernest Wilimowski, their star striker of German extraction, had bagged seven in his last four games. The Polish team showed two changes from the one that had hammered Ireland, and their forward line bragged a total of 38 international goals between them.

Unfortunately for the huge crowd, the Polish team did not perform to expectations. The Irish, most of whom had played in Warsaw, began determinedly to erase the memories of that 0-6 hammering six months previously. Dunne headed on a Carey cross for O'Flanagan to shoot into the side netting, and then Dunne himself had a curling shot saved by Madejski. Dunne would enjoy another fine game for Ireland but it was O'Flanagan who set up the first goal. Madejski came out to claim a cross from the Bohs right-winger but was clattered in the air by Bradshaw. The ball ran to Carey, who would have scored had not Galecki blocked on the line. Instead it was left to Fallon to put the chance away.

Two minutes later the home side won a corner which was flung over by Fallon for Carey to head home. He became the 25th player to score for Ireland. The Polish goalkeeper had started nervously and it was about to get worse for him. Fallon floated over a cross to O'Flanagan who thundered into Madejski. As the ball ran free, Bradshaw put it into the net. Dr Bauwens, refereeing his fourth Irish game, disallowed the goal for offside, which was a relief for the Poles until they discovered that their goalkeeper was unable to continue. Roman Mrugala, their reserve, who had only played once before for Poland, took his place.

When all was sorted, the Poles went on the attack and reduced the arrears with their first effort on goal. Wostal let fly with a stinging shot that McKenzie could not hold and Wilimowski capitalised to take him within one goal of the all-time Polish scoring record.

That would be as good as it got for the visitors, because the Irish had all the subsequent play and should have gone in at the break with a more convincing lead. Certainly Bradshaw was unlucky not to have netted. Soon after the Poles scored, the centre-forward was sent free in the box but shot across the goal and wide. He then missed two sitters that he would normally have gobbled up before Dunne sent in a shot which had the substitute goalkeeper at full stretch to save.

The Poles made a better fist of it in the second half, which turned out to be a battle of the inside-forwards. Both Wilimowski and Piontek played well but were overshadowed by Carey and Dunne who, along with the half-backs, won the game for Ireland. Dunne threaded a ball through to Bradshaw. Mrugala came out from his goal and got to the ball a fraction before Bradshaw. The Irish forward was in full flight and clattered into Mrugala who had to be assisted off the field. Both Polish goalkeepers had now been put out of action, but in this unusual circumstance Madejski was allowed to resume in Mrugala's place.

The substitution roused the visitors as Piec escaped Hoy to set up Piontek, who delayed his shot and Lunn charged down his effort. Next Wilimowski, at last living up to his reputation, was set up, only for O'Reilly to snatch the ball off his toe as he was about to shoot. Lunn, full of tricks, ran rings around the Polish defence and forced a corner. O'Flanagan swung it over and Dunne – as he had done against the Swiss – headed into the back of the net.

Poland hit back when McKenzie dropped a shot by Wilimowski, allowing Piontek to prod the ball over the line. The Poles began to exert themselves and when McKenzie weakly punched a cross from Piec, Wilimowski almost got an equaliser with an overhead kick which flew wide. Late on Wilimowski received the ball out on the right, turned inside Gorman, dribbled past O'Mahoney and squeezed by McKenzie, only to lose control and make the Irish goalie's job a lot easier to save at his feet.

Match No. 28 **REPUBLIC OF IRELAND** (1) 2 *Sunday, 19th March 1939* *Cork*
HUNGARY (1) 2 Bradshaw 14, Carey 87
Ref: H Nattrass (England) Kollath 35, Zsengeller 50
  The Mardyke Att: 18,000

IRELAND (2-3-5)		A-G	HUNGARY (2-3-5)	
George McKenzie	Southend Utd	7–1/17	Antal Szabo	(Hungaria)
Bill Gorman	Brentford	11–0	Lajos Koranyi	(Ferencvaros)
Mick Hoy	Dundalk	4–0	Sandor Biro	(Hungaria)
Joe O'Reilly	St James's Gate	18–2	Gyula Lazar	(Ferencvaros)
Charlie Turner	West Ham	10–0	Bela Sarosi	(Ferencvaros)
Ned Weir	Clyde	1–0	Istvan Balogh	(Ujpest)
Kevin O'Flanagan	Bohemians	5–1	Sandor Adam	(Ujpest)
Jimmy Dunne	Shamrock Rov	13–13	Gyula Zsengeller	(Ujpest)
Paddy Bradshaw	St James's Gate	3–3	Ferenc Kollath	(Szolnok)
Johnny Carey	Manchester Utd	6–2	Istvan Kiszely	(Ferencvaros)
Tommy Foy	Shamrock Rov	2–0	Laszlo Gyetvai	(Ferencvaros)

MANAGERS: Committee (28) Dr Karoly Dietz
CAPTAINS: Jimmy Dunne Gyula Lazar

For the visit of the 1938 World Cup runners-up, the Football Association of Eire chose host the match outside Dublin for the first time. The venue chosen was the Mardyke, which was then the home of Cork City. At the time, football in Munster was at a low ebb, and the boost that such a prestigious fixture would give the province was seen by the powers that be as worth the risk. There is no doubt that the Hungarians were a top attraction, and in view of the buzz surrounding Irish football at that moment there was every possibility that Dalymount Park would have been sold out. As it was, the match in Cork attracted a huge crowd, which filled the ground to capacity, even though the 18,000 present represented the second lowest pre-war home crowd to see Ireland play. Only a week before, the domestic game had been boosted when the League of Ireland representative side beat both the Irish League and the Scottish league. A crowd nearly double that at the Mardyke witnessed the first-ever meeting with the Scottish League at Dalymount Park.

Hungary were one of the top sides in Europe and as runners-up to Italy in the World Cup finals the previous year could claim to be the second best side in the world. Italy had deservedly won the crown, but Hungary's lack of finish and distaste for over-physical contact was something that probably denied them the chance of winning it.

They would show the same failing against Ireland. Their record since their last visit was one win in every two games played and six-plus goals scored. For a perceived lack of finish, their forwards displayed a fondness for scoring goals and Dr Gyorgy Sarosi and Gyula Zsengeller had shared 32 of Hungary's 58 goals. The good doctor would be missing from the line-up in Cork, and only Gyetvai had a goal to his name from the forwards who lined up. This was Hungary's third visit to Ireland – no other country had visited more often – and for goalkeeper Antal Szabo it was his fourth game against the men in green, also a record.

Irish football was still glowing from victories against Switzerland and Poland. The League of Ireland team had also recorded memorable wins against the Irish League (for the first time in Belfast), and the Scottish League (in the first ever contest between the two). The man in form for Ireland was Paddy Bradshaw who had scored four goals in his last four games for both Ireland and the LOI, not to mention topping the League's scoring charts. He was due to be joined in the forward line by a Corkman, Owen Madden from Birmingham City at outside-left. Madden was injured, so another Corkonian, Tim O'Keeffe, from Raith Rovers, was called up. In the event O'Keeffe, a hero in Cork footballing circles, missed a train connection and arrived too late to play. Ned Weir, who had turned out for Northern Ireland in midweek, became the 100th player capped by Ireland. He would tie down the troublesome left-half spot for Ireland for the rest of the season.

Given the passion most Corkmen exhibit for their sports, it was surprising that the following day's newspapers were scathing in their criticism of the lack-lustre support that Ireland had received from the big crowd. WP Murphy of the *Irish Independent* began his report with this searing criticism: 'Before one of the most apathetic crowds I have ever seen at an International' and followed up with 'the spectators must take the blame for ... [our failure] to record our first victory over Hungary'. Harsh word, indeed, but given the level of actual support Ireland were to receive in the latter spell of Jack Charlton's reign, perhaps, honest. Would that WP had been around then!

Ireland got off to a fine start but the lack of vocal backing from the crowd probably played on the minds of the players, so the game gradually deteriorated into an end-of-season friendly, which, in fact it was. The new boy, Weir, set up Ireland's first attack, which gave Bradshaw an opening that was thwarted by Biro at the expense of a corner. The flag-kick was taken by Foy. The ball found Carey, whose effort was saved by Szabo on the goal-line. O'Flanagan almost nipped in but again that man Biro swooped to intercept.

Gyetvai, who ran rings around Gorman in the first half, instigated Hungary's first attack, eluding his man again only to see his effort fly off target. Carey got on the end of another corner, this time by O'Flanagan, but his headed effort went wide. Gyetvai once more skinned Gorman and crossed for the unmarked Zsengeller, who was offside. Ireland should have gone in front after ten minutes when Bradshaw flicked on a Carey cross for Foy, but the winger's shot was badly off-target. Hungary came back with Gyetvai who fired in a thunderbolt shot which McKenzie, untroubled until then, dealt with.

Dunne was his usual industrious self and his ageing legs were responsible for Ireland's opening goal. The captain tried to get his forward line moving and lobbed a centre into the box. The ball was covered by Szabo but Koranyi intervened, heading it across the open goal and out for a corner-kick. Foy trotted across to take it and placed a perfect ball for Bradshaw to score with a stooping header.

Stung by this setback, Hungary began a spell of attacking which exposed Ireland's defensive limitations. Gorman was second best to Gyetvai while the aging Turner, not having a great time in London with the his club, West Ham, was clearly out of it. Kiszely, kept quiet for most of the game by O'Reilly, evaded Ireland's most capped player and crossed, but Gyetvai's shot was smothered by McKenzie. The left-winger then had two shots blocked before he set up Kiszely, whose effort was again saved by Gorman.

Kollath was surprisingly quiet, given Turner's lack of match practice, but he nearly equalised when his shot curled around McKenzie but hit a post. The rebound fell for Adam but, with the goal at his mercy, the winger blazed horribly over. A minute later Kollath burst clear of Hoy, lobbed the ball over Turner and would have scored a brilliant solo goal had he not lost control of the falling ball and the chance was gone.

The visitors were not to be denied, however, and levelled with ten minutes of the half left. Adam, who had been kept at bay by Hoy, wriggled free of the Dundalk man and pulled the ball back for Kollath who raced in, controlled it with his foot, and slipped it past McKenzie.

Hungary made a change in the second half. Dunne was causing more problems then Carey, so the half-backs, Lazar and Balogh, swapped positions. And it was Lazar who started the move that put the visitors ahead. Kollath received a ball from his captain and quickly played it into Zsengeller, who shot past the advancing goalkeeper just as McKenzie crashed into him. The Hungarian forward was angered by the goalkeeper's challenge, and tempers became frayed a few minutes later when Adam was flattened by Hoy.

The Hungarians, not afraid to use elbows and feet to stop the Irish, began to get a taste of their own medicine and for five minutes the match denigrated into a vicious bout of fouling. Adam's injury necessitated him leaving the field for a while but when he returned normality was restored. Gyetvai, the dangerman of the first half, never got a look in after the break as Gorman took his measure. This seemed to blunt the Hungarian attack and when they did break through their finishing left a lot to be desired. Their best chance of the half fell to Kiszely, who shook off O'Reilly to have a snap shot saved by McKenzie.

Ireland found themselves drawn into the roughhouse tactics of the visitors in the second half and never really threatened until, late on, they roused themselves to save the match. Dunne, at 33 and still fresh, sent the ball to Carey. Foy, overlapping, was played in by the inside-left and crossed for Bradshaw to tee up Carey.. Carey thus became only the third player to score in consecutive home games, following the example of Davis and Dunne.

This would be Ireland's last home game for seven years and the last time Cork hosted an Ireland international for another 46 years.

Match No. 29   *Thursday, 18th May 1939*   *Budapest*
HUNGARY (1) 2   Kollath 41, 86
REPUBLIC OF IRELAND (0) 2   K O'Flanagan 53, 80
Ref: P Bauwens (Germany)   *MTK Stadium*   *Att: 15,000*

IRELAND (2-3-5)		A-G	HUNGARY (2-3-5)	
George McKenzie	Southend Utd	8–1/19	Antal Szabo	(Hungaria)
William O'Neill	Dundalk	10–0	Karoly Kis	(Hungaria)
Mick Hoy	Dundalk	5–0	Sandor Biro	(MTK)
Joe O'Reilly	St James's Gate	19–2	Antal Szalay	(Ujpest)
Matt O'Mahoney	Bristol Rov	5–0	Gyorgy Szucs	(Ujpest)
Ned Weir	Clyde	2–0	Istvan Balogh	(Ujpest)
Kevin O'Flanagan	Bohemians	6–3	Jozsef Szanto	(Szolnok)
Jimmy Dunne	Shamrock Rov	14–13	Gyorgy Sarosi	(Ferencvaros)
Paddy Bradshaw	St James's Gate	4–3	Ferenc Kollath	(Szolnok)
Johnny Carey	Manchester Utd	7–2	Istvan Kiszely	(Ferencvaros)
Bill Fallon	Sheffield Wed	8–2	Antal Nagy	(Szeged)
MANAGERS:	Committee (29)		Dr Karoly Dietz	
CAPTAINS:	Jimmy Dunne		Dr Gyorgy Sarosi	

Ireland's previous tour of Europe had started with a 2-2 draw and a year on from that game in Czechoslovakia they started this one with another 2-2 draw. The squad that the selectors picked for this trip was the strongest Ireland was to field for some time, with a total of 78 caps and 23 goals. For all but two of the players it would be their last involvement in international football. This was especially disappointing for players like Mick Hoy, Ned Weir and Paddy Bradshaw who were only just beginning their international careers, but the successful tour did bring to a glorious end the careers of Jimmy Dunne, Ireland's record goalscorer, and evergreen Joe O'Reilly, Ireland's most capped player. Dunne was 33 but still had a few more years of football in him, but O'Reilly was really only reaching his football peak at 27. He quit playing football in 1944 to concentrate on raising a family and work but, like Dunne, was still playing representative football two years before he retired.

    The Hungarians had not played at home in well over a year, so the visit of Ireland was greeted with much enthusiasm by the home crowd, most of whom were seeing their World Cup runners-up in action for the first time. A crowd of between 15,000 and 25,000 (depending on which report you read) greeted their heroes with a tremendous reception on a stiflingly hot day in the Hungarian capital.

    As befitting their status, the home side were early into the attack and forced the Irish back on the defensive for much of the early play. Ireland soaked up this pressure and began to attack themselves, showing surprising fitness in a fast game in withering heat. Fallon was concussed following a hard knock and was forced to leave the field but, even down to ten men, Ireland still had more of the play until Fallon returned. It was the left-winger who set up Ireland's best chance. Shaking off the effects of the concussion, Fallon broke up the wing and crossed for Dunne, who was denied by a diving save from Szabo. Kollath, as in the match in Cork, was proving a handful, unleashing a powerful shot which McKenzie turned aside with his outstretched hand. A few minutes later Kollath tried his luck once more, but again the Irish goalkeeper was equal to it. Ireland suffered a further injury blow when O'Neill was knocked unconscious in blocking another Kollath shot and had to be carried from the field. Down to ten men for a second time, Ireland asked O'Reilly to drop back and fill in at right-back. It was the fourth position the versatile O'Reilly had filled for Ireland.

Four minutes before the break Kollath finally beat McKenzie from close range to put the home side one up. There was time for Ireland to equalise when Bradshaw went on a mazey run and beat three defenders, but he delayed his shot and Kis got back to clear.

There was no let-up in the heat or the tempo in the second half. O'Neill was back but still feeling groggy. The Irish defence played solidly and restricted the home side to pot shots early on. Then O'Flanagan moved infield and received a pass from Dunne. The Irish captain, who had played against the Magyars in Budapest three years previously, had obviously instructed his charges to shoot on sight, given the success he had enjoyed against Szabo on Ireland's last visit. O'Flanagan, top scorer for Bohs in a poor season for the amateurs, took his captain's advice and unleashed a 25-yarder which Szabo saw too late. It was a great goal for the 20-year-old who would better it before the end of the match.

However, urged on by a passionate crowd, Hungary did all the pressing and should have restored their lead. Hungary's old failing of not being able to put away their chances would cost them dear. Szanto missed a gaping goal and Kiszely somehow contrived to send a sitter straight at McKenzie. The Irish goalkeeper, winning a record eighth cap, stood firm behind an Irish defence which kept the home side at bay.

In a breakaway, Carey sent the ball up to the restored O'Flanagan. The Bohemians winger gathered the ball on the run and hared towards goal. Again, remembering his captain's instructions, the medical student renowned at Dalymount for his speed and shooting, unleashed a thunderbolt from 25 yards which gave Szabo no chance. It was Ireland's 30th away goal in 16 games.

Soon afterwards, O'Neill, who had been struggling since his injury, collapsed in the heat and was taken from the field, with O'Reilly again covering. The home side pressed but the depleted Irish held out until the Dundalk man returned. Yet four minutes from time a fine move up the right involving Szanto and Sarosi allowed Kollath to score again from close in.

Match No. 30		*Tuesday, 23rd May 1939*		*Bremen*
GERMANY	(1) 1	Schoen 38		
REPUBLIC OF IRELAND	(0) 1	Bradshaw 65		
Ref: O Remke (Denmark)		*Weser Stadium*		*Att: 35,000*

IRELAND (2-3-5)		A-G	GERMANY (2-3-5)	
George McKenzie	Southend Utd	9–1/20	Hans Jakob	(Jahn Regensburg)
William O'Neill	Dundalk	11–0	Paul Janes	(Fortuna Dusseldorf)
Mick Hoy	Dundalk	6–0	Jakob Streitle	(Bayern Munich)
Joe O'Reilly	St James's Gate	20–2	Andreas Kupfer	(Schweinfurt 05)
Matt O'Mahoney	Bristol Rov	6–0	Hans Rohde	(TV Eimsbuttel)
Ned Weir	Clyde	3–0	Albin Kitzinger	(Schweinfurt 05)
Kevin O'Flanagan	Bohemians	7–3	Ernst Lehner	(Schwaben Augsburg)
Jimmy Dunne	Shamrock Rov	15–13	Wilhelm Hahnemann	(Admira)
Paddy Bradshaw	St James's Gate	5–4	Josef Gauchel	(TuS Neuenddorf)
Johnny Carey	Manchester Utd	8–2	Helmut Schoen	(Dresdner SC)
Bill Fallon	Sheffield Wed	9–2	Willi Arlt	(SV Riesa)

MANAGERS:	Committee (30)	Sepp Herberger
CAPTAINS:	Jimmy Dunne	Paul Janes

The overland journey from Hungary to Germany would normally have gone via Czechoslovakia or Austria, but by May 1939 neither of these two countries existed any more. Germany had first absorbed Austria, and then western parts of Czechoslovakia. Then, with the help of Hungary, Hitler had gobbled up the rest of that country. In footballing terms it was a windfall for Greater Germany who, like a schoolyard bully, now had the pick of the best footballers from all three countries. Austrian players were drafted in, but the Czechs, now a state within Germany called Bohmen-Mahren, retained a sense of national pride and refused. In fact, in preparation for the Irish visit, the Germans had played three games against the semi-autonomous region, including one with an all-Austrian line-up.

However, all was not well with the Greater German football team. They had gone to France for the World Cup with a strong squad and fell at the first hurdle to the Swiss. And in their last full international before taking on the Irish, they had been beaten by – of all teams – Luxembourg.

Following the disastrous trip to the World Cup, German eyes were firmly focused on the 1940 Olympics, preparations for which seemed to be going well until the short hop to Luxembourg, where they did admittedly field an experimental line-up. For the match against the Irish, Sepp Hergerger recalled most of his experienced players, including a former Austrian, Wilhelm Hahnemann. Germany had played 25 matches since their defeat by Ireland three years earlier, and had only lost four. Their home record was good – only one loss since their other disastrous campaign, the 1936 Olympics. This would be the first full international to be played in the northern city of Bremen.

The Irish selectors, concerned about their players' fitness following the Hungarian match, delayed naming their side to face Germany until very late. The problem was that both O'Neill and Fallon were carrying knocks and the two reserves were not exactly direct replacements. Mick McCarthy was a goalkeeper and, with McKenzie in fine form, there was little chance of him playing. The other reserve was Sonny Molloy of Shamrock Rovers, who was a forward. A rejig of the forward line could accommodate him in place of Fallon, but should O'Neill not recover then Ireland's lineout would be reliant on Carey playing in an unfamiliar position, although he would become used to it in the future. As it was, the five-day break was enough to get both Fallon and O'Neill back to full fitness and the selectors named an unchanged team for only the third time.

A huge crowd turned up at the Weser Stadium and they nearly saw the home side take the lead in the first minutes. A right-wing move by Janes and Kupfer found Schoen in the middle. Schoen, who had scored four goals in his first five internationals and was later to manage Germany, found Hahnemann with an astute pass and the inside-right shot high past the advancing McKenzie, only to see his effort bounce off the crossbar and back into play.

The German strength was in their passing, whereas the Irish were strong in the air, which made for an interesting contest. Gauchel, who had scored eleven goals in eleven games for Germany, was starved of the ball and when he did get possession he met a brick house in Matt O'Mahoney. Up front, Ireland's most capped winger came up against Germany's most experienced player, Janes, and got little change from him. O'Flanagan's marker was the less experienced Streitle but the newcomer still kept the hero of Budapest quiet. It was the inside pairing of Dunne and Carey which carried the most danger and, in Bradshaw, they had a willing workhorse.

Ireland's first real chance on goal came from a foul by Rohde on Bradshaw on the edge of the box. This was normally O'Reilly territory but, on instructions from Dunne, Bradshaw took a quick free-kick and almost caught out Jakob. The German goalkeeper scrambled across his goal and got his hands to the ball but only succeeded in knocking it down for the inrushing Dunne. The Irish captain couldn't miss, and didn't, but somehow Jakob recovered to divert the goalbound shot for a corner. Dunne, hands on hips, could not believe it. Jakob had been in goal in 1936 when Ireland knocked five past him at Dalymount. He had let in seven in his last two games but seemed determined to keep a clean sheet for the first time since 1937. His tormentor in chief was Bradshaw who, along with Carey, caused the Germans all sort of problems. It was Carey who set up Bradshaw for a shot, which was sailing towards the bottom corner of the net until Jakob pushed it around the post for an inconclusive corner.

The Irish were gradually gaining the upper hand until an unfortunate accident resulted in them playing most of the game a player down. Dunne shook off his marker and chased a long ball out of defence. Rohde came out to cover and with both players' eyes on the ball it resulted in a sickening collision. The German defender was quickly on his feet but not Dunne, who stayed down. He was in no condition to continue and had to leave the field. It would have been possible to use the sub, Molloy but, it seems, Dunne demanded to continue, which he did after 'treatment', which in those days amounted to no more then a sponge and some cold water. Dunne's quiet demeanour hid a passion for Ireland which meant only a broken leg would stop him from playing on, so Molloy sat it out as the trainer worked on his club boss.

Meanwhile, the Germans took advantage of their extra man and dominated the remaining ten minutes of the half. They broke through when Ernst Lehner, who had played in both previous games against Ireland, got in a shot which McKenzie saved but could not hold. The ball rolled to Kupfer on the wing, whose cross was headed on by Gauchel for Schoen to volley Germany's first goal at the Weser Stadium. They might have had another, but ten-man Ireland held firm until the break.

Dunne was still not fit to resume for the second half and so Ireland continued to play a man shy. After the excitement of the first half, the second proved a little dull in comparison. An early chance fell to Gauchel but he hesitated and O'Mahoney hustled him off the ball. When Dunne finally reappeared it seemed to give his teammates heart. Normally, in these situations, an injured player would be farmed out to the wing so as to contribute to the team while not exposing it to danger should he lose the ball. So Dunne trotted out to the right and told O'Flanagan to take up the centre-forward position, with Bradshaw moving to inside-right. For the young Bohs player this was nothing new, but Dunne and Bradshaw were playing in unaccustomed positions and, strangely, both prospered. In fact, Bradshaw – as was noted in the reports of the game – was Ireland's best forward before and after the switch.

Soon it was all Ireland, who were faster to the ball and battled with such determination that the home side were visibly shaken. After 58 minutes, Kupfer and Jakob collided in going for a cross and the ball fell for Carey who would have levelled except that Jakob was on his feet quickly to push the ball out for a corner.

It seemed that the German goalkeeper was not to be beaten today, until he made one error which invariably cost a goal. Jakob, like most Continental goalkeepers, appeared weak on crosses. The Irish exploited this by giving their wingers every chance to test him. Fallon, one of Ireland's better crossers, was sent scurrying up the wing by Carey and his cross caught Jakob in two minds – come for it or stay. He decided on the former but that slight hesitation was fatal as Bradshaw reached the ball first and headed into the empty net. It was his third straight headed goal for Ireland. The visitors pressed for a winner as the Germans wilted. Most of the danger stemmed from the left, where Carey and, especially, Fallon, were having a field day. That Ireland did not win was due to a superb display for the subsequently flawless Jakob and some fine interceptions from the full-backs, Janes and Streitle.

Four months later the Second World War broke out. Ireland, who remained neutral, would not play international football until after its conclusion. Ireland's pre-war record made for interesting reading. Of the 30 matches played they had won eleven and lost eleven with a near equal goal-difference. They had played twelve nations, had failed to beat five of these, while not losing to four others. Joe O'Reilly would hold the record as most capped player until 1949, when Johnny Carey would surpass it. Jimmy Dunne's record of 13 goals would not be bettered until Noel Cantwell scored in his last appearance for Ireland in 1967. Ireland had capped exactly 100 players and just over two thirds of them were from the League of Ireland. Only 21 were from the English League and eleven each from the Irish and Scottish Leagues. Ireland's failure to reach the 1934 and 1938 World Cup finals would come back to haunt them but, at the time, they were viewed as no more then just another competition. Ireland would have to wait 64 years until they could claim a place in the world's greatest sporting event, outside the Olympics.

Mick O'Brien captained Ireland for the second and last time against the Dutch in Amsterdam in 1932

THE REPUBLIC OF IRELAND SOCCER TEAM 143

Bill Gorman, who won his eighth cap against Poland in 1938

The Irish team which beat Switzerland 1-0 in 1937. Standing (left to right): Johnny Feenan, Mick McCarthy (reserve goalkeeper), Joe O'Reilly, Charlie Turner, Tommy Breen and Con Moulson. Kneeling (left to right): Johnny Brown, Davy Jordan, Jimmy Dunne, William O'Neill, Paddy Farrell and Bill Fallon.

144　　　　　　　　Freestaters 1921-1939

Ireland's Tommy Breen gathers the ball under the watchful eyes of Con Moulson and Charlie Turner and just in front of Switzerland's Alfred Bickel

Charlie Dowdall was involved in some 'afters' with Bob Fullam at the end of the 1921 FAI Cup final

Paddy Bradshaw scores Ireland's opening goal against Hungary in Cork.
Beside him is Johnny Carey

The Irish team in Norway to kick off their 1938 World Cup campaign. Players standing (left to right): Joe Williams, Billy Jordan, Andy Maguire (Bohemians, reserve), Joe O'Reilly, Mick McCarthy (Shamrock Rovers, reserve), Charlie Turner, Tom Donnelly and Mick Hoy. Players kneeling (left to right): Owen Kinsella, George McKenzie, Jimmy Dunne, Joey Donnelly and Matty Geoghegan

Bob Fullam was top LOI goalscorer for 1922-23 and played against Gallia

The Republic of Ireland Soccer Team

The Irish team that played Hungary in Cork in 1939. Players standing (left to right): Joe O'Reilly, Bill Gorman, Tommy Foy, George McKenzie, Mick Hoy and Charlie Turner. Players sitting (left to right): Ned Weir, Jimmy Dunne, Paddy Bradshaw, Johnny Carey and Kevin O'Flanagan. Not a Corkman in a team dominated by 'Jackeens'

148   FREESTATERS 1921-1939

The Irish team which suffered a heavy defeat by the Netherlands in 1935. Players standing (left to right): Bill McGuire, Joey Donnelly, Paddy Andrews, William Harrington, Joe O'Reilly and William O'Neill. Seated (left to right): Joe Kendrick, Fred Horlacher, William 'Sacky' Glen, Plev Ellis and Paddy Moore. William O'Neill seems to have lost his first cap

Tom Farquharson won his fourth and last cap against Spain but conceded 5 goals

THE REPUBLIC OF IRELAND SOCCER TEAM 149

Ireland's Billy Lacey stops Belgium's Michel Vanderbauwhede in Brussels in 1930

Bill Fallon scores the first goal against Poland in 1938

The Mardyke stadium in Cork

Paddy Moore gets ahead of Germany's Josef Rodzinski to have a shot on goal.

The Irish team in Basle prior to playing Switzerland in 1935. Standing (left to right): Charlie Harris (trainer), Paddy Monahan, Joey Donnelly, Freddie Hutchinson, Plev Ellis, Jim 'Fox' Foley, Jimmy Daly, Leo 'Ducky' Dunne, Paddy O'Kane, Alf Rigby, Paddy Gaskins and Charlie Lennon

The first Irish team to play in the World Cup. Players standing (left to right): Miah Lynch, Harry Cannon (Bohemians, reserve), Joe Kendrick, Jim 'Fox' Foley, Patrick 'Sonny' Molloy (Shamrock Rovers, reserve), Tom Burke, Johnny Squires (Shelbourne, reserve), Joe O'Reilly and Paddy Gaskins. Players seated (left to right): Billy Kennedy, David 'Babby' Byrne, Paddy Moore, Tim O'Keeffe and Jimmy Kelly

Players capped by the Free State FA 1926-1939

Popular name	Given name	Caps	Goals
ANDREWS, PADDY (Bohemians) 08.12.1935 v Netherlands	Andrews, Patrick	1	0
ARRIGAN, TOM (Waterford) 07.11.1937 v Norway (World Cup)	Arrigan, Thomas	1	0
BARRY, PADDY (Fordsons) 12.02.1928 v Belgium 20.04.1929 v Belgium	Barry, Patrick	2	0
BERMINGHAM, JIMMY (Bohemians) 20.04.1929 v Belgium	Bermingham, James	1	0
BERMINGHAM, PADDY (St James's Gate) 16.12.1934 v Hungary (1 pen)	Bermingham, Patrick	1	1
BRADSHAW, PADDY (St James's Gate) 18.09.1938 v Switzerland (2 goals) 13.11.1938 v Poland 19.03.1939 v Hungary (1 goal) 18.05.1939 v Hungary 23.05.1939 v Germany (1 goal)	Bradshaw, Patrick	5	4
BRADY, FRANK (Fordsons) 21.03.1926 v Italy 23.04.1927 v Italy B Captain	Brady, Francis	2	0
BREEN, TOMMY (Manchester United) 17.05.1937 v Switzerland (Clean Sheet) 23.05.1937 v France (Clean Sheet)	Breen, Thomas	2	0
BROWN, JOHNNY (Coventry City) 17.05.1937 v Switzerland 23.05.1937 v France (1 goal)	Brown, John 'Jackie'	2	1
BURKE, JOHN (Shamrock Rovers) 20.04.1929 v Belgium Captain	Burke, John 'Tipp'	1	0
BURKE, TOM (Cork) 25.02.1934 v Belgium (World Cup)	Burke, Thomas	1	0
BYRNE, DAVID (Shelbourne) 20.04.1929 v Belgium (1 goal) (Shamrock Rovers) 13.12.1931 v Spain (Coleraine) 25.02.1934 v Belgium (World Cup)	Byrne, David 'Babby'	3	1
BYRNE, JACK (Bray Unknowns) 12.02.1928 v Belgium	Byrne, John 'Squib'	1	0
BYRNE, PADDY (Shelbourne) 26.04.1931 v Spain 08.05.1932 v Netherlands (Drumcondra) 08.04.1934 v Netherlands (World Cup)	Byrne, Patrick 'Babs'	3	0

BYRNE, SEAN (Bohemians) 26.04.1931 v Spain	Byrne, Sean	1	0
CANNON, HARRY (Bohemians) 21.03.1926 v Italy 12.02.1928 v Belgium	Cannon, Harold James	2	0
CAREY, JOHNNY (Manchester United) 07.11.1937 v Norway (World Cup) 18.05.1938 v Czechoslovakia 22.05.1938 v Poland 18.09.1938 v Switzerland 13.11.1938 v Poland (1 goal) 19.03.1939 v Hungary (1 goal) 18.05.1939 v Hungary 23.05.1939 v Germany	Carey, John Joseph 'Jackie'	8	2
CHATTON, HARRY (Shelbourne) 26.04.1931 v Spain (Dumbarton) 13.12.1931 v Spain Captain (Cork) 08.04.1934 v Netherlands (World Cup)	Chatton, James Harold	3	0
COLLINS, FRANK (Jacobs) 23.04.1927 v Italy B	Collins, Francis John	1	0
CONNOLLY, HUGH (Cork) 17.10.1936 v Germany	Connolly, Hugh	1	0
CONNOLLY, JAMES (Fordsons) 21.03.1926 v Italy	Connolly, James 'Sally'	1	0
DALY, JIMMY (Shamrock Rovers) 08.05.1932 v Netherlands 05.05.1935 v Switzerland	Daly, James	2	0
DAVIS, TOM (Oldham Athletic) 17.10.1936 v Germany (2 goals, 1 pen) 06.12.1936 v Hungary (1 pen) (Tranmere Rovers) 18.05.1938 v Czechoslovakia (1 goal) 22.05.1938 v Poland	Davis, Thomas Lawrence	4	4
DONNELLY, JOEY (Dundalk) 16.12.1934 v Hungary (1 goal) 05.05.1935 v Switzerland 08.05.1935 v Germany 08.12.1935 v Netherlands 17.03.1936 v Switzerland 03.05.1936 v Hungary 09.05.1936 v Luxembourg (1 goal) 17.10.1936 v Germany (2 goals) 06.12.1936 v Hungary 10.10.1937 v Norway (World Cup)	Donnelly, Joseph	10	4

DONNELLY, TOM (Drumcondra)   Donnelly, Thomas   2   1
10.10.1937 v Norway (World Cup)
(Shamrock Rovers)
18.09.1938 v Switzerland (1 goal)

DOWDALL, CHARLIE (Fordsons)   Dowdall, Charles   3   0
12.02.1928 v Belgium
(Barnsley)
20.04.1929 v Belgium
(Cork)
26.04.1931 v Spain

DOYLE, DENIS (Shamrock Rovers)   Doyle, Denis 'Dinny'   1   0
21.03.1926 v Italy

DOYLE, LARRY (Dolphin)   Doyle, Laurence   1   0
13.12.1931 v Spain

DUGGAN, HARRY (Leeds United)   Duggan, Henry Anthony   5   1
23.04.1927 v Italy B
11.05.1930 v Belgium
03 05 1936 v Hungary
09.05.1936 v Luxembourg
(Newport County)
07.11.1937 v Norway (World Cup, 1 goal)

DUNNE, JIMMY (Sheffield United)   Dunne, James 'Snowy'   15   13
11.05.1930 v Belgium (2 goals)
(Arsenal)
17.03.1936 v Switzerland (1 goal)
03.05.1936 v Hungary (2 goals)
09.05.1936 v Luxembourg (2 goals)
(Southampton)
17.05.1937 v Switzerland (1 goal)
23.05.1937 v France
(Shamrock Rovers)
10.10.1937 v Norway (World Cup, 1 goal)
07.11.1937 v Norway (World Cup, 1 goal)
18.05 1938 v Czechoslovakia (1 goal)
22.05.1938 v Poland
18.09.1938 v Switzerland (1 goal)   Captain
13.11.1938 v Poland (1 goal)   Captain
19.03.1939 v Hungary   Captain
18.05.1939 v Hungary   Captain
23.05.1939 v Germany   Captain

DUNNE, LEO (Manchester City)   Dunne, Leopold 'Ducky'   2   0
05.05.1935 v Switzerland
08.05.1935 v Germany

EGAN, ROBERT (Dundalk)   Egan, Robert   1   0
20.04.1929 v Belgium

ELLIS, PLEV (Bohemians)   Ellis, Plevna Thomas   7   2
05.05.1935 v Switzerland
08.05.1935 v Germany (1 goal)
08.12.1935 v Netherlands (1 goal)
17.03.1936 v Switzerland
09.05.1936 v Luxembourg
17.10.1936 v Germany
06.12.1936 v Hungary

FAGAN, JACK (Shamrock Rovers)   Fagan, John 'Kruger'   1   0
21.03.1926 v Italy

FALLON, BILL (Notts County)   Fallon, William Joseph   9   2
16.12.1934 v Hungary
03.05.1936 v Hungary
06.12.1936 v Hungary (1 goal)
17.05.1937 v Switzerland
23.05.1937 v France
(Sheffield Wednesday)
18.09.1938 v Switzerland
13.11.1938 v Poland (1 goal)
18.05.1939 v Hungary
23.05.1939 v Germany

FARQUHARSON, TOM (Cardiff City)   Farquharson, Thomas George   4   0
20.04.1929 v Belgium (Clean Sheet)
11.05.1930 v Belgium
26.04.1931 v Spain
13.12.1931 v Spain

FARRELL, PADDY (Hibernian)   Farrell, Patrick   2   0
17.05.1937 v Switzerland
23.05.1937 v France

FEENAN, JOHNNY (Sunderland)   Feenan, John Joseph   2   0
17.05.1937 v Switzerland
23.05.1937 v France

FLOOD, JOHN JOE (Shamrock Rovers)   Flood, John Joseph   5   4
21.03.1926 v Italy
20.04.1929 v Belgium (3 goals)
11.05.1930 v Belgium (1 goal)
26.04.1931 v Spain   Captain
13.12.1931 v Spain

FOLEY, JIM (Cork)   Foley, James 'Fox'   7   0
25.02.1934 v Belgium (World Cup)
08.04.1934 v Netherlands (World Cup)
(Glasgow Celtic)
16.12.1934 v Hungary
05.05.1935 v Switzerland
08.05.1935 v Germany
17.10.1936 v Germany
06.12.1936 v Hungary

FOLEY, MICK (Shelbourne)   Foley, Michael John 'Boxer'   1   0
21.03.1926 v Italy   Captain

FOY, TOMMY (Shamrock Rovers)   Foy, Thomas Gerard   2   0
07.11.1937 v Norway (World Cup)
19.03.1939 v Hungary

FULLAM, BOB (Shamrock Rovers)   Fullam, Robert   2   1
21.03.1926 v Italy
23.04.1927 v Italy B (1 goal)

GALLAGHER, PATSY (Falkirk)   Gallagher, Patrick   1   0
13.12.1931 v Spain

GASKINS, PADDY (Shamrock Rovers)   Gaskins, Peader   7   0
25.02.1934 v Belgium (World Cup)   Captain
08.04.1934 v Netherlands (World Cup)   Captain
16.12.1934 v Hungary   Captain
05.05.1935 v Switzerland   Captain
08.05.1935 v Germany   Captain
(St James's Gate)
18.05.1938 v Czechoslovakia
22.05.1938 v Poland

GEOGHEGAN, MATTY (St James's Gate)   Geoghegan, Matthew   2   2
17.10.1936 v Germany (1 goal)
10.10.1937 v Norway (World Cup, 1 goal)

GLEN, WILLIAM (Shamrock Rovers)   Glen, William 'Sacky'   8   0
23.04.1927 v Italy B
20.04.1929 v Belgium
11.05.1930 v Belgium
13.12.1931 v Spain
08.12.1935 v Netherlands   Captain
17.03.1936 v Switzerland   Captain
03.05.1936 v Hungary Captain
09.05.1936 v Luxembourg   Captain

GOLDING, JOSEPH (Shamrock Rovers)   Golding, Joseph 'Lye'   2   0
12.02.1928 v Belgium
11.05.1930 v Belgium

GORMAN, BILL (Bury)   Gorman, William Charles   11   0
17.03.1936 v Switzerland
03.05.1936 v Hungary
09.05.1936 v Luxembourg
17.10.1936 v Germany
06.12.1936 v Hungary
07.11.1937 v Norway (World Cup)
18.05.1938 v Czechoslovakia
22.05.1938 v Poland
18.09.1938 v Switzerland
13.11.1938 v Poland
(Brentford)
19.03.1939 v Hungary

GRACE, JOE (Drumcondra)   Grace, Joseph   1   0
21.03.1926 v Italy

GRIFFITHS, BOB (Walsall)   Griffiths, Robert   1   0
16.12.1934 v Hungary

HARRINGTON, WILLIAM (Cork) 08.12.1935 v Netherlands 17.03.1936 v Switzerland (Clean Sheet) 03.05.1936 v Hungary 09.05.1936 v Luxembourg 22.05.1938 v Poland Substitute	Harrington, William	5	0
HORLACHER, FRED (Bohemians) 11.05.1930 v Belgium 13.12.1931 v Spain 08.05.1932 v Netherlands 08.04.1934 v Netherlands (World Cup) Substitute 16.12.1934 v Hungary 08.12.1935 v Netherlands (2 goals) 17.03.1936 v Switzerland	Horlacher, Alfred Frederick	7	2
HOY, MICK (Dundalk) 10.10.1937 v Norway (World Cup) 18.09.1938 v Switzerland 13.11.1938 v Poland 19.03.1939 v Hungary 18.05.1939 v Hungary 23.05.1939 v Germany	Hoy, Michael	6	0
HUTCHINSON, FREDDIE (Drumcondra) 05.05.1935 v Switzerland 08.05.1935 v Germany	Hutchinson, Alfred	2	0
JORDAN, BILLY (Bohemians) 08.04.1934 v Netherlands (World Cup) 10.10.1937 v Norway (World Cup)	Jordan, William	2	0
JORDAN, DAVY (Wolverhampton) 17.05.1937 v Switzerland 23.05.1937 v France (1 goal)	Jordan, David	2	1
KAVANAGH, PETER (Glasgow Celtic) 26.04.1931 v Spain 13.12.1931 v Spain	Kavanagh, Peter James	2	0
KELLY, JIMMY (Derry City) 08.05.1932 v Netherlands 25.02.1934 v Belgium (World Cup) 17.03.1936 v Switzerland 09.05.1936 v Luxembourg (2 goals)	Kelly, James	4	2
KENDRICK, JOE (Everton) 23.04.1927 v Italy B (Dolphin) 25.02.1934 v Belgium (World Cup) 08.04.1934 v Netherlands (World Cup) 08.12.1935 v Netherlands	Kendrick, Joseph	4	0
KENNEDY, BILLY (St James's Gate) 08.05.1932 v Netherlands 25.02.1934 v Belgium (World Cup) 08.04.1934 v Netherlands (World Cup)	Kennedy, William	3	0

KINSELLA, JOE (Shelbourne)　　　　　Kinsella, Joseph 'Barney'　　　1　　0
12.02.1928 v Belgium

KINSELLA, OWEN (Shamrock Rovers)　　Kinsella, Owen　　　　　　　2　　0
08.05.1932 v Netherlands
10.10.1937 v Norway (World Cup)

KIRKLAND, ALEC (Shamrock Rovers)　　Kirkland, Alexander　　　　　1　　0
23.04.1927 v Italy B

LACEY, BILLY (Shelbourne)　　　　　Lacey, William　　　　　　　3　　1
23.04.1927 v Italy B
12.02.1928 v Belgium (1 goal)
11.05.1930 v Belgium

LENNON, CHARLIE (St James's Gate)　　Lennon, Charles 'Skip'　　　　3　　0
16.12.1934 v Hungary
05.05.1935 v Switzerland
08.05.1935 v Germany

LENNOX, GEORGE (Dolphin)　　　　　Lennox, George　　　　　　　2　　0
26.04.1931 v Spain
(Shelbourne)
13.12.1931 v Spain

LUNN, DICK (Dundalk)　　　　　　Lunn, Richard　　　　　　　　2　　0
18.09.1938 v Switzerland
13.11.1938 v Poland

LYNCH, MIAH (Cork Bohemians)　　　Lynch, Jeremiah　　　　　　　1　　0
25.02.1934 v Belgium (World Cup)

McCARTHY, JACK (Bohemians)　　　　McCarthy, John　　　　　　　3　　0
21.03.1926 v Italy
12.02.1928 v Belgium Captain
11.05.1930 v Belgium

McCARTHY, MICK (Shamrock Rovers)　　McCarthy, Michael Anthony　　1　　0
08.05.1932 v Netherlands (Clean Sheet)

McGUIRE, BILL (Bohemians)　　　　　McGuire, William　　　　　　1　　0
08.12.1935 v Netherlands

McKENZIE, GEORGE (Southend United)　McKenzie, George Charle　　　9　　0
10.10.1937 v Norway (World Cup)
07.11.1937 v Norway (World Cup)
18.05.1938 v Czechoslovakia
22.05.1938 v Poland
18.09.1938 v Switzerland (Clean Sheet)
13.11.1938 v Poland
19.03.1939 v Hungary
18.05.1939 v Hungary
23.05.1939 v Germany

McLOUGHLIN, FRANK (Fordsons)　　　McLoughlin, Francis　　　　　2　　0
11.05.1930 v Belgium
(Cork)
13.12.1931 v Spain

MADDEN, OWEN (Cork) 03.05.1936 v Hungary	Madden, Owen	1	0
MAGUIRE, JIM (Shamrock Rovers) 20.04.1929 v Belgium	McGuire, James	1	0
MARTIN, CHRIS (Bo'ness) 23.04.1927 v Italy B	Martin, Christopher 'Christy'	1	0
MEEHAN, PADDY (Drumcondra) 08.04.1934 v Netherlands (World Cup)	Meehan, Patrick 'Wooderer'	1	0
MONAHAN, PADDY (Sligo Rovers) 05.05.1935 v Switzerland 08.05.1935 v Germany	Monahan, Patrick Joseph 'Monty'	2	0
MOORE, PADDY (Shamrock Rovers) 26.04.1931 v Spain (1 goal) 08.05.1932 v Netherlands (1 goal) (Aberdeen) 25.02.1934 v Belgium (World Cup, 4 goals) 08.04.1934 v Netherlands (World Cup, 1 goal) 16.12.1934 v Hungary 08.05.1935 v Germany (Shamrock Rovers) 08.12.1935 v Netherlands 17.10.1936 v Germany 06.12.1936 v Hungary	Moore, Patrick	9	7
MOULSON, CON (Lincoln City) 03.05.1936 v Hungary 09.05.1936 v Luxembourg (Notts County) 06.12.1936 v Hungary 17.05.1937 v Switzerland 23.05.1937 v France	Moulson, Cornelius Christopher	5	0
MULDOON, TOMMY (Aston Villa) 23.04.1927 v Italy B	Muldoon, Thomas Patrick	1	0
O'BRIEN, MICK (Derby County) 23.04.1927 v Italy B (Walsall) 20.04.1929 v Belgium (Norwich City) 11.05.1930 v Belgium Captain (Watford) 08.05.1932 v Netherlands Captain	O'Brien, Michael Terence	4	0
O'FLANAGAN, KEVIN (Bohemians) 07.11.1937 v Norway (World Cup, 1 goal) 18.05.1938 v Czechoslovakia 22.05.1938 v Poland 13.11.1938 v Poland 19.03.1939 v Hungary 18.05.1939 v Hungary (2 goals) 23.05.1939 v Germany	O'Flanagan, Kevin Patrick	7	3

O'KANE, PADDY (Bohemians)   O'Kane, Patrick   3   0
16.12.1934 v Hungary
05.05.1935 v Switzerland
08.05.1935 v Germany

O'KEEFFE, TIM (Cork)   O'Keeffe, Timothy Jim   3   0
25.02.1934 v Belgium (World Cup)
(Waterford)
18.05.1938 v Czechoslovakia
22.05.1938 v Poland

O'MAHONEY, MATT (Bristol Rovers) O'Mahoney, Matthew Thomas   6   0
18.05.1938 v Czechoslovakia
22.05.1938 v Poland
18.09.1938 v Switzerland
13.11.1938 v Poland
18.05.1939 v Hungary
23.05.1939 v Germany

O'NEILL, WILLIAM (Dundalk)   O'Neill, William   11   0
08.12.1935 v Netherlands
17.03.1936 v Switzerland
03.05.1936 v Hungary
09.05.1936 v Luxembourg
17.10.1936 v Germany
06.12.1936 v Hungary
17.05.1937 v Switzerland
23.05.1937 v France
07.11.1937 v Norway (World Cup)
18.05.1939 v Hungary
23.05.1939 v Germany

O'REILLY, JOE (Brideville)   O'Reilly, Joseph   20   2
08.05.1932 v Netherlands (1 goal)
(Aberdeen)
25.02.1934 v Belgium (World Cup)
08.04.1934 v Netherlands (World Cup)
(Brideville)
08.12.1935 v Netherlands
17.03.1936 v Switzerland
03.05.1936 v Hungary (1 goal)
09.05.1936 v Luxembourg
(St James's Gate)
17.10.1936 v Germany
06.12.1936 v Hungary
17.05.1937 v Switzerland
23.05.1937 v France
10.10.1937 v Norway (World Cup)
07.11.1937 v Norway (World Cup)
18.05.1938 v Czechoslovakia
22.05.1938 v Poland
18.09.1938 v Switzerland
13.11.1938 v Poland
19.03.1939 v Hungary
18.05.1939 v Hungary
23.05.1939 v Germany

REID, CHARLIE (Brideville) 26.04.1931 v Spain	Reid, Charles	1	0
RIGBY, ALF (St James's Gate) 16.12.1934 v Hungary 05.05.1935 v Switzerland 08.05.1935 v Germany	Rigby, Alfred	3	0
ROBINSON, JEREMIAH (Bohemians) 12.02.1928 v Belgium (Dolphin) 26.04.1931 v Spain	Robinson, Jeremiah 'Sam'	2	0
SQUIRES, JOHNNY (Shelbourne) 08.04.1934 v Netherlands (World Cup, 1 goal)	Squires, John	1	1
STEVENSON, ALEX (Dolphin) 08.05.1932 v Netherlands	Stevenson, Alexander Ernest	1	0
SULLIVAN, JACK (Fordsons) 12.02.1928 v Belgium (1 pen)	Sullivan, Jack	1	1
TURNER, CHARLIE (Southend United) 17.03.1936 v Switzerland 17.10.1936 v Germany Captain 06.12.1936 v Hungary Captain 17.05.1937 v Switzerland Captain 23.05.1937 v France Captain 10.10.1937 v Norway (World Cup) Captain 07.11.1937 v Norway (World Cup) Captain (West Ham United) 18.05.1938 v Czechoslovakia Captain 22.05.1938 v Poland Captain 19.03.1939 v Hungary	Turner, Charles John	10	0
WATTERS, FRAN (Shelbourne) 21.03.1926 v Italy	Watters, Francis	1	0
WEIR, NED (Clyde) 19.03.1939 v Hungary 18.05.1939 v Hungary 23.05.1939 v Germany	Weir, Edward	3	0
WHITE, JIMMY (Bohemians) 12.02.1928 v Belgium (2 goals)	White, James Joseph	1	2
WILLIAMS, JOE (Shamrock Rovers) 10.10.1937 v Norway (World Cup)	Williams, Joseph	1	0

The Republic of Ireland Soccer Team

Ireland's international record 1926-1939

	P	W	D	L	F	A
Overall:	30	11	8	11	65	66
Home:	13	5	3	5	34	32
Away:	17	6	5	6	31	34

Record of international matches:

#	Date	Venue	Opponent	H/A	Result	Score	Scorers
1.	21.03.1926	Turin	v Italy	A	L	0-3	
2.	23.04.1927	Dublin	v Italy B	H	L	1-2	Fullam
3.	12.02.1928	Liege	v Belgium	A	W	4-2	White (2), Lacey, Sullivan (p)
4.	20.04.1929	Dublin	v Belgium	H	W	4-0	Flood (3), Byrne
5.	11.05.1930	Brussels	v Belgium	A	W	3-1	Dunne (2), Flood
6.	26.04.1931	Barcelona	v Spain	A	D	1-1	Moore
7.	13.12.1931	Dublin	v Spain	H	L	0-5	
8.	08.05.1932	Amsterdam	v Netherlands	A	W	2-0	O'Reilly, Moore
9.	25.02.1934	Dublin	v Belgium(WC)	H	D	4-4	Moore (4)
10.	08.04.1934	Amsterdam	v N'lands(WC)	A	L	2-5	Squires, Moore
11.	16.12.1934	Dublin	v Hungary	H	L	2-4	J Donnelly, Bermingham (p)
12.	05.05.1935	Basle	v Switzerland	A	L	0-1	
13.	08.05.1935	Dortmund	v Germany	A	L	1-3	Ellis
14.	08.12.1935	Dublin	v Netherlands	H	L	3-5	Ellis, Horlacher (2)
15.	17.03.1936	Dublin	v Switzerland	H	W	1-0	Dunne
16.	03.05.1936	Budapest	v Hungary	A	D	3-3	Dunne (2), O'Reilly
17.	09.05.1936	Luxembourg	v Luxembourg	A	W	5-1	Dunne (2), J Donnelly, Kelly (2)
18.	17.10.1936	Dublin	v Germany	H	W	5-2	J Donnelly (2), Davis (2, 1p), Geoghegan
19.	06.12.1936	Dublin	v Hungary	H	L	2-3	Fallon, Davis (pen)
20.	17.05.1937	Berne	v Switzerland	A	W	1-0	Dunne
21.	23.05.1937	Paris	v France	A	W	2-0	Jordan, Brown
22.	10.10.1937	Oslo	v Norway(WC)	A	L	2-3	Geoghegan, Dunne
23.	07.11.1937	Dublin	v Norway(WC)	H	D	3-3	Dunne, K O'Flanagan, Duggan
24.	18.05.1938	Prague	v Czechoslovakia	A	D	2-2	Davis, Dunne
25.	22.05.1938	Warsaw	v Poland	A	L	0-6	
26.	18.09.1938	Dublin	v Switzerland	H	W	4-0	Bradshaw (2), Dunne, T.Donnelly
27.	13.11.1938	Dublin	v Poland	H	W	3-2	Fallon, Carey, Dunne
28.	19.03.1939	Cork	v Hungary	H	D	2-2	Bradshaw, Carey
29.	18.05.1939	Budapest	v Hungary	A	D	2-2	K O'Flanagan (2)
30.	23.05.1939	Bremen	v Germany	A	D	1-1	Bradshaw

Ireland's international record against other nations 1921-1939

	Overall	Home	Away
Number of nations played:	12	9	12
Number of nations that Ireland have never beaten:	5	5	7
Number of nations that Ireland are unbeaten against:	4	5	6
Number of nations never drawn with Ireland:	6	6	8
Number of nations Ireland have never scored against:	0	1	2
Number of nations that have never scored against Ireland:	1	1	1

FREESTATERS 1921-1939

					Total			Home					Away			
		P	W	D	L	F	A	P	W	D	L	F	A	P	W	D	L	F	A
Belgium		4	3	1	0	15	7	2	1	1	0	8	4	2	2	0	0	7	3
12 02 1928	Liege				W	4-2
20 04 1929	Dublin				W	4-0
11 05 1930	Brussels				W	3-1
25 02 1934	Dublin(WC)				D	4-4	Belgium were the second nation Ireland played.

					Total			Home					Away			
		P	W	D	L	F	A	P	W	D	L	F	A	P	W	D	L	F	A
Czechoslovakia		1	0	1	0	2	2	0	0	0	0	0	0	1	0	1	0	2	2
18 05 1938	Prague				D	2-2	Czechoslovakia were the eleventh nation Ireland played.

					Total			Home					Away			
		P	W	D	L	F	A	P	W	D	L	F	A	P	W	D	L	F	A
France		1	1	0	0	2	0	0	0	0	0	0	0	1	1	0	0	2	0
23 05 1937	Paris				W	2-0	France were the ninth nation Ireland played.

					Total			Home					Away			
		P	W	D	L	F	A	P	W	D	L	F	A	P	W	D	L	F	A
Germany		3	1	1	1	7	6	1	1	0	0	5	2	2	0	1	1	2	4
08 05 1935	Dortmund				L	1-3
17 10 1936	Dublin				W	5-2
23 05 1939	Bremen				D	1-1	Germany were the seventh nation Ireland played.

					Total			Home					Away			
		P	W	D	L	F	A	P	W	D	L	F	A	P	W	D	L	F	A
Hungary		5	0	3	2	11	14	3	0	1	2	6	9	2	0	2	0	5	5
16 12 1934	Dublin				L	2-4
03 05 1936	Budapest				D	3-3
06 12 1936	Dublin				L	2-3
19 03 1939	Cork				D	2-2	Hungary were Ireland's most frequent pre-war opponents.
18 05 1939	Budapest				D	2-2	Hungary were the fifth nation Ireland played.

					Total			Home					Away			
		P	W	D	L	F	A	P	W	D	L	F	A	P	W	D	L	F	A
Italy		2	0	0	2	1	5	1	0	0	1	1	2	1	0	0	1	0	3
21 03 1926	Turin				L	0-3
23 04 1927	Dublin (B)				L	1-2	Italy were the first nation Ireland played.

					Total			Home					Away			
		P	W	D	L	F	A	P	W	D	L	F	A	P	W	D	L	F	A
Luxembourg		1	1	0	0	5	1	0	0	0	0	0	0	1	1	0	0	5	1
09 05 1936	Luxembourg				W	5-1	Luxembourg were the eighth nation Ireland played.

					Total			Home					Away			
		P	W	D	L	F	A	P	W	D	L	F	A	P	W	D	L	F	A
Netherlands		3	1	0	2	7	10	1	0	0	1	3	5	2	1	0	1	4	5
08 05 1932	Amsterdam				W	2-0
08 04 1934	Amsterdam(WC)				L	2-5
08 12 1935	Dublin				L	3-5	The Netherlands were the fourth nation Ireland played.

					Total			Home					Away			
		P	W	D	L	F	A	P	W	D	L	F	A	P	W	D	L	F	A
Norway		2	0	1	1	5	6	1	0	1	0	3	3	1	0	0	1	2	3
10 10 1937	Oslo(WC)				L	2-3
07 11 1937	Dublin(WC)				D	3-3	Norway were the tenth nation Ireland played.

Poland

		P	W	D	Total L	F	A	P	W	Home D	L	F	A	P	W	Away D	L	F	A
Poland		2	1	0	1	3	8	1	1	0	0	3	2	1	0	0	1	0	6
22 05 1938	Warsaw				L	0-6
13 11 1938	Dublin				W	3-2	Poland were the twelfth nation Ireland played.

Spain

		P	W	D	Total L	F	A	P	W	Home D	L	F	A	P	W	Away D	L	F	A
Spain		2	0	1	1	1	6	1	0	0	1	0	5	1	0	1	0	1	1
26 04 1931	Barcelona				D	1-1
13 12 1931	Dublin				L	0-5	Spain were the third nation Ireland played.

Switzerland

		P	W	D	Total L	F	A	P	W	Home D	L	F	A	P	W	Away D	L	F	A
Switzerland		4	3	0	1	6	1	2	2	0	0	5	0	2	1	0	1	1	1
05 05 1935	Basle				L	0-1
17 03 1936	Dublin				W	1-0
17 05 1937	Berne				W	1-0
18 09 1938	Dublin				W	4-0	Switzerland were the sixth nation Ireland played.

Records:
Biggest Win: Overall: 5-1   09 05 1936 v Luxembourg
                Home: 5-2   17 10 1936 v Germany
                            4-0   20 04 1929 v Belgium
                                   18 09 1938 v Switzerland
                Away: 5-1   09 05 1936 v Luxembourg

Heaviest Defeat: Overall: 0-6   22 05 1938 v Poland
                 Home: 0-5   13 12 1931 v Spain
                 Away: 0-6   22 05 1938 v Poland

Ireland's most capped pre-war players.

	Overall	Total Caps
Number of Irish players capped 1926-1939:	100	332
Number of League of Ireland players capped by Ireland:	76 (76%)	211 (63.6%)
Number of English League players capped by Ireland:	21 (21%)	95 (28.6%)
Number of Scottish League players capped by Ireland:	9 (9%)	21 (6.3%)
Number of Irish League players capped by Ireland:	2 (2%)	5 (1.5%)

Ireland's most capped pre-war players (minimum of five caps):

Caps	Player	Debut	International career
20	Joe O'Reilly	08 05 1932 v Netherlands	1932-1939
15	Jimmy Dunne	11 05 1930 v Belgium	1930-1939
11	Bill Gorman	17 03 1936 v Switzerland	1936-1939
11	William O'Neill	08 12 1935 v Netherlands	1935-1939
10	Joey Donnelly	16 12 1934 v Hungary	1934-1937
10	Charlie Turner	17 03 1936 v Switzerland	1936-1939
9	Bill Fallon	16 12 1934 v Hungary	1934-1939
9	George McKenzie	10 10 1937 v Norway	1937-1939
9	Paddy Moore	26 04 1931 v Spain	1931-1936
8	Johnny Carey	07 11 1937 v Norway	1937-1939
8	William Glen	23 04 1927 v Italy B	1927-1936
7	Plev Ellis	05 05 1935 v Switzerland	1935-1936
7	Jim Foley	25 02 1934 v Belgium	1934-1936
7	Paddy Gaskins	25 02 1934 v Belgium	1934-1938
7	Fred Horlacher	11 05 1930 v Belgium	1930-1936
7	Kevin O'Flanagan	07 11 1937 v Norway	1937-1939
6	Mick Hoy	10 10 1937 v Norway	1937-1939
6	Matt O'Mahoney	18 05 1938 v Czechoslovakia	1938-1939
5	Paddy Bradshaw	18 09 1938 v Switzerland	1938-1939
5	Harry Duggan	23 04 1927 v Italy B	1927-1937
5	John Joe Flood	21 03 1926 v Italy	1926-1931
5	William Harrington	08 12 1935 v Netherlands	1935-1938
5	Con Moulson	03 05 1936 v Hungary	1936-1937

League of Ireland players capped by Ireland 1926-1939
(These records include Joe Grace who was then a Leinster Senior League player)

Number of League of Ireland players capped by Ireland:	76
Total number of caps won by League of Ireland players:	211
Most Capped League of Ireland player:	Joe O'Reilly, 18
Number of League of Ireland goalscorers for Ireland:	18
Total Number of goals scored by League of Ireland players:	39
Leading League of Ireland scorer for Ireland:	Jimmy Dunne, 5 goals
Number of League of Ireland players who have captained Ireland:	8
Number of times League of Ireland players have captained Ireland:	19
League of Ireland player who has captained Ireland most times:	Paddy Gaskins, 5
All League of Ireland Irish sides: 3	21 03 1926 v Italy
	12 02 1928 v Belgium
	08 12 1935 v Netherlands

Irish sides with no League of Ireland players: 0

First League of Ireland players capped by Ireland:
 Frank Brady, Harry Cannon, James Connolly, Denis Doyle, Jack Fagan, John Joe Flood, Mick Foley, Bob Fullam, Joe Grace, Jack McCarthy, Fran Watters v Italy 1926

First League of Ireland scorer for Ireland:	Bob Fullam v Italy B 1927
First League of Ireland Captain:	Mick Foley v Italy 1926
Club which supplied most players for Ireland:	Shamrock Rovers, 19
Club which provided most goalscorers for Ireland:	Shamrock Rovers, 5
Club which supplied most captains for Ireland:	Shamrock Rovers, 5
Club whose players captained Ireland most times:	Shamrock Rovers, 16 times
Club with most caps for Ireland:	Shamrock Rovers, 51 caps
Club with most goals for Ireland:	Shamrock Rovers, 13 goals

League of Ireland goalkeepers:
1. Harry Cannon   Bohemians   2   0/5
2. Frank Collins   Jacobs   1   0/2
3. Mick McCarthy   Shamrock Rovers   1   1/0
4. Jim Foley   Cork   2   0/9
5. William Harrington Cork   5   1/10

Mick McCarthy of Shamrock Rovers was the first League of Ireland goalkeeper to keep a clean sheet for Ireland.

League of Ireland clubs supplying players for Ireland: 15
 Shamrock Rovers (19), Bohemians (13), Cork FC (9), Shelbourne (9), St James's Gate (8), Fordsons (6), Dolphin (5), Drumcondra (5), Dundalk (5), Brideville (2), Waterford (2) Bray Unknowns (1), Cork Bohemians (1), Jacobs (1), Sligo Rovers (1)

League of Ireland clubs that never had a player capped by Ireland (1926-1939) are as follows:
 Athlone Town, Brooklyn, Cork City, Dublin United, Frankfort, Limerick, Midland Athletic, Olympia, Pioneers, Rathmines Athletic, Reds United, Shelbourne United and the YMCA.)

Bohemians

Total players Capped:	13
Most Capped player:	Plev Ellis, Fred Horlacher, Kevin O'Flanagan, 7
Number of goalscorers for Ireland:	4
Leading goalscorer:	Kevin O'Flanagan, 3 goals
Number of Captains:	1
Number of times a player has captained Ireland:	1
Total Caps won by Bohemians players:	37
Total goals scored by Bohemians players:	9
Most representation in an Ireland side:	4 12 02 1928 v Belgium
First Players Capped by Ireland:	Harry Cannon and Jack McCarthy v Italy 1926
First goalscorer for Ireland:	Jimmy White v Belgium 1928
First captain:	Jack McCarthy v Belgium 1928

Players Capped 1926-1939:
 Paddy Andrews 1, Jimmy Bermingham 1, Sean Byrne 1, Harry Cannon   2, Plev Ellis 7 (2), Fred Horlacher 7 (2), Billy Jordan 2, Jack McCarthy 3, Bill McGuire 1, Kevin O'Flanagan 7 (3), Paddy O'Kane 3, Jeremiah Robinson 1, Jimmy White 1 (2).

Bray Unknowns

Total players Capped:	1
Most Capped player:	Jack Byrne, 1
Number of goalscorers for Ireland:	0
Number of Captains:	0
Total Caps won by Bray Unknowns players:	1
First Player Capped by Ireland:	Jack Byrne v Belgium 1928

Players Capped 1926-1939:
 Jack Byrne 1

Brideville

Total players Capped:	2
Most Capped player:	Joe O'Reilly, 5
Number of goalscorers for Ireland:	1
Leading goalscorer:	Joe O'Reilly, 3 goals
Number of Captains:	0
Total Caps won by Brideville players:	6
Total goals scored by Brideville players:	2
Most representation in an Ireland side:	1 (6 times)
First player Capped by Ireland:	Charlie Reid v Spain 1931
First goalscorer for Ireland:	Joe O'Reilly v Netherlands 1932

Players Capped 1926-1939:
 Charlie Reid 1, Joe O'Reilly 5 (2)

Cork Football Club

Total players Capped:	9
Most Capped player:	William Harrington, 5
Number of goalscorers for Ireland:	0
Number of Captains:	0
Total Caps won by Cork FC players:	14
Most representation in an Ireland side:	3 25 02 1934 v Belgium
First player Capped by Ireland:	Charlie Dowdall v Spain 1931

Players Capped 1926-1939:
 Tom Burke 1, Harry Chatton 1, Hugh Connolly 1, Charlie Dowdall 1, Jim Foley 2, William Harrington 5, Frank McLoughlin 1, Owen Madden 1, Tim O'Keeffe 1

Cork Bohemians
Total players Capped:	1
Most Capped player:	Miah Lynch, 1
Number of goalscorers for Ireland:	0
Number of Captains:	0
Total Caps won by Cork Bohemians players:	1
First player Capped by Ireland:	Miah Lynch v Belgium 1934

Players Capped 1926-1939:
    Miah Lynch 1

Dolphin
Total players Capped:	5
Most Capped player:	Joe Kendrick, 3
Number of goalscorers for Ireland:	0
Number of Captains:	0
Total Caps won by Dolphin players:	7
Most Representation in an Ireland side:	2 26 04 1931 v Spain
First players capped by Ireland:	George Lennox and Jeremiah Robinson v Spain 1931

Players Capped 1926-1939:
    Larry Doyle 1, Joe Kendrick 3, George Lennox 1, Jeremiah Robinson 1, Alex Stevenson 1

Drumcondra
Total players Capped:	5
Most capped player:	Freddie Hutchinson, 2
Number of goalscorers for Ireland:	0
Number of Captains:	0
Total Caps won by Drumcondra players:	6
Most Representation in an Ireland side:	2 08 04 1934 v Netherlands
First player capped by Ireland:	Joe Grace v Italy 1926

Players Capped 1926-1939:
    Paddy Byrne 1, Tom Donnelly 1, Joe Grace 1, Freddie Hutchinson 2, Paddy Meehan 1
    Note: The above records also include Joe Grace who was capped by Ireland when the club was still playing in the Leinster Senior League.

Dundalk
Total players Capped:	5
Most Capped player:	William O'Neill, 11
Number of goalscorers for Ireland:	1
Leading goalscorer:	Joey Donnelly, 4 goals
Number of Captains:	0
Total Caps won by Dundalk players:	30
Total goals scored by Dundalk players:	4
Most representation in an Ireland side:	2 (11 Times)
First player Capped by Ireland:	Robert Egan v Belgium 1929
First goalscorer for Ireland:	Joey Donnelly v Hungary 1934

Players capped 1926-1939:
    Joey Donnelly 10 (4), Robert Egan 1, Mick Hoy 6, Dick Lunn 2, William O'Neill 11

Fordsons

Total players Capped:	6
Most Capped players:	Paddy Barry and Frank Brady, 2
Number of goalscorers for Ireland:	1
Leading goalscorer:	Jack Sullivan, 1 goal
Number of Captains:	1
Number of times a player has captained Ireland:	1
Total Caps won by Fordsons players:	8
Total goals scored by Fordsons players:	1
Most representation in an Ireland side:	3 12 02 1928 v Belgium
First players Capped by Ireland:	Frank Brady and James Connolly v Italy 1926
First goalscorer for Ireland:	Jack Sullivan v Belgium 1928
First Captain:	Frank Brady v Italy B 1927

Players Capped 1926-1939:
   Paddy Barry 2, Frank Brady 2, James Connolly 1, Charlie Dowdall 1, Frank McLoughlin 1, Jack Sullivan 1 (1).

Jacobs

Total players capped:	1
Most capped player:	Frank Collins, 1
Number of goalscorers for Ireland:	0
Number of Captains:	0
Total Caps won by Jacobs players:	1
First player Capped by Ireland:	Frank Collins v Italy B 1927

Players Capped 1926-1939:
   Frank Collins 1

St James's Gate

Total players capped:	8
Most Capped player:	Joe O'Reilly, 13
Number of goalscorers for Ireland:	3
Leading goalscorer:	Paddy Bradshaw, 4 goals
Number of Captains:	0
Total Caps won by St James's Gate players:	32
Total goals scored by St James's Gate players:	7
Most representation in an Ireland side:	3 16 12 1934 v Hungary
First player Capped by Ireland:	Billy Kennedy v Netherlands 1932
First goalscorer for Ireland:	Paddy Bermingham v Hungary 1934

Players Capped 1926-1939:
   Paddy Bermingham 1 (1), Paddy Bradshaw 5 (4), Paddy Gaskins 2, Matty Geoghegan 2 (2), Billy Kennedy 3, Charlie Lennon 3, Joe O'Reilly 13, Alf Rigby 3

Shamrock Rovers

Total players capped:	19
Most Capped player:	Jimmy Dunne, 9
Number of goalscorers for Ireland:	5
Leading goalscorer:	Jimmy Dunne, 5 goals
Number of Captains:	5
Number of times a player has captained Ireland:	16
Total Caps won by Shamrock Rovers players:	51
Total goals scored by Shamrock Rovers players:	13
Most representation in an Ireland side:	4 (Three times)
First players Capped by Ireland:	Denis Doyle, Jack Fagan, John Joe Flood, Bob Fullam
First goalscorer for Ireland:	Bob Fullam v Italy 1927
First Captain:	John Burke v Belgium 1929

Players Capped 1926-1939:
John Burke 1, David Byrne 1, Jimmy Daly 2, Tom Donnelly 1 (1), Denis Doyle 1, Jimmy Dunne 9 (5), Jack Fagan 1, John Joe Flood 5 (4), Tommy Foy 2, Bob Fullam 2 (1), Paddy Gaskins 5, William Glen 8, Joseph Golding 2, Owen Kinsella 2, Alec Kirkland 1, Mick McCarthy 1, Jim Maguire 1, Paddy Moore 5 (2), Joe Williams 1

Shelbourne

Total Players Capped:	9
Most Capped player:	Billy Lacey, 3
Number of goalscorers for Ireland:	3
Leading goalscorer:	David Byrne, Billy Lacey, Johnny Squires, 1 goal
Number of Captains:	1
Number of times a player has captained Ireland:	1
Total Caps won by Shelbourne players:	12
Total goals scored by Shelbourne players:	3
Most representation in an Ireland side:	2 (Three times)
First players Capped by Ireland:	Mick Foley and Fran Watters v Italy 1926
First goalscorer for Ireland:	Billy Lacey v Belgium 1928
First Captain:	Mick Foley v Italy 1926

Players Capped 1926-1939:
David Byrne 1 (1), Paddy Byrne 2, Harry Chatton 1, Mick Foley 1, Joe Kinsella 1, Billy Lacey 3 (1), George Lennox 1, Johnny Squires 1 (1), Fran Watters 1

Sligo Rovers

Total players Capped:	1
Most Capped player:	Paddy Monahan, 2
Number of goalscorers for Ireland:	0
Number of Captains:	0
Total Caps won by Sligo Rovers players:	2
Most representation in an Irish side:	1 (Twice)
First player Capped by Ireland:	Paddy Monahan v Switzerland 1935

Players Capped 1926-1939:
Paddy Monahan 2

Waterford

Total players Capped:	2
Most Capped player:	Tim O'Keeffe, 2
Number of goalscorers for Ireland:	0
Number of Captains:	0
Total Caps won by Waterford players:	3
Most representation in an Ireland side:	1 (Three times)
First player Capped:	Tom Arrigan v Norway 1937

Players Capped 1926-1939:
Tom Arrigan 1, Tim O'Keeffe 2

English League players capped by Ireland 1926-1939

Number of English League players capped by Ireland:	21
Total number of caps won by English League players:	95
Most Capped English League player:	Bill Gorman, 11
Number of English League goalscorers for Ireland:	7
Total Number of goals scored by English League players:	19
Leading English League scorer for Ireland:	Jimmy Dunne, 8 goals
Number of English League players who have captained Ireland:	2
Number of times English League players have captained Ireland:	9
English League player who has captained Ireland most times:	Charlie Turner, 8
All English League Irish sides:	0

Irish teams with no English League players: 5
- 21 03 1926 v Italy
- 12 02 1928 v Belgium
- 25 02 1934 v Belgium
- 08 04 1934 v Netherlands
- 08 12 1935 v Netherlands

First English League players capped by Ireland:
   Harry Duggan, Joe Kendrick, Tommy Muldoon, Mick O'Brien v Italy B 1927

First English League scorer for Ireland: Jimmy Dunne v Belgium 1930

First English League Captain: Mick O'Brien v Belgium 1930

Club which supplied most players for Ireland:
   Manchester United, Notts County, Southend United, Walsall, 2

Club which provided most goalscorers for Ireland:	One player from nine clubs scored for Ireland
Club which supplied most captains for Ireland:	One player from four clubs captained Ireland
Club whose players captained Ireland most times:	Southend United, 6 times
Club with most caps for Ireland:	Southend United, 16 caps
Club with most goals for Ireland:	Arsenal, 5 goals

English League goalkeepers:
1. Tom Farquharson   Cardiff City   4   1/7
2. Tommy Breen   Manchester United   2   2/0
3. George McKenzie   Southend United   9   1/20

Tom Farquharson was the first English League goalkeeper to keep a clean sheet for Ireland.

English League clubs supplying players for Ireland: 28
   Manchester United (2), Notts County (2), Southend United (2), Walsall (2), Arsenal (1), Aston Villa (1), Barnsley (1), Brantford (1), Bristol Rovers (1), Bury (1), Cardiff City (1), Coventry City (1), Derby County (1), Everton (1), Leeds United (1), Lincoln City (1), Manchester City (1), Newport County (1), Norwich City (1), Oldham Athletic (1), Sheffield United (1), Sheffield Wednesday (1), Southampton (1), Sunderland (1), Tranmere Rovers (1), Watford (1), West Ham United (1), Wolverhampton Wanderers (1)

THE REPUBLIC OF IRELAND SOCCER TEAM

Arsenal
Number of Captains: 0
Total players Capped: 1
Players Capped 1926-1939:
Number of goalscorers for Ireland: 1
Jimmy Dunne 3 (5)

Aston Villa
Number of Captains: 0
Total players Capped: 1
Players Capped 1926-1939:
Number of goalscorers for Ireland: 0
Tommy Muldoon 1

Barnsley
Number of Captains: 0
Total players Capped: 1
Players Capped 1926-1939:
Number of goalscorers for Ireland: 0
Charlie Dowdall 1

Brentford
Number of Captains: 0
Total players Capped: 1
Players Capped 1926-1939:
Number of goalscorers for Ireland: 0
Bill Gorman 1

Bristol Rovers
Number of Captains: 0
Total players Capped: 1
Players Capped 1926-1939:
Number of goalscorers for Ireland: 0
Matt O'Mahoney 6

Bury
Number of Captains: 0
Total players Capped: 1
Players Capped 1926-1939:
Number of goalscorers for Ireland: 0
Bill Gorman 10

Cardiff City
Number of Captains: 0
Total players Capped: 1
Players Capped 1926-1939:
Number of goalscorers for Ireland: 0
Tom Farquharson 4

Coventry City
Number of Captains: 0
Total players Capped: 1
Players capped 1926-1939:
Number of goalscorers for Ireland: 1
Johnny Brown 2 (1)

Derby County
Number of Captains: 0
Total players Capped: 1
Players Capped 1926-1939:
Number of goalscorers for Ireland: 0
Mick O'Brien 1

Everton
Number of Captains: 0
Total players capped: 1
Players Capped 1926-1939:
Number of goalscorers for Ireland: 0
Joe Kendrick 1

Leeds United
Number of Captains: 0
Total players capped: 1
Players Capped 1926-1939:
Number of goalscorers for Ireland: 0
Harry Duggan 4

Lincoln City
Number of Captains: 0
Total players capped: 1
Players Capped 1926-1939:
Number of goalscorers for Ireland: 0
Con Moulson 2

Manchester City
Number of Captains: 0
Total players capped: 1
Players Capped 1926-1939:
Number of goalscorers for Ireland: 0
Leo Dunne 2

Manchester United Total players capped: 2
Number of goalscorers for Ireland: 1
Most Capped player: Johnny Carey, 8
Leading scorer: Johnny Carey, 2 goals
Number of Captains: 0 Total Caps won by Manchester United players: 10
Total goals scored by Manchester United players: 2. Most representation in an Ireland side: 1 (10 times)
First player Capped by Ireland: Tommy Breen v Switzerland 1937. First goalscorer for Ireland: Johnny Carey v Poland 1938   Players Capped 1926-1939:   Tommy Breen 2, Johnny Carey 8

Newport County
Number of Captains: 0
Total Players Capped 1
Players Capped 1926-1939:
Number of goalscorers for Ireland: 1
Harry Duggan 1 (1)

Norwich City
Number of Captains: 1
Total Players Capped: 1
Players Capped 1926-1939:
Number of goalscorers for Ireland: 0
Mick O'Brien 1

Notts County Total Players Capped: 2
Number of goalscorers for Ireland: 1
Most Capped player: Bill Fallon, 5
Leading goalscorer: Bill Fallon, 1 goal
Number of Captains: 0   Total Caps won by Notts County players: 8
Total goals scored by Notts County players: 1Most representation in an Ireland side: 2 (three times)
First player Capped by Ireland: Bill Fallon v Hungary 1934. First goalscorer for Ireland: Bill Fallon v Hungary 1936   Players Capped 1926-1939:   Bill Fallon 5 (1), Con Moulson 3

Oldham Athletic
Number of Captains: 0

Total Players Capped: 1
Players Capped 1926-1939:

Number of goalscorers for Ireland: 1
Tom Davis 2 (3)

Sheffield United
Number of Captains: 0

Total Players Capped: 1
Players Capped 1926-1939:

Number of goalscorers for Ireland: 1
Jimmy Dunne 1 (2)

Sheffield Wednesday
Number of Captains: 0

Total Players Capped: 1
Players Capped 1926-1939:

Number of goalscorers for Ireland: 1
Bill Fallon 4 (1)

Southampton
Number of Captains: 0

Total Players Capped: 1
Players Capped 1926-1939:

Number of goalscorers for Ireland: 1
Jimmy Dunne 2 (1)

Southend United Total Players Capped: 2   Most Capped player: G'ge McKenzie, 9
Number of goalscorers for Ireland: 0
Number of Captains: 1   Number of times a player has captained Ireland: 6
Total Caps won by Southend United players: 16   Most representation in an Ireland side: 2 (twice)
First player Capped by Ireland: Charlie Turner v Switzerland 1936. First Captain: Charlie Turner v Germany 1936   Players Capped 1926-1939:   George McKenzie 9, Charlie Turner 7

Sunderland
Number of Captains: 0

Total Players Capped: 1
Players Capped 1926-1939:

Number of goalscorers for Ireland: 0
Johnny Feenan 2

Tranmere Rovers
Number of Captains: 0

Total Players Capped: 1
Players Capped 1926-1939:

Number of goalscorers for Ireland: 1
Tom Davis 2 (1)

Walsall   Total Players Capped: 2   Most Capped players: Bob Griffiths,
Mick O'Brien, 1   Number of goalscorers for Ireland: 0
Number of Captains: 0
Total Caps won by Walsall players: 2   Most representation in an Ireland side: 1 (twice)
First player Capped by Ireland: Mick O'Brien v Belgium 1929
            Players Capped 1926-1939:   Bob Griffiths 1, Mick O'Brien 1

Watford
Number of Captains: 1

Total Players Capped: 1
Players Capped 1926-1939:

Number of goalscorers for Ireland: 0
Mick O'Brien 1

West Ham United Total Players Capped: 1   Number of goalscorers for Ireland: 0
Number of Captains 1   Number of times a player has captained Ireland: 2
         Players Capped 1926-1939:   Charlie Turner 3

Wolverhampton Wand's Total Players Capped: 1   Number of goalscorers for Ireland: 1
Number of Captains: 0   Players Capped 1926-1939:   Davy Jordan 2 (1)

Scottish League players capped by Ireland 1926-1939:

Number of Scottish League players capped by Ireland:	9
Total number of caps won by Scottish League players:	21
Most Capped Scottish League player:	Jim Foley, 5
Number of Scottish League goalscorers for Ireland:	1
Total Number of goals scored by Scottish League players:	5
Leading Scottish League scorer for Ireland:	Paddy Moore, 5 goals
Number of Scottish League players who have captained Ireland:	1
Number of times Scottish League players have captained Ireland:	1
Scottish League player who has captained Ireland most times:	Harry Chatton, 1
All Scottish League Irish sides:	0
Irish teams with no Scottish League players:	15
First Scottish League player capped by Ireland:	Christopher Martin v Italy B 1927
First Scottish League scorer for Ireland:	Paddy Moore v Belgium 1934
First Scottish League Captain:	Harry Chatton v Spain 1931
Club which supplied most players for Ireland:	Aberdeen and Glasgow Celtic, 2
Club which provided most goalscorers for Ireland:	Aberdeen, 1
Club which supplied most captains for Ireland:	Dumbarton, 1
Club whose players captained Ireland most times:	Dumbarton, once
Club with most caps for Ireland:	Glasgow Celtic, 7 caps
Club with most goals for Ireland:	Aberdeen, 5 goals

Scottish League goalkeepers:
1. Jim Foley   Glasgow Celtic   5   0/13

Scottish League clubs supplying players for Ireland: 7
    Aberdeen (2), Glasgow Celtic (2), Bo'ness (1), Clyde (1), Dumbarton (1), Falkirk (1), Hibernian (10

Aberdeen   Total Players Capped: 2   Most Capped player: Paddy Moore, 4
Number of goalscorers for Ireland: 1   Leading goalscorer: Paddy Moore, 5
Number of Captains: 0   Total Caps won by Aberdeen players: 6
Total goals scored by Aberdeen players: 5   Most representation in an Ireland side: 2 (twice)
First players Capped by Ireland: Paddy Moore, Joe O'Reilly v Belgium 1934
First goalscorer for Ireland: Paddy Moore v Belgium 1934
                           Players Capped 1926-1939:   Paddy Moore 4 (5), Joe O'Reilly 2

Bo'ness   Total Players Capped: 1   Number of goalscorers for Ireland: 0
Number of Captains: 0   Players Capped 1926-1939:   Christopher Martin 1

Clyde   Total Players Capped: 1   Number of goalscorers for Ireland: 0
Number of Captains: 1   Players Capped 1926-1939:   Ned Weir 3

Dumbarton   Total Players Capped: 1   Number of goalscorers for Ireland: 0
Number of Captains: 1   Players Capped 1926-1939:   Harry Chatton 1

Falkirk   Total Players Capped: 1   Number of goalscorers for Ireland: 0
Number of Captains: 0   Players Capped 1926-1939:   Patsy Gallagher 1

Glasgow Celtic Total Players Capped: 2 Most Capped player: Jim Foley, 5
Number of goalscorers for Ireland: 0
Number of Captains: 0 Total Caps won by Glasgow Celtic players: 7
Most representation in an Irish side: 1 (7 times) First player Capped by Ireland: Peter Kavanagh v Spain 1931
Players Capped 1926-1939: Jim Foley 5, Peter Kavanagh 2

Hibernian Total Players Capped: 1 Number of goalscorers for Ireland: 0
Number of Captains: 0 Players Capped 1926-1939: Paddy Farrell 2

Irish League players capped by Ireland 1926-1939

Number of Irish League players capped by Ireland:	2
Total number of caps won by Irish League players:	5
Most Capped Irish League player:	Jimmy Kelly, 4
Number of Irish League goalscorers for Ireland:	1
Total Number of goals scored by Irish League players:	2
Leading Irish League scorer for Ireland:	Jimmy Kelly, 2 goals
Number of Irish League players who have captained Ireland:	0
Number of times Irish League players have captained Ireland:	0
Irish League player who has captained Ireland most times:	0
All Irish League Irish sides:	0
Irish teams with no Irish League players:	26
First Irish League player capped by Ireland:	Jimmy Kelly v Netherlands 1932
First Irish League scorer for Ireland:	Jimmy Kelly v Luxembourg 1936
First Irish League Captain:	None
Club which supplied most players for Ireland:	Coleraine and Derry City, 1
Club which provided most goalscorers for Ireland:	Derry City, 1
Club which supplied most captains for Ireland:	None
Club whose players captained Ireland most times:	None
Club with most caps for Ireland:	Derry City, 4
Club with most goals for Ireland:	Derry City, 2 goals
Irish League clubs supplying players for Ireland: 2	Coleraine (1), Derry City (1)

Coleraine
Number of Captains: 0
Total players Capped: 1
Players Capped 1926-1939:
Number of goalscorers for Ireland: 0
David Byrne 1

Derry City
Number of Captains: 0
Total players Capped: 1
Players Capped 1926-1939:
Number of goalscorers for Ireland: 1
Jimmy Kelly 4 (2)

Ireland's scorers 1926-1939

Scorers	(25)	WC	FR	Home	Away	Pen
Jimmy Dunne	13	2	11	4	9	0
Paddy Moore	7	5	2	4	3	0
Paddy Bradshaw	4	0	4	3	1	0
Tom Davis	4	0	4	3	1	2
Joey Donnelly	4	0	4	3	1	0
John Joe Flood	4	0	4	3	1	0
Kevin O'Flanagan	3	1	2	1	2	0
Johnny Carey	2	0	2	2	0	0
Plev Ellis	2	0	2	1	1	0
Bill Fallon	2	0	2	2	0	0
Matty Geoghegan	2	1	1	1	1	0
Fred Horlacher	2	0	2	2	0	0
Jimmy Kelly	2	0	2	0	2	0
Joe O'Reilly	2	0	2	0	2	0
Jimmy White	2	0	2	0	2	0
Paddy Bermingham	1	0	1	1	0	1
Johnny Brown	1	0	1	0	1	0
David Byrne	1	0	1	1	0	0
Tom Donnelly	1	0	1	1	0	0
Harry Duggan	1	1	0	1	0	0
Bob Fullam	1	0	1	1	0	0
Davy Jordan	1	0	1	0	1	0
Billy Lacey	1	0	1	0	1	0
Johnny Squires	1	1	0	0	1	0
Jack Sullivan	1	0	1	0	1	1
Own Goals	0	0	0	0	0	
Total	65	11	54	34	31	4

Leading scorers against Ireland 1926-1939

Scorers against: 41

		Total	WC	EC
Reidar Kvammen	Norway	4	4	0
Arocha	Spain	3	0	0
Beb Bakhuys	Netherlands	3	2	0
Ferenc Kollath	Hungary	3	0	0
Leonard Piontek	Poland	3	0	0
Kick Smit	Netherlands	3	2	0
Istvan Avar	Hungary	2	0	0
Ludwig Damminger	Germany	2	0	0
Alf Martinsen	Norway	2	2	0
Federico Munerati	Italy B	2	0	0
Oldrich Nejedly	Czechoslovakia	2	0	0
Luis Regueiro	Spain	2	0	0
Gyorgy Sarosi	Hungary	2	0	0
Francois Vanden Eynden	Belgium	2	2	0
Joop van Nellen	Netherlands	2	0	0
Jeno Vincze	Hungary	2	0	0
Ernest Wilimowski	Poland	2	0	0
Gerard Wodarz	Poland	2	0	0
Own Goals		0	0	0

Goals scored against

1st.	Adolfo Baloncieri	Italy	1926
10th.	Luis Regueiro	Spain	1931
20th.	Beb Bakhuys	Netherlands	1934
25th.	Jeno Vincze	Hungary	1934
30th.	Ludwig Damminger	Germany	1935
40th.	Leon Mart	Luxembourg	1936
50th.	Reidar Kvammen	Norway	1937
60th.	Leonard Piontek	Poland	1938

Attendances

Home (Top 5)   Total 341,404   Average at home 26,262
35,000 v Spain 1931   Dalymount Park
34,295 v Poland 1938   Dalymount Park
32,000 v Switzerland 1936   Dalymount Park
31,000 v Switzerland 1938   Dalymount Park
28,000 v Belgium 1934   Dalymount Park World Cup
Lowest
15,000 v Belgium 1929   Dalymount Park

Away (Top 5)   Total 385,688   Average away 22,688
40,000 v Netherlands 1934 World Cup
35,000 v Spain 1931
35,000 v Germany 1935
35,000 v Germany 1939
30,000 v Netherlands 1932
Lowest:
8,000 v Luxembourg 1936

Overall   Total 727,092   Average 24,236

Dalymount Park Records

	P	W	D	L	F	A
Matches at Dalymount Park	11	5	2	4	31	28
World Cup	2	0	2	0	7	7
Friendlies	9	5	0	4	24	21

Scorers:
4   Jimmy Dunne, Paddy Moore
3   Tom Davis, Joey Donnelly, John Joe Flood
2   Paddy Bradshaw, Bill Fallon, Fred Horlacher
1   Paddy Bermingham, David Byrne, Johnny Carey, Tom Donnelly, Harry, Duggan, Plev Ellis, Matty Geoghegan, Kevin O'Flanagan

Hat-tricks at Dalymount Park
1. John Joe Flood   v Belgium   20 04 1929   3 goals   57 mins
2. Paddy Moore   v Belgium   25 02 1934   4 goals   29 mins

Ireland games at Dalymount Park (pre-1921)
26 03 1904 v Scotland   D   1–1   Paddy Sheridan
17 03 1906 v Scotland   L   0–1
14 03 1908 v Scotland   L   0–5
10 02 1912 v England   L   1– 6   Mickey Hamill
15 03 1913 v Scotland   L   1– 2   James McKnight
Note-Robert Hamilton of Scotland scored the first international goal at Dalymount Park.

Lansdowne Road Records

	P	W	D	L	F	A
Matches at Lansdowne Road	1	0	0	1	1	2
World Cup	0	0	0	0	0	0
Friendlies	1	0	0	1	1	2

Scorers: Bob Fullam 1

Ireland games at Lansdowne Road (pre-1921)
17 03 1900 v England   L   0-2
Note-William Johnson of England scored the first international goal at Lansdowne Raod.

Home records at other grounds

	P	W	D	L	F	A
Matches at the Mardyke	1	0	1	0	2	2
World Cup	0	0	0	0	0	0
Friendlies	1	0	1	0	2	2

Scorers:
Paddy Bradshaw 1   Johnny Carey 1

Penalties (For)

Penalties awarded to Ireland:	No	Scored	Saved	Missed
Tom Davis	2	2	0	0
Paddy Bermingham	1	1	0	0
Joe O'Reilly	1	0	1	0
Jack Sullivan	1	1	0	0
	5	4	1	0

Penalties (Against)

Penalties against Ireland: 7

					Scored	Saved	Missed
					4	2	1
1.	Gorostiza	Spain	26 04 1931	Farquharson 1	0	1	0
2.	Weiler	Switzerland	05 05 1935	Foley 1	1	0	0
3.	Sarosi	Hungary	03 05 1936	Harrington 1	1	0	0
4.	Mart	Luxembourg	09 05 1936	Harrington 2	1	0	0
5.	Lauri	France	23 05 1937	Breen 1	0	1	0
6.	Holmberg	Norway	10 10 1937	McKenzie 1	0	0	1
7.	Nejedly	Czechoslovakia	18 05 1938	McKenzie 2	1	0	0

Goalkeepers' Penalty Records:	Pens	Saved	Missed	Conceded
Tom Farquharson	1	1	0	0
Jim Foley	1	0	0	1
William Harrington	2	0	0	2
Tommy Breen	1	1	0	0
George McKenzie	2	0	1	1

Ireland team records 1926-1939

Record Win:	5-1 09 05 1936 v Luxembourg
Home:	5-2 17 10 1936 v Germany
Away:	5-1 09 05 1936 v Luxembourg
Record Defeat:	0-6 22 05 1938 v Poland
Home:	0-5 13 12 1931 v Spain
Away:	0-6 22 05 1938 v Poland
Most Capped Player:	Joe O'Reilly, 20
Leading goalscorer:	Jimmy Dunne, 13
Most goals in one game:	Paddy Moore, 4 v Belgium, 1934
Most Scorers in one game: 3	v Bel 1928, Lux 1936, Ger 1936, Nor 1937, Swit 1938, Pol 1938
Most Scorers v ROI in a game:: 4	by Netherlands 1935, Poland 1938

Irish goalkeeping records

Irish goalkeepers:	Caps	CS	GC	Pen
1. Harry Cannon	2	0	5	0
2. Frank Collins	1	0	2	0
3. Tom Farquharson	4	1	7	0(1)
4. Mick McCarthy	1	1	0	0
5. Jim Foley	7	0	22	1
6. William Harrington	5	1	10	2
7. Tommy Breen	2	2	0	0(1)
8. George McKenzie	9	1	20	1(1)
Totals		6	66	4(3)

Minutes without conceding a goal		from	to
180	Tommy Breen	1937 SWIT	1937 FRA
117	George McKenzie	1938 POL (a)	1938 POL (h)
110	Tom Farquharson	1929 BEL	1930 BEL
108	Tom Farquharson	1930 BEL	1931 SPA
99	William Harrington	1935 HOL	1936 HUN

Consecutive Runs

Appearances:	17	Joe O'Reilly
Home:	8	Joe O'Reilly
Away:	9	Joe O'Reilly, Jimmy Dunne
Goalscoring:	5	Jimmy Dunne 1930-1937
Home:	4	Jimmy Dunne 1936-38
Away:	4	Jimmy Dunne
Wins:	3	1928-1930
Home:	2	1938
Away:	3	1936-1937
Draws:	3	1939
Home:	1	Bel 1934, Nor 1937, Hun 1939
Away:	2	1939
Defeats:	5	1934-1935
Home:	2	1934-1935
Away:	3	1934-1935
Without Defeat:	5	1938-1939
Home:	4	1937-1939
Away:	4	1928-1932 & 1936-1937
Without a win:	6	1934-1935
Home:	4	1931-1935
Away:	5	1937-1939
Without conceding a goal:	2	1937
Home:	1	Bel 1929
Away:	2	1937
Without Scoring:	1	Italy 1926 & Spain 1931
Home:	1	Spain 1931
Away:	1	Italy 1926 & Swit 1935
Scoring Games:	12	1935-1938
Home:	10	1934-1939
Away:	7	1935-1938
GK clean sheets:	2	180 mins by Tommy Breen 1937

Won from behind, lost from in front

Won from behind: 3 (BEL 1928, BEL 1930, GER 1936)
Lost from in front: 6 (ITA 'B' 1927, HOL 1934, GER 1935, HOL 1935, HUN 1936, NOR 1937)

Goals scored/conceded in the first and second halves

		Home	Away
Goals scored:	65		
First Half:	29	18	11
Second Half:	36	16	20
Goals Conceded:	66	Home	Away
First Half:	34	17	17
Second Half:	32	15	17

Most games played against Ireland

Szabo, Antal	Hungary	5	1934-1939
Minelli, Severino	Switzerland	4	1935-1938
Aeby, Georges	Switzerland	3	1936-1938
Anderiesen, Wim	Netherlands	3	1932-1935
Braine, Pierre	Belgium	3	1928-1930
Cseh II, Laszlo	Hungary	3	1934-1936
Hoydonckx, Nikolaas	Belgium	3	1928-1930
Lehner, Ernst	Germany	3	1935-1939
Sarosi, Gyorgy	Hungary	3	1936-1939
Szucs II, Gyorgy	Hungary	3	1934-1939
Van Heel, Puck	Netherlands	3	1932-1935
Vincze, Jeno	Hungary	3	1934-1936
Weber, Mauk	Netherlands	3	1932-1935
Wels, Frank	Netherlands	3	1932-1935

Ireland's captains

Captain:			W	D	L
1. Mick Foley		1	0	0	1
2. Frank Brady		1	0	0	1
3. Jack McCarthy		1	1	0	0
4. John Burke		1	1	0	0
5. Mick O'Brien		2	2	0	0
6. John Joe Flood		1	0	1	0
7. Harry Chatton		1	0	0	1
8. Paddy Gaskins		5	0	1	4
9. William Glen		4	2	1	1
10. Charlie Turner		8	3	2	3
11. Jimmy Dunne		5	2	3	0

Consecutive Caps: (Minimum of 5 consecutive appearances)

Joe O'Reilly	17	1935-1939
Jimmy Dunne	11	1937-1939
Joey Donnelly	9	1934-1936
George McKenzie	9	1937-1939
Johnny Carey	8	1937-1939
William O'Neill	8	1935-1937
Charlie Turner	8	1936-1938
Bill Gorman	6	1937-1939
Kevin O'Flanagan	6	1937-1939
Paddy Bradshaw	5	1938-1939
Jim Foley	5	1934-1935
Paddy Gaskins	5	1934-1935
Bill Gorman	5	1936
Mick Hoy	5	1938-1939

Scoring first stats
Matches where Ireland score first:
Total:	15	9	3	3
Home:	9	5	2	2
Away:	6	4	1	1

Matches where the Opposition score first:
Total:	15	2	5	8
Home:	4	0	1	3
Away:	11	2	4	5

Players who have scored on their international debuts:

1.	Jimmy White	Bohemians	55 Mins (2)	v Belgium, 1928	A	W	4-2
2.	Jack Sullivan	Fordsons	79 Mins (p)	v Belgium, 1928	A	W	4-2
3.	David Byrne	Shelbourne	73 Mins	v Belgium, 1929	H	W	4-0
4.	Jimmy Dunne	Sheffield United	32 Mins (2s)	v Belgium, 1930	A	W	3-1
5.	Paddy Moore	Shamrock Rovers	35 Mins	v Spain, 1931	A	D	1-1
6.	Joe O'Reilly	Brideville	20 Mins	v Netherlands, 1932	A	W	2-0
7.	Johnny Squires	Shelbourne	42 Mins	v Netherlands, 1934	A	L	2-5
8.	Joey Donnelly	Dundalk	35 Mins	v Hungary, 1934	H	L	2-4
9.	Paddy Bermingham	St James's Gate	62 Mins (p)	v Hungary, 1934	H	L	2-4
10.	Tom Davis	Oldham Athletic	35 Pen (2)	v Germany, 1936	H	W	5-2
11.	Matty Geoghegan	St James's Gate	59 Mins	v Germany, 1936	H	W	5-2
12.	Kevin O'Flanagan	Bohemians	62 Mins	v Norway, 1937	H	D	3-3
13.	Paddy Bradshaw	St James's Gate	20 secs (2)	v Switzerland, 1938	H	W	4-0

Goalkeepers who have kept Clean Sheets on their international debuts:

1.	Tom Farquharson	Cardiff City	v Belgium, 1929
2.	Mick McCarthy	Shamrock Rovers	v Netherlands, 1932
3.	Tommy Breen	Manchester United	v Switzerland, 1937

Players who have been captain on their international debuts:

1.	Mick Foley	Shelbourne	v Italy, 1926
2.	John Burke	Shamrock Rovers	v Belgium, 1929
3.	Paddy Gaskins	Shamrock Rovers	v Belgium, 1934

Youngest and oldest

Youngest player to play for Ireland:	Kevin O'Flanagan	18 years, 150 days
Youngest player to score for Ireland:	Kevin O'Flanagan	18 years, 150 days
Oldest player to play for Ireland :	Billy Lacey	40 years, 229 days
Oldest player to score for Ireland:	Billy Lacey	38 years, 141 days

Goalscoring Records

First goal scored:	Bob Fullam v Italy B 1927
First home goal:	Bob Fullam v Italy B 1927
First goal at Dalymount Park:	John Joe Flood v Belgium 1929
First goal outside Dalymount Park:	Bob Fullam v Italy B 1927 at Lansdowne Road
First World Cup goal:	Paddy Moore v Belgium 1934
First away goal:	Jimmy White v Belgium 1928
Most number of goals in a game:	4 by Paddy Moore v Belgium 1934
Most number of scorers in a game:	3 (6 times)
Longest run of scoring in consecutive games:	3 by Paddy Moore and Jimmy Dunne
Longest run of scoring in consecutive apps:	5 by Jimmy Dunne (1930-1937)
Fastest goal scored by Ireland:	20 seconds by Paddy Bradshaw v Switzerland 1938
Goals direct from a corner:	0
Goals direct from a free kick:	1 Joe O'Reilly v Hungary 1936

Record of the Irish soccer team from the First World War up to the Split

25 10 1919	Belfast	v England	H	D	1-1	Ferris	
14 02 1919	Belfast	v Wales	H	D	2-2	McCandless, Emerson	
13 03 1919	Glasgow	v Scotland	A	L	0-3		
23 10 1920	Sunderland	v England	A	L	0-2		
26 02 1921	Belfast	v Scotland	H	L	0-2		
09 04 1921	Swansea	v Wales	A	L	1-2	Chambers	

The Soccer tournament of the 1924 Summer Olympic Games, Paris, France

Preliminary Round
25 05 1924	Czechoslovakia	5-2	Turkey
25 05 1924	Italy	1-0	Spain
25 05 1924	Switzerland	9-0	Lithuania
25 05 1924	USA	1-0	Estonia
26 05 1924	Hungary	5-0	Poland
26 05 1924	Uruguay	7-0	Yugoslavia

First Round
27 05 1924	France	7-0	Latvia
27 05 1924	Netherlands	6-0	Romania
28 05 1924	Bulgaria	0-1	Ireland
28 05 1924	Czechoslovakia	1-1	Switzerland (after extra time)
29 05 1924	Egypt	3-0	Hungary
29 05 1924	Italy	2-0	Luxembourg
29 05 1924	Sweden	8-1	Belgium
29 05 1924	Uruguay	3-0	USA
replay			
30 05 1924	Switzerland	1-0	Czechoslovakia

Quarter-finals
01 06 1924	Sweden	5-0	Egypt
01 06 1924	France	1-5	Uruguay
02 06 1924	Netherlands	2-1	Ireland (after extra time)
02 06 1924	Switzerland	2-1	Italy

Semi-finals
05 06 1924	Switzerland	2-1	Sweden
06 06 1924	Uruguay	2-1	Netherlands

Bronze Medal game
08 06 1924	Netherlands	1-1	Sweden (after extra time)
replay			
09 06 1924	Sweden	3-1	Netherlands

Final
09 06 1924	Uruguay	3-0	Switzerland

Medals:
GOLD: Uruguay, SILVER: Switzerland, BRONZE: Sweden

Games played: 24, Goals scored: 96, Top goalscorer: Pedro Petrone (Uruguay), 8

Irish appearances (+goals)
Players Used: 12
P Duncan 2 (1), JJ Dykes 2, M Farrell 2, F Ghent 1 (1), D Hannon 2, J Kendrick 1, H Kerr 2, J McCarthy 2, E McKay 2, T Muldoon 2, J Murray 2, P O'Reilly 2.

20 Players capped by both the IFA and the FAI (up until the end of 1939)

BREEN, Tommy   11 Caps

9 CAPS FOR NORTHERN IRELAND
Belfast Celtic
1. 06 02 1935 v England   A L 1-2   2. 27 03 1935 v Wales   A L 1-3
3. 31 10 1936 v Scotland   H L 1-3   4. 18 11 1936 v England   A L 1-3
Manchester United
5. 17 03 1937 v Wales   A L 1-4   6. 23 10 1937 v England   H L 1-5
7. 10 11 1937 v Scotland   A D 1-1   8. 08 10 1938 v Scotland   H L 0-2
9. 15 03 1939 v Wales   A L 1-3

2 CAPS FOR THE REPUBLIC OF IRELAND
Manchester United
1. 17 05 1937 v Switzerland A W 1-0   2. 23 05 1937 v France   A W 2-0

BROWN, Johnny   12 Caps   (2 goals)

10 CAPS (1 GOAL) FOR NORTHERN IRELAND
Wolverhampton Wanderers
1. 06 02 1935 v England   A L 1-2   2. 27 03 1935 v Wales   A L 1-3
3. 19 10 1935 v England   H L 1-3 (1)
Coventry City
4. 18 11 1936 v England   A L 1-3   5. 17 03 1937 v Wales   A L 1-4
6. 10 11 1937 v Scotland   A D 1-1   7. 16 03 1938 v Wales   H W 1-0
Birmingham City
8. 08 10 1938 v Scotland   H L 0-2   9. 16 11 1938 v England   A L 0-7
10. 15 03 1939 v Wales   A L 1-3

2 CAPS (1 GOAL) FOR THE REPUBLIC OF IRELAND
Coventry City
1. 17 05 1937 v Switzerland A W 1-0   2. 23 05 1937 v France   A W 2-0 (1)

CHATTON, Harry   6 Caps

3 CAPS FOR NORTHERN IRELAND
Partick Thistle
1. 22 10 1924 v England   A L 1-3   2. 28 02 1925 v Scotland   H L 0-3
3. 24 10 1925 v England   H D 0-0

3 CAPS FOR THE REPUBLIC OF IRELAND
Shelbourne
1. 26 04 1931 v Spain   A D 1-1
Dumbarton
2. 13 12 1931 v Spain   H L 0-5
Cork
3. 08 04 1934 v Netherlands A L 2-5

COLLINS, Frank   2 Caps

1 CAP FOR NORTHERN IRELAND
Glasgow Celtic
1. 04 03 1922 v Scotland   A L 1-2

1 CAP FOR THE REPUBLIC OF IRELAND
Jacobs
1. 23 04 1927 v Italy B   H L 1-2

DAVIS, Tom   5 Caps   (5 goals)

4 CAPS (4 GOALS) FOR THE REPUBLIC OF IRELAND
Oldham Athletic
1. 17 10 1936 v Germany   H   W   5-2 (2)   2.   06 12 1936 v Hungary   H   L   2-3 (1)
Tranmere Rovers
3. 18 05 1938 v Czech.   A   D   2-2 (1)   4.   22 05 1938 v Poland   A   L   0-6

1 CAP (1 GOAL) FOR NORTHERN IRELAND
Oldham Athletic
1. 18 11 1936 v England   A   L   1-3 (1)

DUGGAN, Harry   13 Caps   (1 goal)

5 CAPS (1 GOAL) FOR THE REPUBLIC OF IRELAND
Leeds United
1. 23 04 1927 v Italy B   H   L   1-2   2.   11 05 1930 v Belgium   A   W   3-1
3. 03 05 1936 v Hungary   A   D   3-3   4.   09 05 1936 v Luxembourg A   W   5-1
Newport County
5. 07 11 1937 v Norway   H   D   3-3 (1)

8 CAPS FOR NORTHERN IRELAND
Leeds United
1. 19 10 1929 v England   H   L   0-3   2.   20 10 1930 v England   A   L   1-5
3. 22 04 1931 v Wales   A   L   2-3   4.   17 10 1932 v England   A   L   0-1
5. 14 10 1933 v England   H   L   0-3   6.   20 10 1934 v Scotland   H   W   2-1
7. 27 03 1935 v Wales   A   L   1-3   8.   13 11 1935 v Scotland   A   L   1-2

DUNNE, Jimmy   22 Caps   (17 goals)

7 CAPS (4 GOALS) FOR NORTHERN IRELAND
Sheffield United
1. 04 02 1928 v Wales   H   L   1-2   2.   20 10 1930 v England   A   L   1-5 (1)
3. 22 04 1931 v Wales   A   L   2-3 (1)   4.   19 09 1931 v Scotland   A   L   1-3 (1)
5. 17 10 1931 v England   H   L   2-6 (1)   6.   17 10 1932 v England   A   L   0-1
7. 07 12 1932 v Wales   A   L   1-4

15 CAPS (13 GOALS) FOR THE REPUBLIC OF IRELAND
Sheffield United
1. 11 05 1930 v Belgium   A   W   3-1 (2)
Arsenal
2. 17 03 1936 v Switzerland H W   1-0 (1   3.   03 05 1936 v Hungary   A   D   3-3 (2)
4. 09 05 1936 v Luxembourg A   W   5-1 (2)
Southampton
5. 17 05 1937 v Switzerland A W   1-0 (1)   6.   23 05 1937 v France   A   W   2-0
Shamrock Rovers
7. 10 10 1937 v Norway   A   L   2-3 (1)   8.   07 11 1937 v Norway   H   D   3-3 (1)
9. 18 05 1938 v Czech.   A   D   2-2 (1)   10.   22 05 1938 v Poland   A   L   0-6
11. 18 09 1938 v Switzerland H W   4-0 (1)   12.   13 11 1938 v Poland   H   W   3-2 (1)
13. 19 03 1939 v Hungary   H   D   2-2   14.   18 05 1939 v Hungary   A   D   2-2
15. 23 05 1939 v Germany   A   D   1-1

FARQUHARSON, Tom   11 Caps

7 CAPS FOR NORTHERN IRELAND
Cardiff City
1. 03 03 1923 v Scotland   H L 0-1
2. 14 04 1923 v Wales   A W 3-0
3. 20 10 1923 v England   H W 2-1
4. 01 03 1924 v Scotland   A L 0-2
5. 15 03 1924 v Wales   H L 0-1
6. 22 10 1924 v England   A L 1-3
7. 28 02 1925 v Scotland   H L 0-3

4 CAPS FOR THE REPUBLIC OF IRELAND
Cardiff City
1. 20 04 1929 v Belgium   H W 4-0
2. 11 05 1930 v Belgium   A W 3-1
3. 26 04 1931 v Spain   A D 1-1
4. 13 12 1931 v Spain   H L 0-5

FARRELL, Paddy   3 Caps

2 CAPS FOR THE REPUBLIC OF IRELAND
Hibernian
1. 17 05 1937 v Switzerland A W 1-0
2. 23 05 1937 v France   A W 2-0

1 CAP FOR NORTHERN IRELAND
Hibernian
1. 16 03 1938 v Wales   H W 1-0

GALLAGHER, Patsy   12 Caps

2 CAPS FOR IRELAND
Glasgow Celtic
1. 25 10 1919 v England   H D 1-1
2. 13 03 1920 v Scotland   A L 0-3

9 CAPS FOR NORTHERN IRELAND
Glasgow Celtic
3. 04 03 1922 v Scotland   A L 1-2
4. 03 03 1923 v Scotland   H L 0-1
5. 14 04 1923 v Wales   A W 3-0
6. 01 03 1924 v Scotland   A L 0-2
7. 15 03 1924 v Wales   H L 0-1
8. 22 10 1924 v England   A L 1-3
9. 28 02 1925 v Scotland   H L 0-3
10. 18 04 1925 v Wales   A D 0-0
Falkirk
11. 26 02 1927 v Scotland   H L 0-2

1 CAP FOR THE REPUBLIC OF IRELAND
Falkirk
1. 13 12 1931 v Spain   H L 0-5

KAVANAGH, Peter   3 Caps

1 CAP FOR NORTHERN IRELAND
Glasgow Celtic
1. 19 10 1929 v England   H L 0-3

2 CAPS FOR THE REPUBLIC OF IRELAND
Glasgow Celtic
1. 26 04 1931 v Spain   A D 1-1
2. 13 12 1931 v Spain   H L 0-5

KELLY, Jimmy   15 Caps   (6 goals)

11 CAPS (4 GOALS) FOR NORTHERN IRELAND
Derry City
1. 17 10 1931 v England   H L 2-6 (1)   2. 05 12 1931 v Wales   H W 4-0 (2)
3. 19 09 1932 v Scotland   H L 0-4   4. 17 10 1932 v England   A L 0-1
5. 07 12 1932 v Wales   A L 1-4   6. 04 11 1933 v Wales   H D 1-1
7. 19 10 1935 v England   H L 1-3   8. 13 11 1935 v Scotland   A L 1-2 (1)
9. 11 03 1936 v Wales   H W 3-2   10. 31 10 1936 v Scotland   H L 1-3
11. 18 11 1936 v England   A L 1-3

4 CAPS (2 GOALS) FOR THE REPUBLIC OF IRELAND
Derry City
1. 08 05 1932 v Netherlands A W 2-0   2. 25 02 1934 v Belgium   H D 4-4
3. 17 03 1936 v Switzerland H W 1-0   4. 09 05 1936 v Luxembourg A W 5-1 (2)

LACEY, Billy   26 Caps   (4 goals)

20 CAPS (3 GOALS) FOR IRELAND
Everton
1. 10 02 1909 v England   A L 0-4   2. 15 03 1909 v Scotland   A L 0-5
3. 20 03 1909 v Wales   H L 2-3 (1)   4. 12 02 1910 v England   H D 1-1
5. 19 03 1910 v Scotland   H W 1-0   6. 11 04 1910 v Wales   A L 1-4
7. 28 01 1911 v Wales   H L 1-2   8. 11 02 1911 v England   A L 1-2
9. 18 03 1911 v Scotland   A L 0-2   10. 10 02 1912 v England   H L 1-6
Liverpool
11. 18 01 1913 v Wales   H L 0-1   12. 19 01 1914 v Wales   A W 2-1
13. 14 02 1914 v England   A W 3-0 (2)   14. 14 03 1914 v Scotland   H D 1-1
15. 25 10 1919 v England   H D 1-1   16. 14 02 1920 v Wales   H D 2-2
17. 13 03 1920 v Scotland   A L 0-3   18. 23 10 1920 v England   A L 0-2
19. 26 02 1921 v Scotland   H L 0-2   20. 09 04 1921 v Wales   A L 1-2

3 CAPS FOR NORTHERN IRELAND
21. 22 10 1921 v England   H D 1-1   22. 04 03 1922 v Scotland   A L 1-2
New Brighton
23. 22 10 1924 v England   A L 1-3

3 CAPS (1 GOAL) FOR THE REPUBLIC OF IRELAND
Shelbourne
1. 23 04 1927 v Italy B   H L 1-2   2. 12 02 1928 v Belgium   A W 4-2 (1)
3. 11 05 1930 v Belgium   A W 3-1

MADDEN, Owen   2 Caps

1 CAP FOR THE REPUBLIC OF IRELAND
Cork
1. 03 05 1936 v Hungary   A D 3-3

1 CAP FOR NORTHERN IRELAND
Norwich City
1. 23 10 1937 v England   H L 1-5

MARTIN, Christopher   2 Caps

1 CAP FOR NORTHERN IRELAND
Bo'ness United
1. 28 02 1925 v Scotland   H L 0-3

1 CAP FOR THE REPUBLIC OF IRELAND
Bo'ness United
1. 23 04 1927 v Italy B   H L 1-2

MOORE, Paddy   10 Caps   (7 goals)

9 CAPS (7 GOALS) FOR THE REPUBLIC OF IRELAND
Shamrock Rovers
1. 26 04 1931 v Spain   A D 1-1 (1)   2. 08 05 1932 v Netherlands A W 2-0 (1)
Aberdeen
3. 25 02 1934 v Belgium   H D 4-4 (4)   4. 08 04 1934 v Netherlands A L 2-5 (1)
5. 16 12 1934 v Hungary   H L 2-4   6. 08 05 1935 v Germany   A L 1-3
Shamrock Rovers
7. 08 12 1935 v Netherlands H L 3-5   8. 17 10 1936 v Germany   H W 5-2
9. 06 12 1936 v Hungary   H L 2-3

1 CAP FOR NORTHERN IRELAND
Aberdeen
1. 17 10 1932 v England   A L 0-1

O'BRIEN, Mick   14 Caps

1 CAP FOR IRELAND
Queen's Park Rangers
1. 26 02 1921 v Scotland   H L 0-2

9 CAPS FOR NORTHERN IRELAND
Leicester City
2. 04 03 1922 v Scotland   A L 1-2   3. 01 04 1922 v Wales   H D 1-1
4. 01 03 1924 v Scotland   A L 0-2   5. 15 03 1924 v Wales   H L 0-1
Hull City
6. 22 10 1924 v England   A L 1-3   7. 28 02 1925 v Scotland   H L 0-3
8. 18 04 1925 v Wales   A D 0-0   9. 13 02 1926 v Wales   H W 3-0
Derby County
10. 09 04 1927 v Wales   A D 2-2

4 CAPS FOR THE REPUBLIC OF IRELAND
Derby County
1. 23 04 1927 v Italy B   H L 1-2
Walsall
2. 20 04 1929 v Belgium   H W 4-0
Norwich City
3. 11 05 1930 v Belgium   A W 3-1
Watford
4. 08 05 1932 v Netherlands A W 2-0

O'MAHONEY, Matt   7 Caps

6 CAPS FOR THE REPUBLIC OF IRELAND
Bristol Rovers
1. 18 05 1938 v Czech.   A D 2-2   2. 22 05 1938 v Poland   A L 0-6
3. 18 09 1938 v Switzerland H W 4-0   4. 13 11 1938 v Poland   H W 3-2
5. 18 05 1939 v Hungary   A D 2-2   6. 23 05 1939 v Germany   A D 1-1

1 CAP FOR NORTHERN IRELAND
1. 08 10 1938 v Scotland   A L 0-2

STEVENSON, Alex 15 Caps (4 goals)

1 CAP FOR THE REPUBLIC OF IRELAND
Dolphin
1. 08 05 1932 v Netherlands A W 2-0

14 CAPS (4 GOALS) FOR NORTHERN IRELAND
Glasgow Rangers
1. 16 09 1933 v Scotland   A W 2-1   2. 14 10 1933 v England   H L 0-3
3. 04 11 1933 v Wales   H D 1-1
Everton
4. 20 10 1934 v Scotland   H W 2-1   5. 06 02 1935 v England   A L 1-2 (1)
6. 13 11 1935 v Scotland   A L 1-2   7. 11 03 1936 v Wales   H W 3-2 (1)
8. 18 11 1936 v England   A L 1-3   9. 17 03 1937 v Wales   A L 1-4 (1)
10. 23 10 1937 v England   H L 1-5 (1) 11. 16 03 1938 v Wales   H W 1-0
12. 08 10 1938 v Scotland   H L 0-2   13. 16 11 1938 v England   A L 0-7
14. 15 03 1939 v Wales   A L 1-3

WEIR, Ned 4 Caps

1 CAP FOR NORTHERN IRELAND
Clyde
1. 15 03 1939 v Wales   A L 1-3

3 CAPS FOR THE REPUBLIC OF IRELAND
Clyde
1. 19 03 1939 v Hungary   H D 2-2   2. 18 05 1939 v Hungary   A D 2-2
3. 23 05 1939 v Germany   A D 1-1

Total players capped by the IFA and FAI:	20
Most capped player for IFA and FAI:	Billy Lacey 26
Capped by the IFA before the FAI:	13
Capped by the FAI before the IFA:	7
First players capped by both IFA and FAI:	4 Frank Collins, Billy Lacey, Christopher Martin, Mick O'Brien
Won More Caps for IFA then FAI:	9
Won More Caps for FAI then IFA:	7
Total number of scorers for both IFA and FAI:	5
Highest scorer for IFA and FAI:	Jimmy Dunne 17
First to score for both:	Billy Lacey
Scored on his debut for both:	0
Scored more goals for IFA then FAI:	3 Jimmy Kelly, Billy Lacey, Alex Stevenson
Scored more goals for FAI then IFA:	4 Tom Davis, Harry Duggan, Jimmy Dunne, Paddy Moore
First GK to keep a clean sheet for IFA and FAI:	Tom Farquharson
First player to captain both Ireland's:	Mick O'Brien
Played in the World Cup for both IFA and FAI:	0
Scored in the World Cup for both IFA and FAI:	0
League of Ireland players capped by NI & ROI:	0
Irish League players capped by ROI & NI:	1 Jimmy Kelly

Printed in Great Britain
by Amazon